# Six Million Crucifixions

*How Christian Teachings About Jews*
*Paved the Road to the Holocaust*

GABRIEL WILENSKY

D1581818

QWERTY Publishers
P.O. Box 927784
San Diego, CA 92192-7784
U.S.A
http://www.qwertypublishers.com

QWERTY books may be purchased for educational, business, or sales promotional use. For more information please write QWERTY Publishers, P.O. Box 927784, San Diego, CA 92192-7784 or orders@qwertypublishers.com.

FIRST EDITION


Publisher's Cataloging-in-Publication (Provided by Quality Books, Inc.)

Wilensky, Gabriel, 1964-
    Six million crucifixions : how Christian teachings
  about Jews paved the road to the Holocaust / Gabriel
  Wilensky. -- 1st ed.
      p. cm.
    Includes bibliographical references and index.
    LCCN 2009911617
    ISBN-13: 978-0-9843346-7-4
    ISBN-10: 0-9843346-7-X

    1. Christianity and antisemitism. 2. Judaism
(Christian theology)--History of doctrines.
3. Holocaust, Jewish (1939-1945) 4. Christianity and other
religions--Judaism. 5. Judaism--Relations--
Christianity. 6. World War, 1939-1945--Religious
aspects--Christianity.   I. Title.

BM535.W55 2010              261.2'6
                        QBI09-600206

# Six Million Crucifixions

*Dedicated to all present and future Christians with the courage to confront the past in order to forge a better future.*

*The world is a dangerous place to live; not because of the people who are evil, but because of the people who don't do anything about it.*

Albert Einstein

*The struggle against the Jews has always been a mark of inferior, envious and cowardly natures. Whoever takes part in it must have something of the plebeian mentality about him.*

Friedrich Nietzsche

*Whoever saves a single life is as if one saves the entire world.*

Talmud

# Table of Contents

## Part I: Historical Background

# Epilogue

# Appendices

# Foreword

On July 23, 1998, the Holocaust historian Yehuda Bauer interviewed his Christian friend Franklin Littell at Yad Vashem in Jerusalem, where the two scholars frequently led seminars on the Holocaust. The interview provides an overview of Littell's primary concerns in Holocaust studies, and concludes with remarks that succinctly capture the character, outlook, and aspirations of this remarkable man, who died on May 23, 2009, at the age of 91. Underscoring that his motivation in writing and teaching about the Holocaust was above all to prevent "premature closure," Littell ended the 1998 interview by declaring his intent "to keep this thing [the memory of the Holocaust] irritating—you know, be the harpoon that the fish can't escape."[1]

His aim clear, his thrust sure, Littell and his harpoon rarely missed their targets, including, first and foremost, Littell's own Christian tradition. He often referred to the Holocaust as an "alpine event," his way of identifying that disaster's unprecedented, watershed significance. In Littell's view, the Holocaust produced the most severe "credibility crisis"—one of his favorite terms—to afflict the Christian tradition. That tradition's "teaching of contempt" about Judaism and Jews had contributed mightily to genocide against the Jewish people, he believed. Only profound contrition and reform, including fundamental theological revision that tackled the New Testament's anti-Judaic themes, could restore integrity to post-Holocaust Christianity.

Whether Franklin Littell and Gabriel Wilensky ever met, I do not know. Clearly, however, both have wielded harpoons that find their marks; each has been determined to make sure that the fish do not escape and that no premature closure diminishes the Holocaust and Christian responsibility for it. The title of Wilensky's book, *Six Million Crucifixions*, echoes Littell's important 1975 study, *The Crucifixion of the Jews*. More than that, Wilensky's Jewish outlook complements Littell's Christian perspective. Both writers, for example, drive home a point as tragic as it is fundamental: Absent Christianity, no Holocaust would have taken place. Christianity alone did not cause the Holocaust, but the Christian tradition's centuries-long hostility toward Judaism and Jews was a necessary condition—the nitroglycerin in the dynamite, as Wilensky puts it—for the genocide that Nazi Germany perpetrated against the European Jews. If given its way, that destruction process would have utterly destroyed the Jewish people and their traditions, which highlight the most basic ethical imperative of all: "Thou shalt not murder."

Wilensky dedicates his book "to all present and future Christians" but with a crucial qualification. The dedication is not for Christians who remain forgetful, complacent, or indifferent about their tradition's relationship to the Holocaust, although Wilensky hopes that his book will awaken, shake, and trouble them. Instead Wilensky dedicates his book to Christians who have "the courage to confront the past in order to forge a better future," particularly a better future regarding Christian-Jewish relationships. As a Christian, I can say that indeed courage is needed to grapple with the challenges that Wilensky thinks Christians must face to improve the odds in favor of that better future.

By now, numerous books by Christians, Jews, and others have taken Christianity to task for its many failures before, during, and after the Holocaust. But few, if any, hit harder than Wilensky's. Quite literally, he would put Christianity and at least some Christians on trial for Holocaust-related crimes, including human rights abuses and crimes against humanity. The fact that such judicial proceedings will not take place provides meager comfort, however, because so many of his indictments rightly sting.

Post-Holocaust Christianity never will match Wilensky's wishes. But for Christianity to advance in confronting the Holocaust for the sake of a better future, honesty of the kind that his book displays always will be necessary. If we Christians can be fully honest about our tradition—candidly facing and attempting to correct its dark side even as we embrace and honor the goodness that Christianity contains and can inspire—that maturity will be a sign that we Christians have at least some of the courage that Wilensky hopes we will find. If steps in those directions continue to take place, then a growing number of Christians will join Littell and Wilensky to keep memory of the Holocaust properly irritating as they thrust well-aimed harpoons that injustice and antisemitism in particular must not escape.

John K. Roth

Edward J. Sexton Professor Emeritus of Philosophy
Founding Director,
The Center for the Study of the Holocaust,
Genocide, and Human Rights
Claremont McKenna College

# Introduction

*"Father, forgive them; for they know not what they do."*

*Jesus (Lk. 23:34)*

## Purpose of this Book

This book is meant to be used as a resource for increasing the understanding of the root causes of antisemitism that led to the extermination of millions of European Jews in the Second World War. I followed the following objectives in writing this book:

1. To perform historical research to provide a complete understanding of the oral and written teachings that created, promoted and/or encouraged the negative perception of the Jewish people over the last two millennia that culminated in the genocidal antisemitism that engulfed Germany and other European nations during the Second World War;

2. To gather evidence that might make possible the identification of members of the Christian churches who through their acts of commission or omission may have had a role in the extermination of the Jews; to determine the extent and nature of said role; and to suggest what the appropriate legal actions against those responsible would have been;

3. To recommend changes to Christian traditions, doctrine, liturgy and lectionaries to prevent further grave acts of incitement,

demonization and segregation caused by the supersessionistic, vicious and defamatory anti-Jewish polemic included in some of those Christian teachings.

## What This Book Comprises

*Six Million Crucifixions* is composed of five parts. The first provides an overview of the historical background of key events spanning the time between the death of Jesus up to the end of the Second World War. By necessity this section is short and can thus only focus on a few relevant events out of the immense amount of material in the almost two thousand year old history. The second part focuses on various specific aspects of Christian Antisemitism. Part III goes into some detail into the role of the Catholic and Protestant Churches during the Nazi era and its aftermath. The fourth part provides an overview of the criminal activities that individual clergy as well as the Churches as such may be guilty of and provides some remedial recommendations. Lastly, the Epilogue gives an account of developments since the conclusion of the war until present time.

## Defining Antisemitism

According to the current edition of Merriam-Webster's dictionary, which continues to use an 1882 definition, antisemitism is "hostility toward or discrimination against Jews as a religious, ethnic, or racial group." As will be described below, antisemitism took two main forms over the last two millennia, shifting from a theologically based enmity against Jews to a secular and racial hatred.

*A note on style*: in this book I will spell the term "antisemitism," as opposed to "anti-Semitism," as there is no such thing as "Semitism" and thus should not be capitalized or spelled with a hyphen. Also, when referring to "the Church" I mean both the Catholic and Protestant churches unless one of them is specifically identified.

## A Personal Note

I have been fascinated and amazed by the magnitude and significance of World War II and the Holocaust since I was a teenager. When reading about the Holocaust I was baffled, as I was unable to comprehend how one people could hate another people so much, and in such scale, as the Germans and other European peoples hated the Jews. Think about it: how can you have so much hate in you that every day you get up, you drag thousands of men, women and children to a forest, and shoot them in the head at close range one by one, getting blood, pieces of brain and splinters of cranial bone splattered all over you after each victim, and continue to do it all day long, day after day? Less than half of one percent of Germany's population before the war was Jewish, so a large majority of the perpetrators probably never even saw a Jew until they invaded Poland! Despite all the books I read over the years, I still could not fathom what it was that motivated that level of hatred. There had to be something else besides relentless racial propaganda. When I finally understood, it motivated me to want to help others understand as well.

Antisemitism is on the rise again. Never since the end of the Second World War have there been so many antisemitic incidents worldwide. The world suffers from amnesia and often disregards the lessons from the past. Film director Mel Gibson releases *The Passion of the Christ,* a passion play watched by more people than all the previous passion play productions put together, and equally if not more damning of the Jewish people. A senior Vatican cardinal compares the Gaza Strip with a big concentration camp. A Swedish newspaper updates the old Christian Ritual Murder canard and accuses the Israeli Defense Forces—as a proxy for "The Jew"—of killing young Palestinians to harvest their organs. Holocaust denial has become more common, and no amount of lawsuits and debunking seem to make it disappear. Even a shunned, excommunicated Catholic bishop openly denied the Holocaust ever happened, and he was rewarded by Pope Benedict XVI by bringing him back into the Catholic fold. A pope who believes Pope Pius XII "spared no effort in intervening in their [the Jews'] favour either directly or through instructions given to other individuals or to institutions of the Catholic Church"[2] during the war. And this is the same Pope who seems to be interested in eroding the progress made by the Second Vatican Council and reverting to a more traditional version of Catholicism, a version that taught for almost two millennia that Jews were Christ-killers and the enemies of Christianity.

*Six Million Crucifixions* examines the root causes of antisemitism in Christianity and how that prepared the soil for the modern/racial antisemitism that culminated in the Holocaust. The point of the book is to present the historical background to explain how the Holocaust could have happened, and to raise awareness of where antisemitism comes from and why it has not yet disappeared. In doing so, and despite my best efforts to be true to the historical record, I will surely outrage some readers who will be unable or unwilling to accept anything negative about their Church or religion. Some readers will surely want to dismiss the book outright without even seeing whether they might agree with the points I'm making. The only thing I ask is that they resist this urge and give the book a chance, to read on with an open mind and determine by themselves if they agree or not with my points. I believe that in so doing those readers might learn something, and we might learn something from them.

Gabriel Wilensky
San Diego, April 2010

# Part I: Historical Background

*"The Jews held Him [Jesus], the Jews insulted Him, the Jews bound Him, they crowned Him with thorns, they dishonored Him by spitting upon Him, they scourged Him, they heaped abuses upon Him, they hung Him upon a tree, they pierced Him with a lance..."*

*St. Augustine*

# 1

# Laying the Foundation

Jesus' ignominious death was a cataclysmic event for his followers. In the terrible times under which they lived, under a brutal
and oppressive Roman occupation, the Jews of first century Judea
eagerly awaited their redeemer—their Messiah—and to a group of
those Jews, Jesus was the one. In the days and weeks after his death,
his followers attempted to console themselves by looking into the
Hebrew Bible for something that would help them understand
what happened. As they told stories and read from Scriptures they
found verses that seemed to fit what they had experienced, or that
made that experience more meaningful. In this way, as they saw
that some of the prophesies in the Hebrew Bible appeared to explain what they had experienced, they began to see the reality of
the crucifixion as fulfillment of biblical prophecy.

Early Christian writers, adept in the art of relaying information
to uneducated and sometimes illiterate believers, weaved key passages from the Hebrew Bible into a coherent narrative that fully
incorporated these prophetic passages. Eventually, as decades
passed and the oral narrative of Jesus' life and Passion was written
down as the Gospels, the history several generations of Christians
recalled shifted from *history remembered* to *prophecy historicized*. In
this way, by using these texts as theological, ideological and peda-
gogic tools these early Christian preachers successfully managed to
capture and direct the loyalties of the uneducated. These texts are
therefore more of a product of the historical context in which they

were written and the needs of those that wrote them than of the people whose stories they purport to portray.[3]

In the decades following Jesus' death, his followers, all of whom were Jewish, started to drift apart from mainline Judaism which did not believe Jesus had been the Messiah. This led to a feeling of ambivalence toward their Jewish brethren. The feeling of ambivalence manifested itself in many ways, for instance when calling the Hebrew Bible "Old Testament," meaning of course old in the ancient sense but also in the superseded sense of not being "New." This pattern of ambivalence was made worse over time as a new generation built on top of the previous generation's mistakes. Strong feelings of rejection in the first century turned to hatred in the fourth century when Christians all but forgot the original conflicts were among Jews, and not among opposing religions. When hatred for the Jews continued to increase as they became the theological permanent other, Jews stopped thinking of the Church as competition and disengaged from Christians. This had the effect of increasing the hatred Christians felt toward Jews, as is typical when one member of a rivalry opts out. This feeling of ambivalence, in which early Christians simultaneously felt love and hatred toward their Jewish brethren, became part of the official political and intellectual doctrine of the Church after Augustine fatefully wrote that Jews may survive, but never thrive. This dictum manifested itself many times with the popes and high-ranking Church leaders sometimes defending the Jews, while instilling venomous teachings about them on the ignorant masses that often persecuted them.[4] A good example of the popes defending the Jews is what Pope Innocent IV said in 1247:

> "They are wrongly accused of partaking of the heart of a murdered child at the Passover. . . Whenever a corpse is found somewhere, it is to the Jews that the murder is wickedly imputed. They are persecuted on the pretext of such fables . . . they are deprived of trial and of regular judgment; in mockery of all justice, they are stripped of their belongings, starved, imprisoned and tortured."[5]

Unfortunately, history shows what little effect words like these had on the community at large. This was because the popes, kings, nobility and bishops had little influence over the populace who had long before absorbed the negative and fantastical conception of the Jew. By the Middle Ages the greatest influence on the people was from ignorant, fanatical and superstitious lesser clergy.[6]

One of the things that had the greatest influence on the creation of the foundational myths of the Christian movement was Jesus' followers' refusal to accept his death and the assertion he had risen from his grave and ascended to heaven to take his place beside God. They believed the Hebrew Bible provided confirmation that Jesus' terrible demise was precisely the fate that had been prophesied to happen to the savior of Israel. To most of the people that knew him, however, Jesus' death and the way he died was a clear indication that he could not have been the messiah. They believed the still unredeemed state of the world clearly showed the savior had still not come. At the same time, a few of his followers interpreted this as an indication that Jesus would return to complete his work of redemption during their lifetimes.[7]

Another important parallel early Christian writers saw was that between the story of the Jewish people's persecution of their prophets as narrated in the Hebrew Bible and the imputed persecution of Jesus and his apostles by his contemporary Jewish brethren. This can be seen in the Gospel according to Matthew (23:33-38) where Matthew has his Jesus indict the scribes and Pharisees. As mentioned before, this reflects Matthew's historical context many decades after Jesus' death, and not Jesus' true historical environment.[8]

Long after the death of Jesus, a Jew from Tarsus called Saul changed his name to Paul and began proselytizing to the Jewish communities outside Judea. To make adoption of his message easier he lifted some of the arduous duties imposed by Jewish Law, particularly the dietary laws and the requirement that all males were circumcised. This made the message spread very quickly among Christian proselytes, God-fearers and the general Gentile population of the Roman Empire. It also caused a rift between traditional Jews (still faithful to the Law of Moses) and Paul's dissidents from Judaism, whom traditional Jews increasingly considered to be dangerous heretics. When Paul's followers realized that their new message was not having an effect on traditional Jews, they made efforts to show the world that God had chosen a new Israel and had forsaken what they perceived to be an obstinate people. To these Christians the destruction of the Jerusalem Temple in 70 CE and the further dispersion of the surviving Jews provided confirmation of this view. As the great French court preacher and bishop Jacques-Benigne Bossuet would say centuries later, "The greatest crime of the Jews is not that they caused the death of the Savior. . . . God, upon the death of his son, left them still forty years without punishing them. . ." This implies that the destruction of the Temple and the further dispersion were providential punishment for the crucifixion and their obdurate refusal to believe in Jesus as the messiah. Most Jews, however, likely believed that the catastrophe was God's punishment to his people for having forsaken their covenant with him.[9]

*The treasures of the Jewish Temple in Jerusalem displayed for the Roman people in the Arch of Titus in Rome.*

The new Christian converts in the pagan world perceived the stubborn Jewish refusal to accept Jesus as the Christ (from the Greek word for the Hebrew term "messiah") and as the only son of God as a challenge to their certainty in Jesus' revelation. In their view, if God's chosen people, the Jews, continued to reject God's promised messiah it could either mean that the Jewish people were extraordinarily mistaken or that the messiah was false. Unable to accept that the object of their veneration could be false, they fully accepted the notion that the Jews were wrong.[10] To distance themselves further from mainstream Jews in front of the pagan world, the early Jewish Christians characterized traditional Jews as Christianity's ontological "other." This distinction slowly evolved into animosity as the Jewish rejection of the new faith continued while the first century came to a close.[11] We find the first explicit charge of deicide (that is, the charge the Jews were responsible for Jesus' death) in Bishop Saint Melito of Sardis in one of his second century homilies: "God has been murdered; the king of Israel has been slain by an Israelite hand."[12] Ultimately, the accusation that the Jews killed Jesus is an amendment to the real charge leveled against the Jews, namely, that they refused to accept the new Christian faith.[13]

Until the time of Emperor Constantine, the fate of Christianity hung in the balance. In 315 CE he reneged on the liberal edict of Milan by issuing a new edict prohibiting the Jews to proselytize, forever limiting their ability to stand in opposition to the new Christian faith.[14] In an attempt to unify the various religious factions in the largely pagan Roman Empire, Constantine converted to Christianity and made it the official religion of the empire. However, having internal quarrels on the nature of Jesus' divinity between Christian factions was problematic. A council was convened in Nicea in 325 CE to settle the issue conclusively. This council produced what is known as the Christian Creed.

There are some interesting changes in the modern creed from the original: "becoming man, suffered and rose again on the third day" was changed to ". . . and became man. For our sake he was crucified under Pontius Pilate; he suffered, died, and was buried. On the third day, he rose again in fulfillment of the Scriptures." The original focused on incarnation, suffering and resurrection, while the second focused on death. The updated creed put the crucifixion at the center of faith and the death of Jesus at the heart of redemption. The crucifixion replaced resurrection as the saving event and, interestingly, blamed Pilate instead of the Jews, as the gospels do. The libelous shift of responsibility from the Romans to the Jews as narrated in the gospels resonated with a hate-filled Christian mob. "Tell me, do you praise the Jews for crucifying Christ, and for, even to this day, blaspheming Him and calling Him a lawbreaker?" sermonized Saint John Chrysostom, bishop of Antioch, around 387 CE. After this many other strongly anti-Jewish sermons led to assaults on synagogues, exclusion of the Jews from public office, and expulsions.[15]

# 2

## The Middle Ages

### The Crusades

After the Saracens took over the Holy Land, Pope Urban II launched the First Crusade in 1095 to liberate the holy city of Jerusalem and the Holy Land. Additionally, his goal was to free Eastern Christians from Islamic rule. Knights, peasants and priests from many nations of western Europe travelled together united by religious fervor. The cross was the unifying symbol that provided the appeal, the ideology and the name to the event. Given this basic role played by the cross, it was natural for Christians to seek vengeance from those they believed to be responsible for the crucifixion. In fact, as the crusaders approached the Holy Land, Jews *as killers of Christ* were brought to the forefront in the minds of Christians incensed by memories of Jesus' Passion.[16]

As the First Crusader stampede trampled on Jews in the eleventh century, they did so on what they imagined Jews to be, and not what they actually were. This imaginary picture of Jews was the result of the portrayal of Jews as still murdering Jesus in Jerusalem in the permanent present tense of the liturgy repeated year after year. Godfrey of Bouillon, who led the First Crusade, swore to "avenge the blood of Christ on Israel and to leave no single member of the Jewish race alive." Gangs of people led by adventurers, ex-priests and inferior monks fell upon the Jews of Rouen, Metz and then the Rhineland with the war cry "Baptism or death."[17] The First Crusade reached Mainz, in the Rhineland, in late May 1096. Despite the bishop's interest in helping, once the crusaders overran the city he fled. According to the chronicler Solomon bar Simson, who lived between the First and Second Crusades, the crusaders declared in clear anti-Jewish theology, "You are the children of those who killed our object of veneration, hanging him from a tree; and he himself said: 'There will yet come a day when my children will come and avenge my blood.' We are his children and it is . . . therefore obligatory for us to avenge him since you are the ones who rebel and disbelieve him."

As Jews in the archbishop's courtyard saw everything was lost, they chose the path of martyrdom rather than converting. Mothers slew their sons and daughters, and men also slaughtered their wives, children and infants before killing themselves.[18] Over eleven hundred Jews were massacred in Mainz alone, and many more thousands would perish before the First Crusade was over. To the masses of Christians stampeding across Europe on the way to the Holy Land the Jew was the worst infidel of all, indeed the Christ-killer himself. The massacres of Jews they conducted were inspired by a religious fanaticism instilled in them by a multitude of low-level clergy among the rabble. Indeed, three priests, Peter the Hermit, Volkmar and Gottschalk were responsible for arousing the masses against Jews and leading the roaming mob. Significantly, there is no record of attacks on Jews anywhere in Europe by the great nobles of the official army.[19]

The First Crusade ignited a tradition of organized violence, extortion and slaughter of Jews, a pattern that would be repeated in subsequent crusades. It is estimated that by the time the Fourth Crusade was over, two hundred years later, about one hundred thousand Jews had been murdered.

Pope Innocent III wrote to the archbishops of Sens and Paris in 1205 that "the Jews, by their own guilt, are consigned to perpetual servitude because they crucified the Lord. . . As slaves rejected by God, in whose death they wickedly conspire, they shall by the effect of this very action, recognize themselves as the slaves of those whom Christ's death set free. . ." Not content with initiating the Fourth Crusade Pope Innocent III also launched the Albigensian massacre, intended to eliminate the Cathar heresy in the south of France.

*Crusaders are killing Jews, identifiable by their conical hats. From a 1250 French Bible.*

## Blaming Jews for Everything

By the time of the Crusades the original animosity between Jewish Christians and traditional Jews had turned into a full-blown antagonism. The "new" Christians produced a new and separate theology that defined itself in part as everything Judaism was not. Over time, Christians felt the need to do everything possible to stand out from Judaism and Jews, and this evolved into a hatred that imputed Jews with all the ills of the world. Reflecting the language used in the Gospels, medieval Christians imputed these superstitious crimes on "the Jews" and not on any particular Jew.

In Norwich, England, in 1144 a new and notorious allegation was concocted. The accusation was that the Jews had "bought a Christian child before Easter, tortured him with all the tortures wherewith our Lord was tortured and on Friday hanged him on a rood in hatred of our Lord." This allegation was that Jews ritually murdered non-Jews, especially Christians, to obtain blood to make Passover bread. It was a complex of deliberate lies, trumped up accusations, and popular beliefs about the murder-lust of the Jews and their bloodthirstiness, based on the conception that Jews hated Christianity and humankind in general. It was combined with the delusion that Jews were in some way not human and had to have recourse to special remedies and subterfuges to appear, at least outwardly, like other men. The blood libel led to trials and massacres of Jews. Its origin was rooted in ancient, almost primordial concepts concerning the potency and energies of blood. It is one of the most terrible expressions of human cruelty and credulity. These blood rituals are expressly forbidden in Judaism.[20]

The Blood Libel charges Jews with playing the same role they did during the crucifixion by murdering a Christian boy and using his blood in perverse rituals. The false charge was made during Holy Week and the "informant" was a Jew, again a Judas Iscariot. This charge spread like a virus and took hold of the Christian imagination as Jews were accused of crucifying boys in Würzburg in 1147, and similar or same crimes in Gloucester in 1168, in Blois in 1171, in Zaragoza in 1182 and repeatedly after that all over Europe into the twentieth century.[21] According to a popular medieval Christian legend, "a secret rabbinical synod convened periodically from all over Europe to determine which community was in turn to commit ritual murder."[22] Even though prelates and other high authorities of the Church often denied the veracity of the stories, local lower level clergy frequently supported and encouraged them while launching profitable pilgrimages to the sites of the alleged murders.

*Accusing Jews of practicing ritual murder to secure the blood of Christian boys to use in Jewish religious rituals, as "reported" by the antisemitic publication Der Stürmer. The May 1939 edition on the left, with the headline "Ritual Murder" shows a reprint of a medieval depiction of a purported ritual murder committed by Jews, while the May 1934 edition, with the headline "Jewish Murder Plan against Gentile Humanity Revealed," shows a contemporary rendition of the same thing.*

A small step detached from the blood libel was that of well poisoning. Christians easily jumped from permanently blaming Jews for murdering Jesus and making the accusation that by murdering Christian boys they were murdering a surrogate Jesus, to the assumption they were also ready and willing to murder all Christians. Jews were believed to be ready to poison wells to accomplish this goal. Because of this belief twenty-seven Jews were executed for well poisoning in Bohemia in 1163. The accusations were repeated in Breslau in 1226 and in Vienna in 1267. When Jews were accused of a conspiracy to poison every well in France in 1321, many Jews were burned at the stake and the Jews of Paris were expelled from the city.[23]

In 1348 the Black Plague hit Europe. The disease spread through the continent from the Southeast leaving twenty to twenty-five million people dead in its wake. By the time it reached England, about one in three people in Europe were dead.[24] It created such a widespread panic that it became almost natural for a Christian population already prepared to blame the Jews to infer the plague was connected to well poisoning. A rumor identified the initiator of a putative Jewish conspiracy to kill Christians as Jacob Pascal, a native of Toledo. The rumor claimed a cabal of Spanish Jews was the supplier of poison to Jewish agents everywhere in Europe. Once a few Jews confirmed this under torture, a reaction resulting in violence far surpassing that of the First Crusade ensued. As in the Crusades, this started in the Rhineland. One chronicler reported twelve thousand deaths, including some from Jews who committed suicide when they saw that all was lost.

An incidental byproduct of the fantastical conception of the Jews during the Black Plague was Shakespeare's Shylock. The figure of the usurer who demands a pound of flesh as payment for a debt was already a familiar character in European medieval tales in which he was a Christian or a heathen. However, circumstances in Europe made the Jew assume that role in the Christian mind, and that was how Shakespeare immortalized him.[25]

The Jews were only protected in Avignon, as that was where Pope Clement VI's court was. He defended the Jews by instructing the curia to do so and went so far as to issue a bull (i.e. a papal communication of public nature) pointing out the obvious fact that Jews were dying like everyone else: "That the Jews have provided the occasion or the cause for such a crime has no plausibility."[26] Meanwhile the plague was wreaking havoc everywhere and despite the Pope's attempt to save Jews, out of control Christian mobs were massacring them wherever they could find them. Many Jewish communities, including those in Trier, Mainz and Cologne were entirely wiped out. Christians acted this way because they felt they were defending themselves from a threat that logically derived from a theological doctrine dramatically reiterated every Holy Week of every year in which Jews were portrayed as murderers.[27]

This belief, and the blood libel, came about as the Christian mob held another widespread belief that the Jews had secret powers, rituals and black magic.[28]

*Burning Jews during the Black Plague, 1349.*

After 1348 the Christian stereotyping of Jews became more vicious as their perception of Jews changed. Jews were then no longer seen simply as an enemy like before but rather as a mortal threat. Popes, bishops and some princes continued to defend Jews from violence and forced conversion as Pope Clement VI had done, but they also continued with an intensified proselytizing program. The political and ecclesiastical authorities failed to understand that the mob was merely acting out in practice what the Church taught in theory and enforced as social degradation at every opportunity.[29]

## The Fourth Lateran Council

Convened by Innocent III in 1215, this was the most important ecumenical gathering up until that point in history. More than four hundred bishops and archbishops, eight hundred priors and abbots, and the ambassadors of Europe's kingdoms and cities were in attendance. The Council established the main elements of Catholic culture as it exists today, and among those elements is the resolute assertion that there is no salvation possible outside the Church: "There is indeed one universal church of the faithful outside of which nobody at all is saved, in which Jesus Christ is both priest and sacrifice."[30] As a consequence, ecclesiastical authorities felt an even stronger need to convert Jews and others.

*Jewish man from Worms wearing a Jewish badge and holding garlic. The badge is yellow and oval in shape; a moneybag and a garlic bulb are antisemitic ethnic stereotypes. Heidelberg, 1551-1600. On the right panel, "He is guilty for the war!" An anti-Jewish poster from 1943 showing a Jew wearing the yellow Star of David.*

This Council is particularly important in the history of Christian persecution of Jews because it was the first one to promulgate resolutions designed to denigrate, restrict and isolate the Jews. Local indignities and insults were now made legitimate, official, and universal. "Jews and Saracens of both sexes in every Christian province, and at all times, shall be marked off in the eyes of the public from other people through the character of their dress." This is the precursor to the Nazi yellow star Jews were forced to wear in the 1930s.

Jews were also banned from taking public office, forbidden to go out during Holy Week and had a compulsory tax payable to the local Catholic clergy imposed on them.[31]

The Council expressly called upon the secular powers to exterminate all heretics. This provision was the basis for a wave of stake burnings during the Inquisition.[32] This was later reinforced at the Council of Florence in 1442, in which an increasing Church paranoia led the council to promulgate:

> "The holy Roman church firmly believes, professes and preaches that all those who are outside the Catholic Church, not only pagans but also Jews and heretics and schismatics, cannot share in eternal life, and will go into the everlasting fire, 'which was prepared for the devil and his angels,' unless they are joined to the Catholic Church before the end of their lives. . . Nobody can be saved no matter how much he has given away alms and even if he has shed his blood in the name of Christ, unless he has persevered in the bosom and unity of the Catholic Church."[33]

A little over a decade after the Fourth Lateran Council, in 1231, Council Pope Gregory IX established the Inquisition. Initially meant to target heretics, it was soon aimed at the Jews as they were increasingly seen as not that much different from heretics. In the fifteen and sixteenth centuries the social and religious upheavals in Europe provoked a shift in the Christian perception of Jews. The Spanish Inquisition provided a clear explanation for the Church's shaken faith when they said that the cause for it was the very presence of the Jews. Pope Paul III brought a Spanish-style Inquisition to Rome in 1542, appointing as its head Gian Pietro Caraffa, who had been papal nuncio in Spain and who presided over the burning at the stake of dozens of Jews.[34]

## Forced Preaching

After the Fourth Lateran Council, Dominican and Franciscan friars were sent out to preach to Jews. They were easier to identify than the heretics, and closer than the Saracens. An edict from King James I of Aragon in 1242 stated, "Likewise we wish and decree that, whenever the archbishop, bishops, or Dominican or Franciscan friars visit a town or a locale where Jews or Saracens dwell and wish to present the word of God to the said Jews or Saracens, these must gather at their call and must patiently hear their preaching. If they do not wish to come of their own will, our officials shall compel them to do so, putting aside all excuses."[35] In justification of the forcing of the Jews to listen to Christian sermons, Pope Innocent IV, who condemned the Talmud, said: "Indeed, we believe that the pope, who is the vicar of Jesus Christ, has authority not only over Christians but also over all infidels, since Christ had authority over all. . . . Therefore, the pope can judge the Jews, if they violate the law of the Gospel in moral matters and their own prelates do not check them, and also if they invent heresies against their own law."[36]

Forced preaching and proselytizing became officially sanctioned when Pope Nicholas III promulgated the customary bull *Sicut Judaeis* (the "Constitution for the Jews"; intended to protect Jews) but altered it by adding a new requirement to the Church mandating "sermons and other means for the conversion of the Jews."[37]

To the friars' surprise, their proselytizing efforts through forced preaching did not bear fruit. Very few Jews were actually converting to Christianity. The failure of the strong conversionist efforts created a considerable level of frustration and anger, which served to reinforce old prejudices of Jewish blindness and obtuseness. That generally the friars doing the preaching came from the mercantile class meant that they reinforced the prejudices related to commerce and money-lending. The friars then attempted to use a new angle by also preaching to Christians about the Jews. A Dominican called Giordano da Rivalto in Florence on November 9, 1304 said, after the customary deicide charge, that the Jews were still murdering Christ: "I say first of all that they repeat it [the crucifixion] in their hearts with ill will—wherefore they are evil at heart and hate Christ with evil hatred; and they would, were they able, crucify him anew every day. . . They are hated throughout the world because they are evil toward Christ, whom they curse." According to him, the Jews cursed Christ by refusing to convert. He also declared in his sermons that the Jews stole the Eucharist host to blaspheme it, and he claimed to have personally witnessed such a desecration and saw with his own eyes an apparition of Jesus that came to stop it. With this "miraculous intervention" Jesus "recruited" the local Christian population to slaughter twenty-four thousand Jews for their evil deed. Giordano also makes use of the Blood Libel by claiming the Jews continue to murder Jesus down to the present by kidnapping and crucifying a Christian boy every year. This is significant because this was not the work of the illiterate mob, but rather that of the official representative of the Church.[38]

The Church attempted to convert Jews because it felt that Jews who refused to convert were a threat to the ultimate fulfillment of salvation theology, and this was a threat that could not be tolerated. In the Catechism it expressed that, "The Jews bear a terrible burden because they willfully insist on being an obstacle to the well-being of the rest of humanity, preventing the arrival of the Messiah and human salvation because of their 'unbelief' in Jesus." Even after the extermination of millions of European Jews during the Second World War and the reforms of the Second Vatican Council the Catechism of the Catholic Church still teaches that the Jews' desire to remain Jews is the greatest impediment to the well being of Christians. In essence, the Church holds that salvation of humanity depends upon the conversion of Jews to Christianity. The Catholic Church continues to hold on to scripture, theology and doctrine that denigrates and censures Jews and Judaism.[39]

Even some of the greatest Christian thinkers of Nazi period could not detach themselves from the position that Jews had to convert and had to accept Jesus as their savior. In 1942, at the height of the exterminatory campaign against the Jews, Karl Barth, perhaps the greatest Christian theologian of the twentieth century, expressed that the reason Jews were suffering the fate imposed on them was as divine punishment for their willful unbelief. Even in 1949, four years after the demise of the Third Reich and after the Nuremberg Trials that brought to light in graphic detail the extent and nature of the genocide, he intimated that the disaster that befell on the Jewish people was "a result of their unfaithfulness." What makes this particularly significant is that Barth was one of the strongest opponents of Nazism and even of antisemitism. This was not uncommon, however. Other German religious leaders who opposed Nazism held on to their ingrained theological inheritance, which ascribed Jewish unbelief in Jesus as Lord to their spiritual blindness, hardness of heart, willful ignorance or partnership with Satan, and thus believed the Holocaust was a form of divine punishment. Ultimately, these Christian thinkers had fully absorbed the Christian supersessionistic view that stipulated that God's covenant with the Jewish people was null and that Christianity was now the true Israel, the community truly chosen by God. None of these Christian thinkers and teachers could conceive of both Judaism and Christianity as equally legitimate ways of worshiping God.[40]

## The Talmud

The rabbinic tradition in Judaism that originated after the destruction of the second Temple of Jerusalem in 70 CE led to a rich oral tradition of study, commentary, legal teachings and instruction of the Torah (the Pentateuch). In the third century, those oral traditions had been assembled into a collection of writings known as the Mishnah. Jews treated this book as a living text, and it inspired further rabbinic interpretations and commentaries that later became the Talmud. Rabbinic Judaism developed an enduring tradition of Talmudic study which went largely ignored by Christianity until the thirteenth century, when they reacted to the unknown text as if it was a dangerous and subversive book capable of not only poisoning Christian's minds, but also those of the Jews. To Christian prelates, this mysterious and voluminous text explained Jewish recalcitrance and aversion to conversion.

The Inquisition soon started to investigate the Talmud, and a convert from Judaism named Nicholas Donin testified to Pope Gregory IX himself in 1236 that these writings were blasphemous and heretical. The Pope was convinced the Talmud was "the chief cause that holds the Jews obstinate in their perfidy." A study of the Talmud led by the University of Paris was charged with determining whether rabbinic commentaries were heretical within the context of Judaism, and not surprisingly that was precisely what they found. This marked an unprecedented effort in Christian theology to establish moral and theological authority over the content of Jewish belief.[41]

However, despite all the findings of these studies, the Talmud is not what these Christian zealots portrayed it to be. Here's an example of what's written in the Talmud:

"Love of humanity is more than charity. The value of charity lies only in love, which lives in it. Love surpasses charity in three respects: Charity is only for the poor; love is for both poor and rich. Charity is only for the living; love is for both living and dead. Love without reproof of error is no love. He who judges his neighbor leniently will himself be judged leniently by God. Let man be always intelligent and affable in his God-fearing. Let him answer softly, curb his wrath and let him live in peace with his brethren and his kin and with every man, yes, even with the pagan on the street, in order that he be beloved in heaven and on earth, and be acceptable to all men. The kindly man is the truly God-fearing man."[42]

After the Church, which had been involved in the violent persecution and repression of every form of heresy, had discovered and understood that Jews had gone beyond the teachings of the Hebrew Bible and that modern Judaism was based on the teachings of the Talmud, it began attacking the Jewish holy book. In the Church's view, the existence of a post-biblical or Talmudic Judaism made no sense, as it no longer served the Augustinian purpose of being witness to the Old Testament legacy that gave birth to the New Testament and Christianity. To Augustine, Jews were blind to Christian revelation but they were useful in the Christian world as witnesses of Christian truth as prophesied in the Hebrew Bible. However, if Jews had moved past the religion of the Bible and now followed the religion of the Talmud, which was not the word of God, then they could no longer be conceived of as blind and therefore that made the entire Augustinian conception of Jews weak.[43]

Gregory IX's successor, Innocent IV, gave an indictment of the Talmud:

"Ungrateful to the Lord Jesus Christ, who, His forbearance overflowing, patiently awaits their conversion, they manifest no shame for their guilt, nor do they reverence the dignity of the Christian faith. Omitting or condemning the Mosaic Law and the Prophets, they follow certain traditions of their elders. . . In Hebrew they call them 'Thalamuth,' and an immense book it is, exceeding the text of the Bible in size, and in it are blasphemies against God and His Christ, and against the blessed Virgin, fables that are manifestly beyond all explanation, erroneous abuses, and unheard-of stupidities—yet this is what they teach and feed their children . . . and render them totally alien to the Law and the Prophets, fearing lest the Truth which is understood in the same Law and Prophets, bearing patent testimony to the only begotten Son of God, who was to come in flesh, they be converted to the faith, and return humbly to their Redeemer."[44]

The faculty of the University of Paris held a trial in the form of a debate between Jewish sages and Dominican friars to determine whether the Talmud was heretical or not, and the verdict was that it was heretical. The assumption was that the Talmud was the reason the Jews were refusing to convert, and thus if it was destroyed they would see the truth about the "fulfillment" arguments from the Hebrew Bible.[45] On July 16, 1242, the men of King Louis IX of France, also known as Saint Louis, invaded Jewish homes and synagogues to confiscate all copies of the Talmud. They brought up to twenty-four cartloads of books, something like twelve thousand volumes to the square in front of Paris' Hôtel de Ville, and burned them in a bonfire that raged for one and a half days.

*On the left, detail from a panel by Berruguete from the 15th century showing the Church burning books it considered dangerous. On the right, at Berlin's Opernplatz, the burning of books and other printed materials considered "un-German" by members of the SA and students from universities and colleges in Berlin. Germany, May 10, 1933.*

Coincidentally, on that day in 1942 the Nazis deported the Jews of Paris, including ten thousand children, to their deaths from a place nearby.[46] In 1553 Pope Paul IV launched an assault against the Talmud as well, invading Jewish homes and synagogues in Rome and confiscating copies of the Talmud and other texts, which were later burned in a huge bonfire in the Campo dei Fiori. The Talmud was placed on the Index of Forbidden Books in

1559.[47] This assault on the Talmud was different from previous assaults on Jews and their property in that the perpetrator was not an illiterate, fanatical mob but rather Christendom's established intellectual and ecclesiastical heads.

## Expulsions

The expulsions of the Jews from most of the European countries in which they lived marked the beginning of an attempt at elimination which culminated with the Nazis' extermination of two thirds of European Jewry. These expulsions were theologically, racially and economically driven. In France the first expulsion took place in 1182. King Philip Augustus ordered it after having arrested the Jews, despoiled them of their money and vestments and subsequently confiscated all their houses, fields, and other immovable property. Subsequent expulsions in 1306 and 1394 followed the same pattern of expulsion followed by confiscation and readmission designed to enrich the crown.

In Austria the Vienna Edict of 1421 resulted in confiscation of Jewish property, forced conversion of Jewish children, and expulsion. Additionally, two hundred and seventy Jews were burned at the stake. The Jews of England and Germany suffered similar fate. In Italy the first papal order for their expulsion from Bologna came in 1569. Pope Pius V offered the Jewish cemetery of Bologna as a gift to the nuns of the convent of Saint Peter the Martyr, telling them "to destroy all graves . . . of the Jews . . . and to take the inscriptions, the memorials, the marble gravestones, destroying them completely, demolishing them . . . and to exhume the cadavers, the bones and the fragments of the dead and to move them wherever they please."[48]

The most important of the European expulsions took place in Spain. The first date in the conflict was June 6, 1391. Before then, in the decade of the 1380s, a vociferous anti-Jewish preacher in Seville called Ferrant Martinez—who happened to be the administrator of the archdiocese—identified Jews as the obstacle to Christian amity and prosperity. He was somewhat restrained by the king and archbishop, but when they both died in 1390, he went on unchecked in his rabble-rousing sermons inciting the massacre of Jews and the conversion of synagogues to churches. Hundreds of Jews were killed by the mob in Seville followed by hundreds more in Valencia and Barcelona, where the Jewish community was in essence eliminated. The violence spread throughout a peninsula imbibed in pent-up hatred.

Rationalism was spreading throughout Europe, which led to a sense of skepticism as well as an anticlericalism that stemmed from a stronger level of assimilation. After two generations of being on the receiving end of enforced preaching, for the first time large numbers of Jews chose conversion to Christianity instead of death.[49]

The violence inspired and led by the preachers in the decade of the 1390s led to the creation of a new class of people, the *conversos* (Spanish for "converts"). The sense of success led to an increase in the proselytizing efforts, as devout Christians felt the imminent coming of the Messiah that the mass conversion of the Jews would supposedly bring. In the first twenty-five years of the century about a third to a half of all Spanish Jews converted to Christianity, bringing the number of *conversos* to perhaps over two hundred thousand. As *conversos* were no longer restricted from most occupations, could now own land, and be part of the king's court or the Church, they rapidly prospered. At a time when Spain was going though an economic crisis, the distressed peasantry naturally increased their hatred of Jews and suspicion of the *conversos*. During hunger riots both converted and unconverted Jews were targeted, adding an ominous racial aspect to the traditional religious hatred. As the decades passed, and from the Church's perspective, the problem was that they started to suspect the sincerity of the conversions. By then the Church was fully aware that large numbers of conversions had been coerced. They defined Judaizing, the usage and mixing of Jewish and Christian elements of faith, cult and calendar, as a heresy. The Church targeted the *conversos* as a class, defined as anyone who had "Jewish blood" irrespective of their religious identity. Starting in 1449 in Castile, Christians were of the belief that intermixing with Jewish blood was defiling the pure blood of Old Christians.[50]

*Expulsion of the Jews from Frankfurt on August 23, 1614. According to the text, "1380 persons old and young were counted at the exit of the gate" and herded onto ships on the river Main.*

In March 1492, just two months after Granada—the last outpost of Moorish population in Spain—was overrun, the Catholic monarchs Ferdinand II and Isabella issued the Alhambra decree, General Edict on the Expulsion of the Jews from Spain. This was the final blow to the spirit of *convivencia*, the spirit of religious tolerance that made Spain under the reign of Alfonso the Wise only a few hundred years before such a unique and culturally and economically prosperous place. The "Catholic Monarchs," as Ferdinand and Isabella were called, now clearly defined Spain by its one religion.

*The Nazis deported the Jews from the Frankfurt area on May 30, 1942 to Majdanek and Sobibór, where they were gassed immediately.*

The rationale in Spain was different from that used elsewhere in Europe, as the Spanish monarchs were motivated to protect the Catholic population from the supposedly corrosive influence of the Jews. The monarchs then decreed,

"We have been informed by the Inquisitors . . . that the mingling of Jews with Christians leads to the worst evils. The Jews try their best to seduce the [New] Christians . . . persuading them to follow the Law of Moses. In consequence, our holy Catholic faith is debased and humbled. We have thus arrived at the conclusion that the only efficacious means to put an end to these evils consists in the definitive breaking of all relations between Jews and Christians, and this can only be obtained by their expulsion from our kingdom."

This was issued in the name of "Their Majesties" and "of the Reverend Prior of the Holy Cross, Inquisitor General" [Torquemada], meaning that the expulsion order was also stamped with the cross.[51]

There were about three hundred thousand Jews in Spain at this time, and about half of them chose to convert rather than be exiled. Ironically, these additional forced conversions made the *converso* problem, which prompted the expulsion on the first place, even worse.

## The Reformation

The Protestant Reformation was a reform movement initiated in 1517 by the German monk and theologian Martin Luther. The movement was an attempt to amend what was perceived to be a corrupt Catholic Church, as well as end false Catholic doctrines and malpractices. It quickly spread, particularly in northern Europe.

The Reformation created a violent reaction from the Catholic Church in the form of the Counter-Reformation. Charles V, King of Spain and Holy Roman Emperor when Luther initiated the Reformation movement, presided at the Diet of Worms in 1521 in which Luther was condemned and then later called the Council of Trent in 1545 to deal with the Reformation. Charles V, grandson of King Ferdinand and Queen Isabella, who had expelled Jews from Spain, was not especially fond of Jews, yet in the context of the Counter-Reformation he felt compelled to protect them. In 1544 he issued a new privilege for Jews that outlawed their expulsion from imperial cities, forbade the obligation to wear distinctive badges or clothing, discouraged the charges of ritual murder and made illegal the closing of synagogues. He also stated that ". . . they shall be allowed to invest and make use of their funds by lending them on interest . . . at much higher rates and greater profit than is permitted to Christians."[52]

All efforts to turn back Protestantism failed, as wars raged and the Council of Trent dragged and failed to produce results. Charles V abdicated in 1556 and entered a monastery where he died two years later.

The consequence of all the political and social turmoil was that the Catholic Church became even more entrenched on the old ideas and felt compelled to establish more uniformity in belief and practice. This also affected the Jews as those who fought heretics internalized the natural consequence of the Iberian expulsion, namely, that the Jews were the source of the corruption. The next logical step was for them to also blame the Jews and Jewish influence for the Reformation. Charles V's son, Philip II, wrote after his accession to the throne that "all the heresies which have occurred in Germany and France have been sown by the descendants of Jews, as we have seen and still see daily in Spain."[53]

## Martin Luther

Martin Luther is a pivotal Christian figure, not only because he was the father of the Protestant movement, but also because as one of history's greatest antisemites he unwittingly contributed to the establishment of the foundation on which Nazi antisemitism was built. Just like Hitler, who constantly invoked him, Luther himself was considered to be a leader by German youth, by scores of monks and nuns who had deserted their monasteries, by spiritually and physically enslaved, proletarianized priests, and by a bourgeois intelligentsia that was yearning for inner freedom.[54]

Luther supported the German princes in the peasant uprising of 1524-1525 against priests and lords, and also against Jews. The peasants felt inspired by Luther's own attack on authority, but now became an out of control liability. The uprising was brutally suppressed. Luther found himself on the side of German rulers fighting not only the Pope, but also the devoutly Catholic Holy Roman

Emperor. At this time Luther's religious aims coincided with the political purpose of the German barons, and at the same time his stature was elevated by the role played by his German translation of the Bible in the birth of German national awareness.

Jews increasingly became the negative other and the recipients of political hatred in Germany, as in the mind of the populace they became associated with the money collected for indulgences through their involvement in finance, and because they were traditionally protected and thus associated with the political enemy, the emperor. As German culture became defined partly through these enmities, the Jews became the embodiment of this enmity.[55]

Luther made a strong effort to convert Jews, but after years of failure he became embittered. He developed an anti-Judaism that was based on his conviction that since Jesus' coming there was no further future for the Jews as Jews. His sermons and writings became increasingly more vitriolic, often expressing things like "The Jews deserve to be hanged on gallows, seven times higher than ordinary thieves" and "We ought to take revenge on the Jews and kill them."[56]

In 1543 he published a book called *On the Jews and Their Lies*. This contained some of his strongest language against Jews, and was used often by antisemites of all stripes all the way to the Nazis:

> "Eject them forever from this country. For, as we have heard, God's anger with them is so intense that gentle mercy will only tend to make them worse and worse, while sharp mercy will reform them but little. Therefore, in any case, away with them! . . . What then shall we Christians do with this damned, rejected race of Jews? First, to set fire to their synagogues and schools. . . Second, I advise that their houses also be razed and destroyed. . . Third, I advise that all their prayer books and Talmudic writings be taken from them. . . Fourth, I advise that their rabbis be forbidden to teach henceforth on pain of loss of life and limb. . . Fifth, I advise that safe-conduct on the highways be abolished completely for the Jews. . . Sixth, I advise that usury be prohibited to them, and that all cash and treasure of silver and gold be taken from them, and put aside for safe-keeping. . . Seventh, I

recommend putting a flail, an ax, a hoe, a spade, a distaff, or a spindle into the hand of young, strong Jews . . . letting them earn their bread in the sweat of their brow. . . [Ultimately] let us apply the same cleverness as the other nations [expulsion]. To sum up, dear princes and nobles who have Jews in your domains, if this advice of mine does not suit you, then find a better one so that you and we may all be free of this insufferable devilish burden—the Jews."[57]

Luther believed the fantastic notion that Jews had control over Christians: "Yes, they hold us Christians captive in our own country. . . . They have captured us and our goods through their accursed usury; mock us and spit on us, because we work and permit them to be lazy squires who own us and our realm; they are therefore our lords, we their servants with our own wealth, sweat and work. Then they curse our Lord, to reward us and to thank us. Should not the devil laugh and dance, if he can have such paradise among us Christians, that he may devour through the Jews—his holy ones—that which is ours, and stuff our mouths and noses as a reward, mocking and cursing God and man for good measure." Luther was not content with Catholicism's ambivalence toward Jews, and this would not be an aspect of politicized Lutheranism. He actually wanted Germany to be *Judenrein* (German for "cleansed of Jews," the expression often used by the Nazis to describe the ultimate goal of the "Final Solution of the Jewish Question"). "They are for us a heavy burden, the calamity of our being; they are like a plague, pestilence, pure misfortune in our country."[58]

Luther is widely considered to have contributed enormously to Nazi ideology on Jews. Heinrich Himmler, chief of the SS, wrote admiringly of his sermons and writings. Julius Streicher, publisher of the notoriously antisemitic newspaper *Der Stürmer*, often quoted Luther and used him as precedent and support for the viciously antisemitic language they themselves used in their paper. Ironically, the newspaper described Luther's *On the Jews and their Lies* as the most radically antisemitic tract ever published.

*An illustration in a book for children depicting an announcement for a talk by Julius Streicher, in which the subject will be: "The Jews are our misfortune!" Under the picture is written: "Those who are fighting against the Jews are struggling with the Devil!"*

The picture of Jews we encounter in Nazi diatribes had been drawn centuries before in the sketch Luther presented. The Nazis, in their time, had little to add to it. Both regarded the Jews as hostile, criminal and parasitic. Thus, Hitler did not need to originate any new propaganda, invent any laws or create a bureaucratic machine as all of that had been developed in Germany for centuries.[59] The Nazis timed the *Kristallnacht* pogrom to be on Luther's birthday, so his request to "set fire to their synagogues" came as a birth-day present to him almost exactly four hundred years later.

Perhaps we can find a synthesis of Luther's thinking in what he said in his last sermon, delivered in Wittenberg on January 17, 1546:

> "Reason must be deluded, blinded, and destroyed. Faith must trample underfoot all reason, sense, and understanding, and whatever it sees must be put out of sight and . . . know nothing but the word of God."

## The Roman Ghetto

After the expulsion of Jews from Spain in 1492, many of them traveled to the Papal territories in Italy, including Rome. When they arrived in Italy they were emaciated. Friars in Genoa welcomed the starving refugees on the docks with bread and crucifixes, offering food in return for conversion. Pope Alexander VI, in the best tradition of papal support for Jews, welcomed them in Rome and pressed the local Jewish community to do so as well. He declared that the Jews in Rome "are permitted to lead their life, free from interference from Christians, to continue in their own rites, to gain wealth, and to enjoy many other privileges." The Jews concentrated in Trastevere, along the Tiber at the foot of Vatican Hill.[60]

In 1555 grand inquisitor Gian Pietro Caraffa was elected as Pope Paul IV. He was an ascetic man with a severe and unbending character, and he immediately had loin-clothes painted on Michelangelo's nudes in the Last Judgment in the Sistine Chapel as well as on Jesus' genitals in a statue at Santa Maria sopra Minerva. Not too long after this he issued the bull *Cum Nimis Absurdum* in which he said:

> "Forasmuch as it is unreasonable and unseemly that the Jews, whom God has condemned to eternal slavery because of their

guilt, should, under the pretense that Christian love cherishes them and endures their dwelling in our midst, show such ingratitude to the Christians as to render them insult for their grace and presume mastery instead of the subjection which beseeches them; and forasmuch as it has come to our notice that in Rome and in other cities their shamefulness is carried so far that they do not only make bold to dwell among Christians, even near their Churches, and without any distinction to their dress, but even rent houses in the distinguished streets and squares of these cities, villages and localities, acquire and possess landed property, keep Christian nurses, maids, and other servants, and do much else that is for a disgrace to the Christian name; therefore do we perceive ourselves constrained to issue the following ordinance."[61]

First and foremost, it mandated the creation of a ghetto, a walled quarter in every city in which all Jews were to live segregated from the Christian community. They were also to have just one synagogue and they were banned from constructing others, and any other ones already built were to be demolished. They could not own any buildings, and any properties they may have already owned, they were forced to sell to Christians.

They were prohibited from having nurses, housekeepers or any other Christian servants. They were prohibited from playing, eating or fraternizing with Christians. They were not allowed to be addressed as superiors even by poor Christians. Physicians among them were prohibited from attending to or taking care of Christians. The latter would continue until the seventeenth century, when the clergy of Würtemberg would still say "it is better to die with Christ than to be cured by a Jew doctor aided by the devil." They were to be recognizable anywhere, thus men were to wear a yellow conical or horned hat and women a yellow shawl or other clearly visible, sewn yellow sign. The conical hat was meant to resemble a horn to further strengthen the association of the Jew with the Devil.[62]

*The Jewish poet Süßkind von Trimberg wearing a yellow Jewish hat (Codex Manesse, 14th century).*

Both the language and the content of this bull are an almost literal antecedent to the anti-Jewish legislation the Germans, Italians and French passed in the 1930s.

Ghettos had existed previously, like in Cologne in 1150, Frankfurt in 1460 and Kazimierz in Kraków, Poland in 1496, immediately after the expelled Jews from Spain started to arrive. The Fourth Lateran Council of 1215 had decreed that Jews were to live in confined quarters, but in no case before were these restrictions articulated and enforced so forcefully, and never before had such language been officially promulgated by a pope.

Pope Paul IV's intent in setting up the Roman Ghetto was probably not to repress, but rather as he intimated in the preface of the bull, it was intended as a temporary measure designed to lead Jews to mass conversion. He had finally and permanently given up on the Augustinian idea that Jews served God's purposes by continuing to live among Christians as degraded "witnesses." Instead, he now proposed the notion that Jews had been allowed to survive to glorify God and the truth of his Church by converting. He believed that by the sheer pain inflicted by life in the squalid conditions of the ghetto, Jews would finally come to recognize the fulfillment of the prophesies of servitude, and because of this recognition, they would finally convert. This conversion would accomplish the completion of salvation history as foretold in Paul's Epistle to the Romans where it is written that the conversion of the Jews will mean "nothing less than a resurrection from the dead!"[63]

Jews were not allowed to rent houses or businesses outside the ghetto unless they had special permission from the Cardinal Vicar; they could not acquire real estate outside the ghetto; higher education was prohibited; the professions of lawyer, druggist, notary, painter and architect were prohibited; a Jewish doctor could not treat Christian patients; and no Jew could hold office. To make things even worse Jews were required to pay taxes like everyone else plus a yearly stipend for the upkeep of the Catholic officials who supervised the ghetto and other special missionary expenses to proselytize Christianity among Jews.[64]

Life inside such a restricted and confined environment, compounded with the limited interaction with the outside world, quickly erode on the physical, emotional and cultural—albeit not religious—lives of the once proud Jewish community, making Ghetto Jews the most degraded people in Europe. Illiteracy, illness, poverty, overcrowding and regular inundations of the foul waters of the Tiber totally devastated the Roman Jews mentally and physically. A cramped population that sometimes exceeded ten thousand was forced to live in such a confined area until the nineteenth century.

*On the left, the gated Jewish ghetto in Rome, circa 1860. Located across the Tiber from the Vatican, it was one of many ghettos established by the Catholic Church to segregate Jews from Christians. This photograph shows the old fish market in via del Portico d'Ottavia, one of the overcrowded ghetto's typically oppressive narrow streets. On the right, the Jewish ghetto in Łódź, Poland, one of many ghettos established by the Germans to segregate Jews from Christians. A sign at the entrance to the ghetto reads: "Jewish residential area. Entrance forbidden."*

The ghetto would continue to exist until the soldiers of the French Republic led by Napoleon invaded Italy and tore down the walls in 1796. At the same time, Napoleon abolished the yellow badge Jews had been forced to wear since the time of the Fourth Lateran Council. In this way, he dramatically showed his authority over the Church. After Napoleon's defeat at Waterloo, however, Pope Pius VII ordered the walls of the ghetto rebuilt. The pattern repeated itself in 1808 and 1816, in 1830 and 1831, in 1848 and 1849.

In thinking about why it was important that the Pope did not speak out in defense of the Jews of Rome when they were deported from there to their deaths in 1943, it must be recalled how those Jews came to be there on the first place. It is important to point out how papal authority was represented by their domination and humiliation of the Jews. This was particularly visible during the throes of the revolutionary convulsions of the nineteenth century in which popes repeatedly celebrated their return to power by rebuilding the ghetto walls, a pattern that would last until 1870 when the Pope lost control of Rome after the secular forces of Italian nationalists took control and finally abolished the ghetto and freed the Jews.[65]

As Bishop Alois Hudal, the head of the German Church in Rome and close friend of Pius XII, lamented in 1937, "The walls of the ghetto had been torn down in the nineteenth century by the liberal state first and not by the Church."

# 3

# Emancipation and the Rise of Modern Antisemitism

## Emancipation

After the French Revolution Jews were emancipated in France. One of the characteristics of the emancipation was that the Jews would enjoy all the benefits and privileges of being a citizen of the state as individuals, but not as a people. However, the notion of Jewish nationhood was rooted in the biblical tradition of kinship. Given that since the time of Emperor Constantine Jews were not allowed to proselytize, their religion could therefore only expand through procreation. The natural consequence of this millennium-long tradition was that over time, and as kinship became a kind of nationhood, the religion became a people.[66]

Jews would subsequently be emancipated in other countries. After Napoleon's fall however, a period of reaction followed in which forces of the old order fought to revert Jews to their previous state of debasement. The Holy Alliance, a group formed by old order forces opposing the new freedoms brought by the French Revolution, fought bitterly against the emancipation of the Jews. After 1815 they prevailed in Germany, Austria and Italy where emancipation collapsed.

In Germany, as well as everywhere else in Europe except for Russia, the religious, political and intellectual revivals of the nineteenth century triggered an exodus from the ghettos. This new-found freedom brought a considerable contribution to science and arts by European Jews. These are some examples, including a number of Nobel Prize winners: Albert Einstein, Heinrich Hertz, Lise Meitner, Niels Bohr (a Dane trained in Germany), Albert Michelson, Georg Cantor, Hermann Minkowski, Sigmund Freud, Alfred Adler, Felix Mendelssohn, Karl Marx, Walther Rathenau and many others. Right up to the beginnings of the Third Reich, the German authors most read outside Germany were Jews, for example Heinrich Heine and Franz Kafka. During the nineteenth and early twentieth centuries, which saw the most fruitful intermingling of German and Jewish culture, Jewish thinkers posed and discussed fundamental intellectual, spiritual and religious problems on a scale that is without parallel anywhere else in the world.[67]

When the walls of the ghettos came down, a flow of Jews came out to integrate with a Christian world not prepared for such an encroachment. During the centuries in which there had been few or no Jews in many areas of Europe, religious instruction and theology had created and instilled in the Christian populace the dangerous image of the devilish Jew, with all the physical characteristics of Satan and of the "Jewish pig," the image of Judas, and of the people who killed Christ.[68]

As Jews had become the most visible beneficiaries of the political, social and cultural revolutions that had taken place since 1789, they were also scapegoated for the negative, or perceived to be negative, consequences of those revolutions. In this way, in the mind of the common people Jews became inextricably associated with revolution, a concept that would be exploited during the Nazi era.

The Church wanted the rescission of the Jews' emancipation, their legal and civic emergence during the nineteenth century from the Church-constructed ghetto. The Germans' eliminationist policies of the 1930s simply reimposed measures first instituted by the Church in the previous few centuries, such as expelling Jews from cities or entire regions, forcing them into squalid, overcrowded ghettos, prohibiting them from holding public office and taking part in all kinds of economic and professional activities.[69]


## Modern Antisemitism

The French philosopher Voltaire was a true product of the Enlightenment. As such, he rejected ancient religious notions that were antithetical to the new order. He denounced the slaughter of Jews as a barbaric act, which was characteristic of figures representative of the Enlightenment. However, as an ex-Christian, his spirit of rational tolerance could only go so far, and he extended it neither to the Jewish religion nor to Jewish people. His hatred of Jews originated on a previous hatred, one that could be traced back through various popes to Saint Augustine, Saint John Chrysostom, Saint Ambrose and all the way to Saint John the Evangelist. This hatred had evolved through centuries of animosity, supersessionism, ignorance and opportunism to the point that, by the time of the Enlightenment, the conception of the Jew in the Christian mind was entirely fantastical. The Middle Ages had produced and bequeathed a larger than life image of the Jew. In this conception, Jews were creatures of the devil whom they worshipped with obscene rites; they presented offerings to demons; they rejected and disrespected the Christian faith and defiled its sacred objects; they were rapacious and greedy; they gathered secretly to plot ways to destroy Christian society; they permanently looked down earthward; they emitted a foul, hellish odor; they adorned their heads with horns and their wives had tails; they commonly wore a goat's beard and in their conventicles they wore a goat's mask; they consumed the flesh and blood of Christian boys in their rituals; they slaughtered Christian children in homage of Satan and they believed that they could prolong their own lives by sacrificing an innocent life.[70]

In Voltaire this was transformed. Since he saw Jews as a fanatical, religious people, and since his goal was to liberate humankind from the grips of irrational, violent religion, it was only natural for him to extend the fight to the Jews, albeit in non-religious terms. His new principle was to hate Jews not because they rejected or killed Christ, but rather because of their innate character. This new principle provided the foundation for Voltaire's and nineteenth century post-Christian antisemitism, a new form that was secular, international and in the name of European culture instead of religion.[71]

Even in France, emancipation only managed to transform antisemitism, not end it. In the nineteenth century, as nationalism became the defining factor in European society, ethnically homogenous societies began to decry the existence of an alien Jewish presence in their midst as the character of antisemitism shifted from religious to racial. In countries where the Jews could be blamed for existing social or political grievances, pseudoscientific theories claiming that the Jewish race was inferior to the so-called Aryan race infused antisemitism with popular support and respectability. Politicians were quick to discover that antisemitism could be used as a powerful political tool.

A similar antisemitism could be traced to Karl Marx, born into an ancient Jewish family in Trier, but baptized in the Lutheran faith. Marx was a strong proponent of the new, secular and anti-religious antisemitism. In the modern world of the nineteenth century, the dichotomy was between the strong anti-Jewish stereotyping Marx so eloquently articulated, and the negative other of "that Jew Marx," in Hitler's phrase.[72] These two opposite and opposing images, already vividly established in the Christian imagination, came to define the modern Jew.

With the emancipation, the Jews in Germany began to rise in society and were able to give their children a higher education in disproportionate numbers to those of the general German middle class, small bourgeoisie and artisan classes. These groups were being overwhelmed by industrialization and were not wealthy enough to provide an education for their offspring. Thus, after just a few decades, the Jewish percentage of lawyers, doctors and other intellectual professions exceeded those of the non-Jewish community. At the same time, Jews became more visible as owners of large stores, high-school teachers and professors. In German society no one dared confront the ruling classes, the big figures in politics, in business and in the church to force them to make changes to improve the people's lives. Instead, they attacked the weakest element in German society, the Jews.[73]

It was not until 1871 that unrestrained and belligerent antisemitism began in Germany, France and Russia. The descendants of those antisemites were to become the butchers of the 1940s.[74] The years between 1874 and 1879 marked the worst European economic crisis of the nineteenth century. This was comparable to the depressions of 1919-24 and 1929-33, which caused the rise of National Socialism. In those periods the Jews became the official "Enemy Number One," a time in which the slogan "The Jews are our misfortune" was coined.[75]

The French believed in national integration of people based on the universal principles of the Enlightenment and the Revolution, whereas in Germany the model of national integration was predicated on the conception of a nation as a closed ethnocultural community. In these models the Jews could become French in France, while despite formal emancipation and equality of civic rights, in Germany the Jews were kept at a distance as they were perceived to belong to a distinct ethnocultural, and increasingly, racial group. The situation in Germany was made worse by the rapid process of modernization that took place in the late nineteenth century, in which the transformation of the country's social structures and the threat to the social hierarchy seemed to endanger the traditional values of the society. Moreover, it seemed to allow the unexplainable social ascent of the Jews who now appeared to be the promoters, carriers and exploiters of that modernization.[76]

The "pope's Jews," that is, the Jews of the Roman Ghetto, were still at this time required to attend sermons intended to convert them. Jewish children were continuously at risk from Church-sanctioned kidnappings and forced baptisms, thus being claimed for Christ. This marked a departure from the racial purity laws that had dominated the Church for centuries and was a return to the old line of thinking that claimed that a religion might be bad, but people as people were not necessarily so. This separated the Church from the virus of racial antisemitism that was by then poisoning Europe, although clearly a root of that racial antisemitism could be traced back to the Inquisition's blood purity idea.

In Germany, a journalist called Wilhelm Marr warned that the Jews were a threat to the superior Aryan race and would take over the world if they could. He coined the term "antisemitism" in 1879 to avoid using the term "anti-Judaism," which had a Christian connotation he wanted to avoid. This putative threat was one of the main axioms of racial antisemitism. The other main feature was the conviction that religious conversion could not alter the identity of a Jew.[77] To Hitler and the Nazis, "Once a Jew, always a Jew."

Beginning with the Enlightenment the old medieval superstitious perception of the Jew transmogrified into a more pernicious and debasing one, as it cloaked itself behind a veneer of modernity which made it more acceptable to more people. Antisemitism gradually became "scientific" and in the process transmuted its lexicon by shedding outmoded medieval notions of sorcery, heresy and satanism. To modern antisemites of all persuasions Jews became Communists, Capitalists or, illogically, both at the same time. Regardless, the aim of the Jews was still perceived to be to subvert Christianity, conquer the world, and enslave its peoples for their own devilish ends.[78]

Hitler clearly managed to grotesquely twist everything that came before him, but there is no question he emerged from the centuries-old teachings about Jews he inherited. When Nazism portrayed Jews as the ontological negative other, it was simply building on a foundation of the European mind firmly based on the teachings of Christianity willing and ready to adapt to the Nazi anti-Jewish ideology. When the Nazis gave free rein to German hate impulses they were only meeting a demand that had been building since 1871. The masses did not ask for antisemitism: they merely wanted to hate. Hitler understood this. He once remarked that if there were no Jews, one would have to invent them.[79]

## Usury

Jews were forced into moneylending during medieval times as that was just about the only thing they were permitted to do. This was because in Christian lands they were barred from owning land and joining guilds. Also, given the constant threat of expulsion and massacre, Jews had to keep their possessions liquid and easily transportable. Rulers quickly realized the fiscal benefit of Jewish moneylending and fostered the practice, as that allowed them to exact a steady stream of taxes.[80]

Moreover, the Church condemned usury, which theoretically prevented Christians from lending money. In reality, this did not prevent many Christians, including prelates, from engaging in the practice. Because of the stigma associated with it, however, many of these Christians encouraged the myth that Jews dominated the money exchange and loan business with the goal of deflecting negative attention away from themselves. And there was plenty of negative reaction to Christian moneylenders. Even when *they* were the ones under attack, Jews still provided the universal standard for odious comparison. The strongest condemnation of a Christian usurer was that he was "worse than Jews." The Church attempted to legislate the practice in the twelfth century and classed it as a crime akin to sorcery, incendiarism, homicide, sacrilege, and fornication. In 1257 Pope Alexander IV issued a bull officially identifying usury with heresy and placed it under the jurisdiction of the Inquisition. From this point on the Inquisition would officially brand Jews as heretics instead of common miscreants and commonly use the formula "Jews shall desist from usury, blasphemy and magic" when dealing with them.

Given the Jewish people's early prominence in the profession of moneylending, after the official identification of usury with heresy the stigma of heresy was associated even more strongly with the Jewish people. In the Christian mind it was clear that the devil's hand was behind all these pernicious activities. In popular medieval tales the devil was presented as an active partner in the Jews' usury. The Council of Paris declared in 1212, by which time the practice of moneylending had been almost entirely taken over by Christian sinners, that "In almost every city, town and village of France the ingrained malice of the devil has firmly established synagogues of usurers and extortionists, commonly called communes; and these diabolical institutions, forbidden by ecclesiastical constitutions, are completely wrecking the ecclesiastical system of jurisdiction."[81]

After the emancipation Christians slanderously claimed that the success Jews had had in the money business was not due to the restrictions and oppression that drove them into that line of work to start with, but rather due to something innate in Judaism. When Karl Marx made this point in his essay *On the Jewish Question*, he was actually reflecting the prevalent view of Jews at the time.

Some Jewish families did indeed become very successful investment bankers, however in the mind of the bigoted and ignorant masses they were perceived as the majority and not the actual minority they really were. At this time the majority of Jews still suffered from the consequences of life in cramped and overcrowded ghettos. As Religion became politics and economics in the nineteenth century, populations living in the conditions imposed by the Industrial Revolution were quick to again make a scapegoat of the Jews by holding them responsible for the economic fate of the entire population. Marx's essay *On the Jewish Question*, when combined with his later writings that promoted the myth of the Jewish financier, were instrumental in establishing the equation between Judaism and exploitative Capitalism. This, like the previous association with revolution, was exploited by Nazi antisemitic propaganda in which Jews were characterized as responsible for both Capitalism and Communism.[82]

### Revolution

Of the many conflicts in nineteenth century Europe, in 1830, 1848 and 1871, in each case Jews were portrayed as responsible regardless of which end of the conflict they were thought to have been part of. The 1871 conflict in Paris solidified the image of the Jew as a revolutionary. The conflict was between a citizen army

joining forces with workers, liberal politicians, so-called bohemi-
ans, intellectuals and others who feared a return of the *ancien régime*, and the victorious Prussians of Otto von Bismark who had
vanquished the forces of Napoleon III in the Franco-Prussian War
of the previous year. These groups were known as the Paris Commune and were declared a revolutionary organization. When the
Commune's uprising was squashed by the regular army, the
Communards engaged in a frenzy of executions and murders. They
especially targeted the Catholic Church and murdered the archbishop of Paris. Karl Marx, at the time living in London, published
a romanticized defense of the Commune that brought him international fame and made him an icon of European revolution. Revolutionaries everywhere now had as their scripture Marx's *Das Kapi-
tal*. To the European monarchists, military, Catholics in general
and clerics in particular, landed gentry, the industrial *nouveau riche*
and much of the middle class, the one thing that stood out about
Marx whom they blamed for much of what they believed was the
intellectual poisoning of the working classes, was that he was "that
Jew."[83]

The phrase typically used to describe the Church's mortal enemies in this time of revolution and turmoil was the triad "Freemasons, Protestants, and Jews."[84] In the popular mind, the former
were perceived to be instruments of the latter. Jewish conspiracies
were at this time at the very top of the conspiratorial hierarchy,
with the clear aim of total domination of the world.[85]

To most Catholics, everyone who despised the Church came to
be represented in the image of the emancipated and resurgent Jew.
The reactionary determination to keep Jews subservient was the
Church's way to confront an age of revolution. After the emancipation, Jews in France were citizens of the state with equal rights. In
their new condition they became prosperous and closely aligned
with the republican spirit. However, defenders of the *ancien régime*,
particularly after the tragic events of Paris in 1871, continued to
regard Jews as emblems of the Revolution and thus held them responsible for the excesses of the Revolution.

## Dreyfus Affair

The highly publicized and notorious "Dreyfus Affair" in late nineteenth century France is important, as it is representative of the extent and consequences of the antisemitic hatred instilled deeply in the minds of French Catholics. Captain Alfred Dreyfus graduated from the elite École de Guerre. He was appointed in 1892 to the army's general staff. After one of his superiors protested his appointment because he was Jewish, the minister of war overruled him by stating that "The army makes no distinction among Jews, Protestants and Catholics, and any such division is a crime against the nation." His appointment stood, but latent hatreds prompted a false accusation that Captain Dreyfus was spying for the Germans. He was arrested and charged for spying in October 1894. The evidence against him was a handwritten letter listing military secrets passed to the Germans. His wife was asked for samples of his handwriting, which she produced, and Dreyfus was brought to trial, convicted (despite the handwriting mismatch) to a life sentence and sent to Devil's Island, the notorious penal colony off the coast of French Guiana. News of the trial and conviction created an explosive anti-Jewish reaction in the press. Dreyfus and his family continued to claim his innocence, while the minister of war now made it a case of honor to uphold the conviction. Most of the population, unable or unwilling to accept the possibility of foul play or that such high-ranking members of the military could have lied, rallied behind the officers. Dreyfus supporters became increasingly more vociferous and were perceived as participants in a conspiracy against the nation. The conflict was now clearly demarcated by fault lines separating right from left, monarchists from republicans, secularists from Catholics, all of which shared a common denominator revolving around the word "Jew."[86]

When an army supporter of Dreyfus found a handwritten document a year and a half later in the hand of a Major Ferdinand Esterhazy matching the handwriting of the document that had convicted Dreyfus, his supporters demanded a new trial. It was denied, but charges were brought against Esterhazy, who was later acquitted. The novelist Emile Zola took up the fight proclaiming

Dreyfus' innocence and published an open letter to the President of France titled "*J'Accuse...!*" (I Accuse) in which he condemned "the odious antisemitism of which the great, liberal, rights-of-man France will die if she is not cured."[87] In this document he also named those ministers and generals that were part of the framing of Dreyfus. This public charge galvanized the population, both in favor and against Dreyfus. After a considerable amount of pressure on the Army, a colonel admitted to having forged supporting evidence and then committed suicide. A new trial took place, but now more than ever the military establishment was determined to protect their honor. Although it had become clear that army officers were covering up what appeared to be a mistake, now France's honor was at stake. When a general population not aware of the details had to choose between the General or the Jew, the choice was simple. Dreyfus was convicted again. The injustice of the conviction was so clear that the president of the French Republic immediately pardoned him. It took seven more years for a civilian court to finally overturn the second conviction, decisively overruling the military.[88]

Jews by then were learning lessons from the Dreyfus Affair. An Austrian Jewish journalist named Theodor Herzl, who wrote about the case, came to the realization that the extreme antisemitism the whole affair had elicited was a clear indication that the goals of emancipation and assimilation were not being met. This took him on a path to establish a national home for the Jewish people, which came to fruition with the founding of the State of Israel in May 1948.

Documents provided by Germany in 1931 finally confirmed that Esterhazy had been the spy, however, the French military was still unwilling to acknowledge that a crime had been committed against the Jewish officer. In 1994, to mark the centenary of Captain Dreyfus' arrest, the French Army finally mustered the strength to state that his "innocence is the thesis now generally accepted by historians," yet they never reversed its two verdicts against him.[89]

*Alfred Dreyfus stripped of rank, January 13, 1895. Henri Meyer (1844-1899).*

The antisemitic frenzy in France was a clear indication that despite the spirit of fraternity and equality of the French Revolution, the latent hatred toward Jews inculcated by hundreds of years of Christian teaching had not disappeared. It also showed that people understood clearly that a war against the Jews could be quite beneficial to those individuals or businesses going through financial trouble. To the French Church, animosity against Jews provided a way to again gather the Christian flock using the tested method of fueling antisemitic sentiments. For some time, Catholic priests all around France attended antisemitic congresses, gave Jew-baiting speeches and inflamed their congregations with incendiary sermons in which they portrayed Jews using the common stereotypes of revolutionaries, financiers, traitors, killers of Christ and ritual murderers of Christian children. The French bishops neither attempted to rein in these priests, nor expressed any protest whatsoever as the injustices of the Dreyfus affair mounted.

In 1896, an article was published in Paris that announced, "How the Dreyfus Affair will end." The author of the article ominously predicted that all the Jews "will be chased from France, disappearing in a cloud of dust and smoke . . . engulfed forever. It is the ruin, the death, the horrible slaughter of a race butchered by the hatred it had created across the centuries." The people who heard these speeches and sermons, or read these articles, became the men who willfully collaborated with the Germans in the roundups and deportation of French Jews to the gas chambers less than half a century later, when this prediction almost became fulfilled.[90]

## Protocols of the Elders of Zion

An unknown author working for the Russian secret police in Paris in 1903 wrote this notorious forgery. It was part of the efforts then underway by the Tsar's secret police to foment antisemitism by presenting the *Protocols of the Elders of Zion* as an authentic text. The document revealed the fabricated protocols of an alleged conference of the leaders of World Jewry in which the Jews conspired to reduce the Gentiles to slavery or extermination. This specter grew out of the myths about well poisoning and plague spreading ever present in the medieval Christian imagination. It was translated into a large number of the world's languages. During the Second World War the Protocols of the Elders of Zion were widely used by Nazi propaganda to implicitly justify the genocide of the Jews. The Nazis relied on the document until the very last days of the Third Reich.

At the same time in the United States, popular radio priest Father Coughlin used the *Protocols* as part of his inflammatory antisemitic radio broadcasts. Henry Ford believed the *Protocols* and published anti-Jewish articles in his rabidly antisemitic weekly newspaper, the *Dearborn Independent* in 1920.

# 4

# Modern Views

## The Pius Popes

### *Pope Pius IX*

Pope Pius IX, known in Italy as Pio Nono, was the nineteenth century father of modern antisemitism. His reign was the longest in history (1846-1878). He began his reign as a liberal pope who ordered that the walls of the Roman ghetto be torn down and the dreaded forced sermons be stopped. However, his relatively good attitude toward Jews was short lived. He excommunicated all the Italian nationalists, including the entire Sardinian House of Savoy, who took control of the streets of Rome after the 1848 revolution and forced the Pope to flee. After he came back from exile and was restored to power by the forces of emperor Louis Napoleon, he was a changed man who scapegoated the Jews and swore enmity to every kind of liberal. Revolutionaries were persecuted, and he promulgated violent regulations against the Jews, including nullifying the Roman Republic's proclamation of civic equality, restoring the old restrictions and imprisoning them again in the Roman Ghetto.

In 1864 he compiled a "Syllabus of Errors," a list of what he perceived to be eighty mistakes of theology, philosophy and politics. This was the Pope's attack against "Modernism," a movement he characterized and condemned as "the synthesis of all heresies."

In this proclamation he denied that "the Roman Pontiff can and ought to reconcile and align himself with progress, liberalism, and modern civilization." Among the other errors he saw in modern times and denounced in this document were belief in freedom of religion, in the separation of Church and state, and in the ending of ecclesiastical control of public schools. Then, regarding the embattled Church he said the war was due to a conspiracy of secret sects, the Masons most notable among them. Fatefully, implicating the Jews as the hidden enemies of the church, he said:

> "It is from them that the synagogue of Satan, which gathers its troops against the Church of Christ, takes its strength" and "These wicked groups think that they have already become masters of the world." They seek nothing less than "to subject the Church of God to the most cruel servitude . . . and, if possible, to make it disappear completely from the earth."

The allusion to the "synagogue of Satan" comes from the New Testament Book of Revelation, where the Jewish places of worship are twice referenced as such.[91] The Pope's mention of it would have a profound influence in the decades to come in the association of Jews and the devil.

Just as the Council of Trent was previously convened to repel the false doctrines of the Reformation, Pope Pius IX convened the First Vatican Council in 1870 as part of his crusade against liberalism and modernism. The object of the First Vatican Council was to strengthen the Pope's position, which was achieved by declaring his infallibility. Just as nationalist movements were defining themselves around strong leaders, the effect of Pius' pronouncements was to establish him as the central figure of a strong Roman Catholic identity. Additionally, they gave credence and support to the ultramontanist movement that looked up to the Pope for support and guidance.[92]

Shortly after Italian forces had freed the Jews of the Roman ghetto in 1871, he declared that by rejecting Christianity Jews had become "dogs" and that "we have today in Rome unfortunately too many of these dogs, and we hear them barking in all the streets, and going around molesting people everywhere."[93]

The rise of Nazism, fascism and other antidemocratic movements in the twentieth century owe a considerable debt to the role Pope Pius IX had in the production of the anti-modern and anti-democratic cultural climate he established in the nineteenth century.

As had happened for a very long time, Christian wet nurses, servants and ruffians roaming the streets of the cities who believed that whoever was responsible for baptizing an infidel gained free passage to Paradise, often surreptitiously baptized Jewish children. As Pope Benedict XIV declared, even if a child was baptized against his or his parent's will, and even if it was done contrary to the procedures of canon law, the child was already a Christian and had to live as one. Once that happened, the Church claimed them as part of their flock and were sent to the House of Catechumens in Rome for forced Christian indoctrination, never to be returned to their rightful Jewish parents.

There was one particular case that would lead to Pius IX's most consequential decision regarding the Jews. In Bologna, a Christian servant had told someone she had secretly baptized the Jewish baby Edgardo Mortara, and that person then denounced the boy. When the Holy Office heard of this, they did the same thing they always did in cases like this: they gave orders to have the police bring the child to the House of Catechumens in Rome. One night in June 1858, the Inquisitor sent the police to take six year old Edgardo from the house of his parents. Pius IX did not stop to think that in 1858, after Jews had already been emancipated in some places, he could no longer do as pontiffs had done since time immemorial, that is, as he pleased. In the past, the Pope knew that an abduction of a Jewish child would only bring protests from the Jews. However, in mid nineteenth century, after the revolutionary liberal movements that brought so much freedom to Europe's oppressed populations, the massive protests in Europe and even in the United States brought about by the Mortara case had been unlike anything the Pope had ever seen. Even the French government (who had restored him to power and was still protecting him) expressed their displeasure. However, even after worldwide protests and after receiving the advice from his own Secretary of State that he was undermining the Vatican's diplomatic position—which was already weak—the Pope refused to return Edgardo Mortara to his parents. Consequently, he was raised in a seminary in Rome and eventually became a priest, never to be returned to his parents.[94]

## Pope Pius XI

Achille Ratti, later to become Pope Pius XI, was an antisemite. Pope Benedict XV had sent him to Poland in 1918 to improve the situation of the Jewish community there, but instead Ratti did everything possible to impede any Vatican action on behalf of the Jews. Rather than alerting the authorities about persecutors of Jews in his reports back to the Vatican, Ratti alerted the Vatican of the dangers posed by the Jews themselves. According to him, Jews in Polish cities "only subsist through small commerce involving contraband, fraud, and usury."[95] He also reported that "one of the most evil and strongest influences that is felt here, perhaps the strongest and most evil, is that of the Jews."

As he confided to Mussolini in 1932, Ratti believed that the Jews were a threat to Christian society and that the persecution of the Church around the world was partly a result of "Judaism's antipathy for Christianity."[96]

He, like his successor Pius XII, was convinced Communism was a mortal enemy of Christianity. He was outspoken about something he perceived as evil and antithetical to the values of Christianity and had no qualms in instructing the faithful not to collaborate with the Communists. After Joseph Stalin's takeover in the Soviet Union, Stalin increased the levels of religious persecution. Pius XI, by then an already staunch opponent of "atheistic Bolshevism," strongly denounced Stalin's actions by referring to them as "a page of history dark with persecution and atrocities inconceivable in the twentieth century." He also expressed "horror and emotion over the acts of persecution and sacrilege that were being perpetrated in Russia," protesting at "the ill treatment and imprisonment of the Catholic clergy." Two weeks before issuing the encyclical (a papal letter sent to all bishops) *Mit brennender Sorge* (German for "With burning concern"), he issued another encyclical called *Divini Redemptoris* in which he declared that Communism "is intrinsically wrong and no one who would save Christian civilization may collaborate with it in any field whatsoever."[97]

Pope Pius XI signed the *Reichskonkordat,* a diplomatic agreement between the Vatican and Nazi Germany, thus making the Vatican the first foreign power to formally acknowledge the Third Reich. This agreement, intended to protect the Church's interests in Germany, was ultimately only beneficial to Hitler (see section on the *Reichskonkordat* for more information).

Despite the prevalent antisemitism so entrenched among their coreligionists, a few righteous Dutch Catholics formed the Society of the Friends of Israel in 1928 in Rome. The group had among its aims to expose the blood libel as an "incredible myth," the abandonment of talk of a curse to the Jews and to discontinue the charge of deicide. The Vatican suppressed it in the same year since according to them "words and deeds have begun to intrude into the Society of the Friends of Israel which deviate from the concepts of the church, the spirit of the holy fathers and the sacred liturgy" and their program did not recognize "the continual blindness of this people." As Pius XI said in a 1937 encyclical, "Jesus received his human nature from a people who crucified him." The fact that the same Pope suppressed the "Friends of Israel" Catholic organization is significant because it means that on the eve of Hitler's rise to power the Vatican forbade any theological or journalistic campaign against antisemitism.[98]

## Pope Pius XII

Vatican Secretary of State Cardinal Eugenio Pacelli had the misfortune to be the pope reigning over the Catholic Church during the darkest period in human history, the Second World War.

In the middle of the conflict he wrote to Bishop Preysing stating that his pontificate was the most difficult of modern times, and he was right. No other pope had to deal with the simultaneous calamities of Communism, world war and genocide. It is unfortunate and lamentable that his priority was with confronting the danger of Communism instead of preventing or at least hindering the extermination of the Jews.[99]

As Pope, he had three official positions. He was head of his church and was in direct communication with bishops everywhere. He was chief of state of the Vatican, with his own diplomatic corps. He was also the Bishop of Rome. In theory, at least, his views could influence four hundred million Catholics, including those in all the occupied eastern territories—the Poles, the peoples of the Baltics, Ukrainians, Croatians, Slovaks, Hungarians and others.

At a time of increased antisemitism in Hungary and when their first antisemitic laws were being passed, he departed from his predecessor's late opposition to racism and antisemitism. When he addressed the International Eucharistic Congress held in Budapest in 1938 he mentioned the Jews, "whose lips," according to him, "curse [Christ] and whose hearts reject him even today."[100]

Also unlike his predecessor, who saw Nazism as the greatest threat to Christianity, Pius XII believed that in reality Communism posed that threat. One of his first actions as a pope was to lift the ban on the fiercely anti-Communist and rabidly antisemitic French movement Action Française. By doing so he initiated a policy that manifested itself a number of times during his reign in which he was willing to sacrifice the lives of Jews if that meant advancing the fight against Communism.[101] Even after the evil nature of Nazism became clear Pius XII continued to conceive of it as not only the lesser of two evils but a bulwark against the greater one. Ultimately, as reported to Berlin by the German ambassador to the Vatican, von Weizsäcker, "Pius XII had friendly feelings for the Reich. He had no more ardent wish for the Führer than to see him gain a victory over Bolshevism." Because of this any time he had to make criticisms of Germany he felt he had to do it in a cautious and negotiatory way.[102]

Immediately after Pacelli became pope, he told Vatican officials that "to me the German question is the most important; I will reserve handling it to myself." He added, "Naturally I will follow German matters closer than all others." To ensure continuity of his previous work as nuncio (that is, papal ambassador) in Germany and Secretary of State, Pius XII chose Eugenio Orsenigo as his own nuncio in Berlin. Orsenigo was a pro-German, pro-Nazi, antisemitic fascist so Pacelli knew he would feel right at home with the Nazi regime in Berlin.[103]

*Archbishop Cesare Orsenigo, the papal nuncio in Berlin, with Hitler in 1935.*

The Pope was a germanophile, and he may have been concerned about the perception people may have had regarding the extent of that fondness. In a passage of Monsignor Angelo Roncalli's diary concerning an audience with Pius XII of October 10, 1941, Roncalli wrote that the Pope "Continued to tell me of his generosity toward the Germans who visit him. He asked me if his silence regarding Nazism was not judged badly."[104] He manifested an obsessive preoccupation with Germany during and after the war. The evidence for this is compelling. The German and French ambassadors to the Vatican, the Italian cardinal Filippo Bernardini, and the American papal nuncio consistently perceived the Pope's fixation with all things German. He surrounded himself with Germans as his personal and closest advisers and confidants, such as Monsignor Ludwig Kaas, Robert Leiber, S.J., Sister Pasqualina Lehnert and Augustin Bea as his confessor.

Pius XII never put *Mein Kampf* in the *Index of Forbidden Books*, where Pope Paul IV had put the Talmud in 1555. The Vatican did find Nazi philosopher Alfred Rosenberg's ideological *Myth of the Twentieth Century* objectionable enough to warrant inclusion in the *Index*, though, showing that even then the Church could do that if it wanted.

In response to Hitler's congratulatory letter when he became pope, Pius XII wrote:

> "At the beginning of Our pontificate we wish to assure you that We remain devoted in our hearts to the German people entrusted to your care, in a spirit of fatherly love for the same, We beseech from Almighty God that true good which draws nourishment from religion. . . . We cherish the hope that Our ardent wish, closely bound up as it is with the welfare of the German people and the sure growth of order of every kind, may with God's help find fulfillment. In the meantime We shall pray for the protection of Heaven and the blessing of the Almighty God for you and all members of your nation."

This was written at a time when the world was on the brink of war and after years of intense persecution of the Jews of Austria and Germany.[105]

When Berlin's Bishop Preysing pressured the Pope to speak out against the murder of the Jews, the Pope replied that to him the most pressing issue was maintaining the Church's unity and the trust of Catholics on either side of the conflict. He also wrote to Preysing that he felt he had to do whatever was necessary, including sacrificing his moral standing, to maintain the safety of Rome. For the Pope the lives of millions of Jewish men, women and children were less important than the "priceless treasures" in the Vatican and what they represented to millions of Catholics around the world. Sir Francis D'Arcy Osborne, the British Ambassador to the Vatican, wrote: "I am revolted by Hitler's massacre of the Jewish race on the one hand and, on the other, the Vatican's apparently exclusive preoccupation . . . with the possibilities of the bombardment of Rome."[106]

Even after the war, Pius XII took steps that were inimical to the surviving Jews and to the memory of those who had been exterminated. He had ample opportunity to address the issue of Christian-Jewish relations, yet he chose to not only ignore the issue of antisemitism, but he also disapproved of Catholic efforts to reconcile with Jews. Not content with seeking clemency and amnesty for convicted war criminals, he allowed organizations affiliated with the Vatican to provide shelter and aid and abet the escape of fugitive war criminals.

The fight against Communism and with ensuring that the Concordat he had signed with Germany in 1933 was upheld at all costs dictated his priorities. When the British and Americans expressed objections to the Concordat, the Pope instructed his envoy to disregard their objections, eventually succeeding in having the occupational authorities recognize it. At the end of the war, the Pope was more absorbed by minute diplomatic and contractual issues than with antisemitism or restitution.

## The Secular Racial Aspect

As we have seen, antisemitism evolved from its theological origins to a contemporary, secular form that was grounded on the notion that Jews where inferior owing to their racial constitution. This transformation served the purpose of allowing the peoples of Europe, who chose to no longer hate based on the teachings of the

Church, to continue to find and hate a scapegoat. These modern bigots, brought up on beliefs like those of Pope Benedict VIII who, blaming Jews for a hurricane and an earthquake had them executed in 1021, could now justify and rationally explain modern problems like social and economic upheavals and revolution using what they perceived to be enlightened, pseudoscientific language.[107]

When Hitler arrived on the political scene in Germany after the terrible defeat in the Great War and the devastating economic collapse of Germany that ensued, he found the minds of ordinary Germans suitably prepared to accept a message that explained Germany's defeat and many other problems by blaming the Jews. He managed to do this because these Germans had heard from their parents, teachers and priests that the Jews were evil and were responsible for everything that was loathsome. The common folk had been brought up hearing stories of how Jews were the enemies of Christianity, had killed Christ, poisoned wells, were responsible for the plague, murdered Christian boys to use their blood in Jewish rituals, and a myriad of other baseless accusations that through persistent repetition across time had become ingrained in the cultural makeup of society. After the Enlightenment it was natural for this society to transform these fantastic notions into those things they saw as detrimental to their well-being and could then relate to: revolution, Socialism, Communism, Capitalism, massive social class conflicts, and war. Hitler's predecessors exploited old hatreds with uncanny ability, building on the ancient theologically based aversion and transforming it into something new in which the Jew continued to be responsible for the world's problems, but now it was because their biological constitution made them that way.

The relentless propaganda portraying Jews as a microbial infection of the societies they lived in or as vermin that had to be exterminated eventually dehumanized the Jew, transforming him into a phantasmagoric image in the modern German's mind. This became worse after the pogroms in the Pale of Settlement in Russia drove many eastern Jews into Germany. As opposed to most assimilated German Jews who were undistinguishable from their Christian German neighbors, these eastern European Jews dressed differently, wore long beards and strange hats, and spoke Yiddish. The Jew became totally anathema to the new German sense of æsthetics and incompatible with the Nazi dream of a newly "beautified" Europe. The Germans who built and operated the gas chambers in the death camps did not necessarily think of them as tools for mass murder, any more than a pest control technician feels the poison he uses to eliminate a rat or termite infestation is a tool for murder. To most of those Germans, the gas chambers were simply anthropological sanitation facilities. An ordinary German, a member of a police battalion during the Second World War, summarized his beliefs about the Jews—and those of his comrades: "The Jew was not acknowledged by us to be a human being."[108]

## Hitler's Religious Outlook and Views on the Church

Adolf Hitler was born and raised as a Catholic but soon became an atheist who did not believe in God, although he did believe in the Devil. Hitler, like most Christians, believed that many evils like leprosy, hunger, pestilence and war were the handiwork of the Devil, who had many helpers in this world, including sorcerers and Jews. As a young man he went to school for two years in the monastery at Lambach, where he declared he wanted to become an abbot. Later he recalled, when thinking of the splendors of the church festivals: "It was only natural that the office of the abbot should seem to me to be an ideal infinitely worth striving for."[109]

By the time he began his political career he realized the importance of projecting an image of religiosity, as expressed in *Mein Kampf:* "I believe today that my conduct is in accordance with the will of the Almighty Creator", "What we have to fight for . . . is the freedom and independence of the fatherland, so that our people may be enabled to fulfill the mission assigned to it by the Creator" and "This human world of ours would be inconceivable without the practical existence of a religious belief."[110] Even in his public speeches he made a point to establish a providential connection between him, his work, and God, as well as remark on the religious support for his fight against the Jews. In a speech delivered to the German *Reichstag* (parliament) in 1936 he said, "I believe today that I am acting in the sense of the Almighty Creator. By warding off the Jews, I am fighting for the Lord's work." The understanding that Hitler was on a divine mission was generalized. As Hermann Göring said in distinctly Christian terms, "God gave the savior to the German people. We have faith, deep and unshakeable faith, that he [Hitler] was sent to us by God to save Germany." Hitler himself admitted having been influenced by Karl Lueger, the leader of the Vatican-supported antisemitic Christian Social movement of Austria where he was born and brought up.

*Hitler in front of the "Church of our Lady" in Nuremberg, September 1934, and praying at the end of a rally in Vienna.*

Hitler understood that to conquer the German masses he would have to appear not only religious, but also friendly to the Churches. In public he cynically declared that the churches were to be an integral part of German life, however in private he vowed to "eradicate" Christianity from Germany: "You are either a Christian or a German. You cannot be both."[111]

*Hitler leaves the Marine Church in Wilhelmshaven.*

Hitler was well aware of the Church's long anti-Jewish record. In a meeting with Bishop Berning and Monsignor Steinmann in April 1933 he complained,

"I have been attacked because of my handling of the Jewish question. The Catholic Church considered the Jews pestilent for fifteen hundred years, put them into ghettos, etc., because it recognized the Jews for what they were. In the epoch of liberalism the danger was no longer recognized. I am moving back toward the time in which a fifteen-hundred-year-long tradition was implemented. I do not set race over religion, but I recognize the representatives of this race as pestilent for the state and for the church and perhaps I am thereby doing Christianity a great service for pushing them out of schools and public functions."

The protocol of the conversation does not record any response from Bishop Berning.[112]

Hitler despised the Catholic Church as a religious institution, but greatly admired it for its longevity, resilience and organization:

"The Catholic Church is indeed a great institution. What organization! It has survived for two thousand years, and we must learn from it. . . . The Church did not content itself with the image of Satan; it felt the need to translate that image into a tangible enemy . . . the Jew . . . it is easier to fight him as flesh and blood that as an invisible demon."[113]

We can see here an often-used parallel between the teachings of Christianity and his antisemitic agenda. As always, Hitler spoke to his listeners in language that was already familiar to them, and resonated with teachings they had already internalized. Hitler was highly indebted to the historic Catholic Church for the model it provided him to tame and subjugate the simpleminded masses.

On the other hand, Hitler had very little respect for Protestant clergy: "They are insignificant little people, submissive as dogs, and they sweat with embarrassment when you talk to them."[114]

The *Deutsche Christen* (German Christians) were a group of Protestant Christians who made a strong effort to find a common ground between Nazism and Christianity. To them Hitler represented much more than a political leader: "In the person of the *Führer* we behold the One sent from God, who places Germany in the presence of the Lord of History . . ."[115] Indeed, as George Orwell wrote, "A totalitarian state is in effect a theocracy, and its ruling caste, in order to keep its position, has to be thought of as infallible."[116]

*Long live Germany! German propaganda poster from the 1930s portraying Hitler in religious imagery ordinary Germans could relate to and understand. Mirroring the dove that descended on Christ when John the Baptist baptized him, what appears to be an eagle hovers against the light of heaven over a messianic Hitler.*

Hitler often referred to the *Protocols of the Elders of Zion*, even though he knew it was at odds with the truth, because to him "the inner truth inherent in it is more persuasive." To Hitler, the veracity of the claims in the book and whether the text corresponded to historical truth were immaterial. To him, as well as to all other revilers of the Jews and Judaism, the prime factor was not the truth of their claims, but rather their goal of vilifying the Jews.[117]

## Vatican Position on Zionism and the Holy Land

After the Dreyfus Affair, Austrian journalist Theodor Herzl came to the realization that harmonious coexistence between European Christians and Jews may not be possible. He began the Zionist movement, intended to provide a homeland for the Jewish people in which they would be safe from persecution. He worked assiduously toward this goal, and that included asking the Catholic Church for help. In 1904 he met with the Vatican Secretary of State, Cardinal Merry del Val, who told Herzl:

> "I do not quite see how we can take any initiative in this matter. As long as the Jews deny the divinity of Christ, we certainly cannot make a declaration in their favor. Not that we have any ill will toward them . . . The history of Israel is our own heritage, it is our own foundation. But in order for us to come out for the Jewish people in the way you desire, they would first have to be converted."

He then met with Pope Pius X, who did not recognize the right of the Jews to exist as Jews: "The Jews have not recognized our Lord, therefore we cannot recognize the Jewish people . . . The Jewish religion was the foundation of our own; but it was superseded by the teachings of Christ, and we cannot concede it any further validity."[118]

The Vatican was generally opposed to Jewish emigration to Palestine before and during the Second World War, as an internal Vatican note written by Undersecretary of State Tardini reveals: "The Holy See has never approved of the project of making Palestine a Jewish home . . . [because] Palestine is by now holier for Catholics than for Jews."[119] Even at the height of the exterminatory campaign in May 1943, when Palestine was one of the last places where persecuted Jews could escape to, Cardinal Secretary of State Maglione said in opposition to the possibility of establishing a Jewish homeland in Palestine that Catholics had a right to the holy places, and that their "religious feelings would be injured and they would justly feel for their rights if Palestine belonged exclusively to the Jews." Maglione's words may have been worse than any of Pius XII's "silences," as they represented the official position of the Vatican.[120] This line of thinking stemmed directly from traditional church teaching. As Cardinal Johannes Willebrands said, because Jews as a people were guilty of Christ's death they had been condemned "to eternal pilgrimage across the world outside the land of Israel."[121]

The Vatican refused to recognize the right of the Jewish people to have their own Jewish state even after the war ended, the extent of the genocide became public knowledge, and Europe was filled with emaciated, homeless and stateless Jewish survivors. In May 1948, after the State of Israel had been declared, *L'Osservatore Romano* published an article opposing the formation of the secular, Jewish State of Israel: "Modern Israel is not the true heir of Biblical Israel, but a secular state . . . Therefore the Holy Land and its sacred sites belong to Christianity, the True Israel." Cardinal Tisserant advised Pope Pius to seek a compromise with the Israelis, but the Pope did not budge. The Vatican was the first state to recognize the Federal Republic of Germany and one of the last to recognize Israel. A high Vatican official is reputed to have said at the time of the founding of the state that "it is unthinkable that the Holy Land finds itself in the hands of Christ's murderers."[122] The same Church that gave legitimacy to Hitler's Germany by signing the Concordat was unable and unwilling to recognize the legitimacy of the country that was to become the home to the survivors of Europe's devastated Jewish communities. The Church's nefarious offenses leading up to the Final Solution and during the mass murder itself did not reduce the Church's supersessionistic attitude toward Jews after the war.[123]

# Part II:
# Christian Antisemitism

*"Know, my dear Christian, and do not doubt that next to the devil you have no enemy more cruel, more venomous and virulent than a true Jew."*

*Martin Luther*

# 5

# Christian Attitudes Toward Jews

## Background

The early Church felt the need to differentiate itself from Jews, triumph over them and sustain, doctrinally and psychologically, its claim to be the true bearer of Jewish tradition and the only path to salvation. To distance itself from Jews and Judaism, the early Church changed the historical record presented orally in their proselytizing efforts as well as in texts that would later become part of the official church canon. As expressed by the American Catholic Bishops after World War II, "after the Church had distanced itself from Judaism, it tended to telescope the long historical process whereby the gospels were set down some generations after Jesus' death. Thus, certain controversies that may actually have taken place between church leaders and rabbis toward the end of the first century were 'read back' into the life of Jesus."[124]

Early Christians also felt the need to show the Romans they were different from the then rebellious Jews as well as to court Rome by minimizing or removing their role in the crucifixion. When Matthew has the Jewish crowd cry, "His blood be on us and on our children!" (Matt. 27:25), he is submitting to the requirements of theology and acting with political opportunism in mind. Instead of telling us anything about the events of the day of Jesus' execution, the cry says much about how the crucifixion became a symbol filled with ulterior meaning to the evangelist in the context of the late first century. In a straightforward exegesis of the verse, Origen (one of the most distinguished of the early fathers of the Christian Church) wrote in the third century that the Jews, who had persecuted and killed the prophets of Israel, also persecuted and killed Jesus and therefore "Guilt for the blood of Jesus fell not only on those who lived then, but also on all subsequent generations of Jews, until the end of the world." Two centuries later, Church Father St. Jerome crystallized the views of the Church Fathers when he said, "The curse has been fulfilled in their eternal damnation."[125]

Christian antisemitism was exceptionally well directed and organized toward the end of rendering the Jews hateful. It achieved this in an official, systematic and unified way, which was fed by theology and borrowed her arguments for what amounted to a long indictment of the Jewish people. The French historian Jules Isaac called this teaching, made up of deep-seated prejudices and of the most odious habits of mind, heart and tongue, the "Teaching of Contempt." This evolved into a need to think ill of the Jews, to hate them and to derive meaning from this emotional stance. Moreover, Christianity adopted the ontological conception of the Jews as standing in opposition to the Christian defined moral order, which led to a strong anti-Jewish feeling. From that point it was a short step to the belief that the Jews were capable of all heinous acts which, over time, inspired intensive persecutions and mass murders.[126]

For a long time the Synagogue continued to exert a powerful attraction not only over the pagans, but also over a large group of Christian converts still prone to "Judaizing," that is, observing the Jewish Law. This compelled Christians to attempt to discredit Jews and Judaism by embarking on a campaign to destroy their prestige. This is already noticeable in many passages of the canonical Gospels and it became even more obvious in the apocryphal Gospels. The drive to stigmatize Judaism reached its height with the Church

Fathers of the fourth century, whose writings provide the foundation upon which Christianity (as we understand it today) stands.[127]

*Ecclesia (Church) and Synagoga (Synagogue), column figures, Notre Dame de Paris Cathedral. These common allegorical figures from the Middle Ages represented the replacement of the Synagogue by the Church. The Church typically wears a crown, carries a cross and holds a chalice, representing the Redeemer's blood. The superseded Synagogue is always a blindfolded figure, the blindfold representing spiritual blindness and ignorance, and often its crown is falling from its inclined head, its staff is broken and the upside down Tablets of the Law are falling from her hand.*

## The Church Fathers

One of the most important of these Church Fathers was Saint Ambrose, the vociferous bishop of Milan, who in 374 CE said,

"The Jews are the most worthless of all men. They are lecherous, greedy, rapacious. They are perfidious murderers of Christ. They worship the Devil. Their religion is a sickness. The Jews are the odious assassins of Christ and for killing God there is no expiation possible, no indulgence or pardon. Christians may never cease vengeance, and the Jew must live in servitude forever. God always hated the Jews. It is essential that all Christians hate them."

St. Ambrose was called the Bishop with the Golden Tongue. He offered to burn the synagogue himself, but he did not have to, as his sermons were incendiary enough to incense the faithful to violent reaction against Jews and their property.[128]

Just a few years later, in 386 CE, the bishop of Antioch, Saint John Chrysostom, showed himself capable of spewing even greater venom. His teachings would become part of the standard Christian anti-Jewish rhetoric, consigning the Jews to live in a Christian Europe that condemned, feared and despised them: "Where Christ-killers gather, the cross is ridiculed, God blasphemed, the father unacknowledged, the son insulted, the grace of the Spirit rejected. . . . If the Jewish rites are holy and venerable, our way of life must be false. But if our way is true, as indeed it is, theirs is fraudulent. I am not speaking of the Scriptures. Far from it! For they lead one to Christ. I am speaking of their present impiety and madness." Here he presents a clear Manichean view that if Christians are right, then Jews must be wrong.[129] In a different sermon he said, again attempting to curb the appeal Judaism still held among God-fearers and recent converts,

"I know that many people hold a high regard for the Jew, and consider their way of life worthy of respect at the present time.

This is why I am hurrying to pull up this fatal notion by the roots. . . A place where a whore stands on display is a whorehouse. What is more, the synagogue is not only a whorehouse and a theater; it is also a den of thieves and a haunt of wild animals. . . No better disposed than pigs or goats, [the Jews] live by the rules of debauchery and inordinate gluttony. Only one thing they understand; to gorge themselves and get drunk."

Ominously, he continued, "When animals have been fattened by having all they want to eat, they get stubborn and hard to manage. . . . When animals are unfit for work, they are marked for slaughter, and this is the very thing which the Jews have experienced. By making themselves unfit for work, they have become ready for slaughter. This is why Christ said, 'As for my enemies, who did not want to reign over them, bring them here and slay them before me.'"

Shortly after these sermons were delivered there were violent outbursts against Jews in Antioch, with its great synagogue demolished.[130]

Perhaps the most influential of the Church Fathers was Saint Augustine. His theological legacy molded Christian thinking for centuries, and this includes his attitude, and therefore Christianity's attitude, toward Jews. Augustine believed the basic Christian principle that the Hebrew Bible "foretold" Jesus and thus served as a source for authentication for the prophecy-based claims of Christianity. The destruction of the Jerusalem Temple in 70 CE and the further dispersion of the Jews of Judea strengthened this belief. The reliance on venerable Hebrew texts also provided Christianity with an apparent ancient character and legitimacy, and therefore he believed it was important to preserve Judaism since Jews still had a role in the salvific plan of God. As he wrote in *The City of God,* "Do not slay them, lest at some time they forget your Law." To Augustine the Jews were to survive to be "as witnesses to the prophecies which were given beforehand concerning Christ." They were to be allowed to survive, but never to thrive; their 'backs' were to be 'bent down always.' Their refusal to acknowledge the veracity of the Church's claims meant they had to be punished, and their homelessness and misery were perceived to be not only the proper retribution, but also another proof of the Church's claims.[131]

Augustine's "Let them survive, but not thrive" underlies the destructive ambivalence that marked Catholic attitudes toward Jews. Many times bishops and popes attempted to protect Jews from expressly Christian mobs that wanted to kill them. Those gangs were incensed by what the same or previous bishops and popes had taught about Jews. This ambivalent policy failed at every juncture in history in which Jews began to thrive economically, culturally, or both. Ultimately, as history shows, such double-edged ambiguity is not sustainable and leads to terrible consequences.[132]

All this made Jews unwilling partners in a theological dialectic in which they played the role of "witness people," in essence reaffirming their tradition of faithfulness to the God of Israel. After Augustine, this shifted to being witness to their own degradation, which in the Christian mind was "proof" of their claims, as Jews denied those claims. Christians expected to receive the opposite of this degradation, that is, salvation, by affirming those claims. Being witness to the Jews' evident punishment further strengthened their expectation. In order for this to be sustained, three things needed to happen. First, as Jews could not be allowed to thrive, they had to live in a state of perpetual punishment and debasement. Second, to prevent their disappearance, the punishment could not be too excessive and, third, popes were compelled to protect the Jews' place within the Christian community to enable each new generation of Christians to benefit from their witness. This was particularly important considering the will and repeated attempt by the Christian masses to kill or expel Jews, both of which violated this system.[133]

The papal bull *Sicut Judaeis* was issued by Pope Callixtus II around 1120 after the First Crusade (and reissued by more than twenty popes during the subsequent four centuries) to defend Jews: he offered Jews "the shield of our protection. We decree," he said,

"that no Christian shall use violence to force them [Jews] into baptism." Despite this defense in the Church's credit, based on
Augustine's previous defense, the cognitive dissonance would prove
too much for most of the Christian population who could not
handle extreme theological derision on the one hand and a request
to respect those held in contempt on the other hand. Thus we see
bishops, popes and kings who would usually attempt to protect
Jews while the lower clergy, townspeople and peasants would usually act violently toward them. As Saint Bernard de Clairvaux, the
main preacher of the Second Crusade said, "The Jews are not to be
persecuted, killed or even put to flight." However, when explaining
why by using Augustine's arguments, he again created the same
sense of ambivalence that led to the violence he intended to curtail:
"The Jews are for us the living words of scripture, for they remind
us always of what our Lord suffered. They are dispersed all over the
world so that by expiating their crime they may be everywhere the
living witnesses of our redemption. Hence the same Psalm [59]
adds, 'only let thy power disperse them' . . . If the Jews are utterly
wiped out, what will become of our hope for the promised salvation, their eventual conversion?" Ultimately, what could be expected from the uneducated mob who heard him preach in a sermon: "While we pray for the Jews, they persecute and curse us"?[134]

During the middle ages clerics believed that if Christianity was
the one true faith and its followers the new Israel, then Judaism
had to be discredited in the eyes of the faithful. As they believed
that Jews threatened the moral order of the Christian world, they
portrayed the Jews as adversaries of the Church in sermons, religious literature, art and plays.[135]

Anti-Jewish hatred reached such a peak during the second half
of the fourteenth century that we can date to this period the establishment of antisemitism in its classic form, the form that later led
the Catholic theologian Erasmus to observe: "If it is the part of a
good Christian to detest the Jews, then we are all good Christians."[136] There is no clearer example of the intensity of this hatred
than the medieval attribution of the crime of bestiality to any

Christian who cohabited or married a Jew. In 1222 in Oxford, a deacon who had converted to Judaism to marry a Jewess was burned at the stake on the charge of bestiality after standing trial in front of the archbishop.[137]

*The Church's supersessionism as depicted in a glass window in the church of Werben, Germany, showing the Church as having replaced the Synagogue: the Church is portrayed as a king riding a lion, while the superseded Synagogue is a blindfolded woman, her staff broken, and the crown sliding off her head.*

In Rome, at the heart of Catholicism, the practice of forcing the Jews to run through jeering crowds during Carnival began in 1468. They ran from the Arch of Domitian to the church of St.

Mark at the end of the Corso (known as Via Lata in sixteenth century Rome). On its opening day eight Jews clothed only in loin clothes were forced to pronounce a declaration of self-contempt. Then, the Conservators and Senators in the Capitol (Roman administrators) placed their foot on the forehead of a kneeling Jew and replied, "Go! For this year we tolerate you," and gave the lead person among the Jews a kick in the behind and then they were made to race along the Via Lata where Christian spectators would jeer and throw anything they could get their hands on at them. The racers were often killed and rabbis were forced to follow them simply to listen to the crowd, and then kiss a statue of a pig at the end of the Corso. The races continued for two hundred years until Pope Clement IX accepted money from the Jewish community in place of its participation.

## Association with the Devil

Also in medieval times the perception of the Jew shifted, as Jews became associated with the Devil in the Christian mind. This occurred as the image of the blind, ignorant Jew conceived by Augustine, Abelard, Anselm and others was gradually replaced by that of modern Talmudic Jews who chose not to believe in Jesus, refused to recognize in him the messiah, recognized him for who he was and chose to kill him for that reason. As Augustine wrote, "They beheld the blatant signs of his divinity, but they corrupted them out of hatred and jealousy of Christ; and they wished not to believe his words, by which he proclaimed himself to be the Son of God."

Medieval Christian thinkers began asking themselves what kind of rational creature would deliberately reject the truth and kill God. They concluded that only someone who was an irrational and inhuman agent of Satan could act that way. This made the deliberate Jewish Christ-killer even more detested, inhuman, grotesque and demonic.[138] As Peter the Venerable, abbot of the Benedictine abbey of Cluny said, "Really I doubt whether a Jew can be human for he will neither yield to human reasoning, nor find satisfaction in authoritative utterances, alike divine and Jewish." In the medieval Christian mind, Jews were conceived of as inhuman demonic creatures that used Satan's weapons to fight the forces of truth and salvation. We must remember that to the medieval Christian, Satan was a very real character, as real on one end of the moral scale as Christ was on the other. He was the archenemy of mankind, bent on destroying it. Even the Jews' inability to understand and accept the Christian message in the Christian Bible was attributed to "the spite of the devil, who puts such absurd nonsense into men's minds."

It becomes easier to understand how the masses as well as their intellectual and spiritual mentors could believe the vilest charges against Jews and rise repeatedly and violently against them when one realizes how often and insistently the charge of satanic nature and allegiance was ascribed to the Jews. This was reflected at all levels, from the pulpit all the way to everyday use. Art reflected the prevalent conception, as Shakespeare wrote in *The Merchant of Venice*: "Let me say 'Amen' betimes lest the devil cross my prayer, for here he comes in the likeness of a Jew" and, summarizing, "Certainly the Jew is the very devil incarnal." Even if sometimes this charge was used as vituperation, there is no doubt that its use—whether as mockery or abuse—left a lasting impression on the suggestible mind of the masses who saw the Jew as a murderer, sorcerer, poisoner, cannibal, blasphemer, and the devil's disciple.[139]

In the Middle Ages most Christians subscribed to the conviction that the Jews worked together with the devil. This explains how it was possible to accept *a priori* every accusation against Jews, regardless of how outrageous it was. They were believed to be as likely to desecrate a church's sacred images in front of a large and hostile audience, to refuse the veracity of Christian miracles, or to publicly express contempt for Christian beliefs, as to despoil the host, murder Christian boys to use their blood in their rituals, spread poison with the wind, and practice depraved sexual acts. These, and many other varied and unreasonable accusations made sense to a medieval mind who understood and accepted as self evident that the nature of the Jews was evil and depraved since they were agents of Satan.[140]

*On the left panel is a detail from an 18th-century engraving showing the antisemitic painting on the Old Bridge Tower of Frankfurt am Main dating to 1475, portraying the Devil wearing a Jewish badge. By the time of the Second World War the association of the Jews and the devil had been taught in the Christian world for many centuries. On the right, the February 1943 edition of* Der Stürmer. *The caption to the photograph of the stereotypical Eastern European Jew reads "Satan." At the bottom of the page is the ubiquitous Nazi slogan, "The Jews are our misfortune," echoing Martin Luther's "[The Jews] are for us a heavy burden, the calamity of our being; they are like a plague, pestilence, pure misfortune in our country."*

Church Fathers had hypothesized that the Antichrist was of Jewish origin, and later preachers had implied a connection between the Antichrist and Satan. To medieval Christians aware of this background, it was logical to conclude that since the Antichrist was of Jewish origin, and the Jews, the Antichrist and Satan all denied the kingdom of Christ, then that must have meant that the Jews belonged to the kingdom of Satan.[141]

## Heresy and Sorcery

In the never-ending stream of accusations heaped upon the Jews, heresy stands out because it pushed the limits of logical understanding past the breaking point. This was because it made no sense to accuse someone of heresy when heresy implies a deviation from an accepted set of norms, rules or course of action and not a refusal to subscribe to said course. The Jews were not and had never been Christian, and therefore no amount of logical acrobatics could make sense of the accusation that they were deviating from a doctrine they had never embraced. The Church recognized this fact, and thus in ecclesiastical documents Judaism is categorized as "perfidy" and not heresy. But the populace was free from the constraints of logical reasoning. Thus, in most of Christendom the Jew was considered to be a heretic.

Everywhere in Europe Christians were obsessed with heresy and deviation from the path set down by the Church. Both common people and the Church were convinced that the Jews, guided by the Devil, were turning Christians away from the true faith. Indeed, the only distinction that could be made between Judaism and heresy was that "the heretics were wrong on some points, whereas the Jews were wrong on all." This belief extended to Jewish sacred texts as well. Berthold of Regensburg, the greatest German preacher of the later Middle Ages, preached in his sermons that the Jews were heretics and that their Talmud was so full of heresies that it was a crime to let Jews live.[142]

In Western Europe, of all the censured groups the two most commonly encountered were Jews and heretics. In that environment, it was natural for the common people to associate the two as members of the same group. This assumption is amply corroborated by the juxtaposed portrayal of clearly badged heretics and Jews in medieval illustrations.[143]

When Pope Alexander IV's bull established the association of magic and heresy in 1257, it triggered a crusade against sorcery. The bull led to the conception of Jews as heretics and, since heretics were sorcerers, Christians could draw the logical conclusion that Jews were sorcerers. This is the source of the medieval picture of the Jew as the supreme sorcerer and agent of the devil. This belief formed the basis for the acceptance of every major superstitious accusation that plagued the Jews.[144]

Once the floodgates were open, it did not take long before medieval authorities on witchcraft began to trace back to the Talmud the obscene and bizarre ceremonial of the Sabbat (a supposed meeting of those who practice witchcraft) itself. These same authorities commonly referred to the congregation of the witches for the Sabbat rites as a "synagogue."[145]

## Distortions of the Historical Record

As expressed above, early Christian preachers and writers distorted the historical record to make it suit their theological and political objectives. These early Christians felt they had to gain the trust and sympathies of the Roman authorities by minimizing the Roman role in the crucifixion, and by clearly standing out from those Jews then actively fighting the Roman Empire.

Although Jesus was born, lived and preached as a Jew, and neither ever taught anything outside Judaism nor intended to start a new religion, Christians made concerted efforts to minimize his connection to Judaism. The gospel he preached in the Temple and the synagogues, and its entire tradition, was deeply rooted in Jewish tradition despite efforts made in an attempt to separate it from Judaism. The name "Jesus" is a Hellenization of a Hebrew name, and the word "christ" comes from the Greek for the Hebrew word "messiah."[146]

The writers of the Gospels and other early Christians commonly portrayed the Jewish religion at the time Jesus lived as having descended into mere legalism without a soul. However, a dispassionate study of the historical record shows that during this period the religious life of Israel was deep and intense.[147]

Even though the historical record shows that Jesus was born under, lived and taught the Jewish law, attempts were made to portray Jesus as intending to abrogate it.[148]

Christian writers typically wrote that the Romans dispersed the Jews after the Jewish War and the destruction of the Second Temple in Jerusalem in 70 CE. As Saint Augustine wrote in *The City of God*: "But the Jews who rejected him, and slew him, . . . after that were miserably spoiled by the Romans . . . and dispersed over the face of the whole earth."[149] However they deliberately omitted the fact that at the time of Christ the Jews had been already dispersed for centuries owing to previous Assyrian and Babylonian invasions and thus the majority of Jews no longer lived in Judea. In fact, when fifty years after the Babylonian exile the Persian conqueror Cyrus allowed the Jewish exiles to go back to the Promised Land, few actually did; the majority were content to stay where they were in the land of exile.[150] Moreover, few Jews were really dispersed after the débâcle in 70 CE. Huge numbers died and many were taken prisoner to be sold as slaves, but comparatively few were exiled. A considerably larger dispersion happened after the second Judean war led by Bar Kochba in 135 CE, a war just as bloody and unremitting as the first and in which the Jewish rebels of Judea resisted for three years the Roman armies at the height of their power. This was certainly not something a few remaining rebels would have been able to do. The Romans, by then eager to erase any connection of the Jews to their land, changed the name of the Judean province to Palestine. But there never was a definitive dispersion: the Jews of Judea recovered enough in the following centuries to rebel again against Emperor Constantine and then Justinian, and several other times until the Ottoman Empire conquered the Promised Land after the Crusades.[151]

The Gospels charge the Jewish People "as a whole" with rejecting Jesus, however it is probable that the Jewish people "as a whole" were not even aware of his existence. Most Jews living outside Judea, who did not even speak Aramaic any more, were most likely unaware of events taking place in Judea and Galilee under Roman occupation. Also, few Jews in Galilee and Judea knew Jesus or of him. Of those that knew him, most took him to their hearts.[152]

Jesus chose to preach his gospel of love and forgiveness to his own people, the Jewish People, yet in the canonical Gospels he is presented condemning them. It is much more likely that the objects of his condemnation were the collaborators and hated ruling class allied with the Roman occupiers.[153]

Christianity taught for over eighteen hundred years that the Jewish people, in full culpability for the crucifixion, perpetrated the inexpiable crime of deicide. As Saint Paul explains to the Thessalonians, ". . . the Jews, who killed the Lord Jesus and the prophets and also drove us out. They displease God and are hostile to all men."[154] However, in the Gospels Jesus named in advance those responsible for the Passion: the chief priests, the elders and the scribes, all members of the oligarchic ruling class. This pernicious accusation caused rivers of innocent blood to be spilled.[155]

It is doubtful that the narrative of Jesus' trial, as portrayed in the Christian Bible, is accurate. According to the Gospels this important event took place hastily, is known only by hearsay (none of which is from contemporary witnesses), and there is no official transcript. Additionally, the three synoptic Gospels, in contradiction with the fourth, place the arrest, judgment, sentencing and execution on the first day of the Jewish festivity of Passover. On this day the faithful and particularly the priests would have been in meditation and consecration and not involved in a trial. Irrespective of what may have truly happened on that day this was a matter conducted without the consent of the Jewish people as a whole, and was orchestrated apart from them, despite them, and against them.[156]

The Gospels, which are the only documents that provide us with any information on the crucifixion, are works of religious teaching and are not bound to historical accuracy. For instance, the Gospels portray Pontius Pilate as hesitant, uncertain about what to do, almost meek. He was nothing of the sort, as there is a record that clearly shows him to have been a brutal, bloodthirsty tyrant, even recalled to Rome to explain his excesses. There are accounts from his contemporaries that describe the massacres, including multiple crucifixions, he ordered. Turning a crucified people into a crucifying people may have served a theological and political purpose, but was clearly not in the interest of historical truth.[157]

*The Roman Pontius Pilate is portrayed in this 13th century Belgian psalm book as a Jew washing his hands of the crime. The Liege Psalm book, Belgium, 13th century.*

The Romans tried Jesus as a subversive dissident. As the sign on the cross clearly indicated, he was accused of being the "King of the Jews." It was as a king, or as a pretender to kingship—the kingship of the Messiah—that Jesus was sentenced and crucified. For the Romans, who believed the messiah was going to liberate the people, that was an act of insurrection. Crucifixion was the most ignominious and painful form of Roman punishment and was used for subversive political prisoners.

The flagellation of Jesus, the crowning with thorns and the crucifixion were the work of the Roman soldiers alone. Jesus died the victim of Roman authority, sentenced by Pilate, and tormented and crucified by Roman soldiers. Neither the cooperation of the Jewish authorities nor anything else can diminish the significance of this historical fact, whose certainty is beyond question.[158]

*Accusing the Jews of deicide: on this image from the Latin breviary (13th century) the men scourging Jesus are Jews, as characterized by the Jewish hats they wear.*

In conclusion, irrespective of whatever other sins the Jewish people may have been guilty of, clearly Jesus neither rejected nor cursed them. Furthermore, they are innocent of the crimes the Christian tradition holds them responsible for, namely, rejecting and crucifying him.[159]


## Racial Antisemitism in the Church

Starting in 1449 in Castile, Spain, Christians were of the belief that intermixing with Jewish blood was defiling the pure blood of Old Christians. The City Council of Toledo passed the first racial statute called *Sentencia-Estatuto* in 1449 decreeing "that no *converso* of Jewish descent may have or hold any office or benefice in the said city of Toledo, or in its territory and jurisdiction." Despite Pope Nicholas V's bull rejecting this notion ("We decree and declare that all Catholics are one body in Christ according to the teaching of our faith.") and his excommunication of the author of said ordinance, two years later the king of Castile approved the regulation formally defining Jews in Spain not by religion but by blood.[160]

The Statute of Toledo of 1547, also known as the *limpieza de sangre*, or blood purity statute, was promulgated by the emboldened archbishop of Toledo after he had successfully rejected Pope Paul III's appointment of a *converso* priest to a clerical position at the cathedral in Toledo. This statute stipulated that no one of Jewish blood could hold office at the cathedral of Toledo. This is a particularly significant statute because although the Pope and most other prelates including many in Spain refused to approve it, the Inquisition soon began extending such *limpieza* statutes to other institutions thus banning people of Jewish ancestry from holding office in various guilds, municipalities, Spanish universities and religious orders. This created a sharp demarcating line between the Inquisition, veering toward a racist policy, and the papacy, holding on to the old tradition of believing anyone could be converted to the Christian faith and that there were no distinctions among the baptized.

The line became blurred a few years later in 1555 when Grand Inquisitor Caraffa became Pope Paul IV and quickly ratified the blood purity statute of Toledo. He created the *Index of Forbidden Books*, banned the Talmud and included it in the Index. The only book he allowed Jews to possess was the Bible. This statute marks the beginning of racial antisemitism, and the *limpieza de sangre* legacy is one of movement from religion-based hatred of Jews to race-based hatred.[61]

*A Nazi flag flies in front of the Cologne Cathedral, 1937. There is a* Juden-sau *in the underside of a choir-stall seat in the cathedral (probably the earliest example).*

The Church's concern that its very own *conversos* were corrupting Christians would shift the perception of Jews to that of successful and assimilated parasites feeding off the host society, a concept that would be repeated *ad nauseam* by modern antisemites including Hitler.[162]

Jesuits during the Fifth General Congregation of the Society of Jesus in 1593 issued the pure blood decree prohibiting all Christians tainted with Jewish blood from joining the order, claiming that "Those, however, who are descended from parents who are recent Christians have routinely been in the habit of inflicting a great deal of hindrance and harm to the Society." Fourteen years later, during the Sixth General Congregation, the restriction was extended from "parents" to "the fifth degree of family lineage." Only in the Twenty-seventh General Congregation, in 1923, was it declared that "The impediment of origin extends to all who are descended from the Jewish race, unless it is clear that their father, grandfather and great-grandfather have belonged to the Catholic Church." The Society of Jesus would not finally repudiate the *limpieza de sangre* restriction until 1946, and even then would do it by stating "Regarding the impediment of origin . . . the present congregation did not wish to retain it as a secondary impediment, but substituted for it a statement reminding the provincials . . . of the cautions to be exercised before admitting a candidate about whom there is some doubt as to the character of his hereditary background."[163] These blood purity regulations were the antecedent of the Nazi Nuremberg Laws.

In his Advent sermons in 1933, the year Hitler took power in Germany, Cardinal Faulhaber observed that the Church did not have "any objection to the endeavor to keep the national characteristics of a people as far as possible pure and unadulterated, and to foster their national spirit by emphasis upon the common ties of blood which unite them."[164] Karl Adam, world-renowned and perhaps the leading German theologian of the time, developed a powerful Nazified Catholic philosophy called *Reichstheologie*, and was expressing Nazi-like sentiments already in 1933. "The myth of the German, his culture and his history are decisively shaped by blood." He argued that not only were National Socialism and Catholicism not in conflict with one another, they belonged together as nature and grace. Speaking about Hitler he said, "Now he stands before us, he whom the voices of our poets and sages have summoned, the liberator of German genius. He has removed the blindfolds from our eyes and, through all political, economic, social and confessional covers, has enabled us to see and love again the one essential thing: our unity of blood, our German self, the *Homo Germanus*." Adam, Schmaus and other well-known Catholic thinkers and leaders, by embracing Hitler and Nazism served to legitimize the regime to Catholics.[165]

The German episcopate's February 1936 official guidelines for religious instruction declared: "Race, soil, blood and people are precious natural values which God the Lord has created and the care of which he has entrusted to us Germans."[166] Just one year later, the German Catholic Church's 1937 *Handbook of Contemporary Religious Questions*, under "race," echoed the Nuremberg Laws and the Statute of Toledo of 1547 by endorsing the rejection of "foreign blood." This was in contravention of fundamental Christian doctrine.[167]

# 6

## Christianity in Print

C hristian antagonism and hatred toward Jews manifested itself in multiple ways. The Church, arrogantly convinced that when it came to Jews it was doing the right thing, had no qualms in using the printed page themselves and through its surrogates to express its antisemitism.

### Encyclicals

In 1937, five years into the Nazi era, Pope Pius XI issued the encyclical *Mit bennender Sorge.* The encyclical was either written or supervised by Cardinal Secretary of State Pacelli (the future Pope Pius XII). This important document, written after the Jews of Germany had already being subjected to a dehumanizing process, demonstrates the antisemitism Pius XI and Pacelli felt. This encyclical, often presented erroneously as Pacelli's, Pius XI's or the Church's antipathy toward Nazism, never mentioned Nazism by name. It objected to violations of the Concordat and treatment of religion in Germany. In only six sentences among forty-three paragraphs it objected to the doctrine of race, not because it was false or inherently pernicious, but rather because some would have it take precedence over the teachings of Christianity. There was no mention of antisemitism or the persecution of the Jews. In fact, Pacelli even referred here to the Jews as people "straying from God," reaffirming the German perception of Jews as outsiders that had to somehow be eliminated from society. He went on to remind the German people that the Jews were "a people that was to crucify" Jesus, and that they, as a people, were his "torturer." This was read from every pulpit on Palm Sunday 1937. This is also interesting in that it shows that Pacelli was not afraid to confront Nazi policies openly.

Pius XI attempted late in his life (1938) to atone for his earlier antisemitism with the draft encyclical, *Humani Generis Unitas* (On the Unity of the Human Race). In this encyclical Pius XI was finally clearly and unambiguously speaking against antisemitism and calling for an end to the Nazis' persecution of the Jews:

> "It becomes clear that the struggle of racial purity ends by being uniquely the struggle against the Jews. Save for its systematic cruelty, this struggle is no different in true motives and methods from persecutions everywhere carried out against the Jews since antiquity."

It is remarkable that a pope, particularly one that evidenced antisemitism before, managed to establish and point out the connection between past persecutions of the Jews, which by implication included those of the Church, and the current onslaught from the Nazis. However, he did not manage to completely break with the past and admit guilt, as he continued in the encyclical with a self-exonerating half-truth: "These persecutions have been censured by the Holy See on more than one occasion, but especially when they have worn the mantle of Christianity."[168]

Also remarkable was that one of the Jesuit fathers who worked on the draft still managed to include a passage that lumped Jews together with the misguided souls who are driven "to ally themselves with, or actively to promote revolutionary movements that aim to destroy society to obliterate from the minds of men the knowledge, reverence and love of God." This can be understood when one knows that that same father taught that permissible antisemitism allows governments to protect themselves against "the 'assimilated' Jews who, being for the most part given to moral nihilism and without any national or religious ties, operate within the camp of world plutocracy as well as within that of international Bolshevism, thus unleashing the darker traits of the soul of the Jewish people expelled from the fatherland."[169]

For Pope Pius XI, telling the truth may have been impossible precisely because he was the pope. Even the outsider he brought in to write the encyclical was unable to deliver a document untainted by racism, bad theology, segregation and anti-Communist hysteria. Even with the best intentions the Vatican still subscribed to the anti-modernist stance bequeathed by Pope Pius IX in the nineteenth century in which the Jews were seen as allied with socialism, secularism, rationalism, banking, libertinism and birth control.[170]

Unfortunately Pius XI died shortly before he managed to issue the *Humani Generis Unitas* encyclical, which meant that it was left to his successor, Pius XII, to decide what to do with it. Pius XII began his papacy by suppressing this remarkable document defending the Jews. The Church hid not only the encyclical itself, as it was never issued, but also its very existence.

## Religious Publications

*La Civiltà Cattolica* was a Jesuit journal and was the official, authoritative and critically important Vatican publication, overseen and approved by the Pope. *La Civiltà Cattolica*'s authors, wrote Pope Leo XIII in 1891, "have in their writings pursued the study of truth combined with the law of justice, and, having employed a great intelligence in their works, have acquired great fame." *La Civiltà Cattolica* and *L'Osservatore Romano* were viewed in the Catholic world as offering the clearest expressions of the Pope's own perspectives on the issues of the day.

In late nineteenth century there was a tendency of Catholic writers to adapt to the tenets of modern antisemitism and start defining Jews as a race. In 1880 they wrote, "Oh how wrong and deluded are those who think that Judaism is just a religion, like Catholicism, Paganism, Protestantism, and not in fact a race, a people, a nation!" In 1887 those writers were even more categorical. Father Ballerini explains: "The Jew remains always in every place immutably a Jew. His nationality is not in the soil where he is born, nor in the language that he speaks, but in his seed."[171]

Old antisemitism found new expression by fully embracing all the new forms of the hatred. In a 1893 article entitled "Jewish Morality," Jesuit Father Saverio Rondina wrote:

> [The Jewish nation] "does not work, but traffics in the property and the work of others; it does not produce, but lives and grows fat with the products of the arts and industry of the nations that give it refuge. It is the giant octopus that with its oversized tentacles envelops everything. It has its stomach in the banks . . . and its suction cups everywhere: in contracts and monopolies, . . . in postal services and telegraph companies, in shipping and in the railroads, in the town treasuries and in state finance. It represents the kingdom of capital . . . the aristocracy of gold . . . It reigns unopposed."

It is hard to see any differences between the language used by this representative of the Church, in the official Vatican publication, and that found in the worst secular antisemitic screeds of the time. Here we can see that the emancipation of the Jews had the effect of transforming the old Church views into modern antisemitism: "With religious liberty proclaimed, and citizenship conceded even to the Jews, the Jews took advantage of it . . . to become our masters. . . . What shapes and reshapes public opinion is the press, and this also is in large part inspired and subsidized by the Jews."

To avoid being accused of antisemitism during the entire period in which the Church contributed to the establishment and spread of modern antisemitism, Church leaders carefully orchestrated a campaign of repudiation and demurrals. Shortly after the "Jewish Morality" article had come out, Father Rondina wrote, "We do not write with any intention of sparking or fomenting any antisemitism in our country. Rather we seek to sound an alarm for

Italians so that they defend themselves against those who, in order to impoverish them, dominate them, and make them their slaves, interfere with their faith, corrupt their morals, and suck their blood."[172]

Even on the eve of the Second World War *Civiltà Cattolica* was spreading an antisemitic ideology meant to preserve Hungary's Catholic makeup, which the Jews were putatively destroying. In an article titled "The Jewish Question in Hungary" from July 1938, *Civiltà Cattolica* wrote of the influence of the Jews in all positions of importance and power and concluded that "The antisemitism of Hungarian Catholics is neither vulgar nor fanatical or racial. It is a movement for the defense of national traditions and true freedom and independence of the Hungarian people."

*L'Osservatore Romano* was the official Vatican newspaper. It was closer to the Pope than *La Civiltà Cattolica* at the end of the nineteenth century. In 1898, at the height of the Dreyfus Affair, *L'Osservatore Romano* also reflected the paranoid, modern antisemitism of their environment: "Jewry can no longer be excused or rehabilitated. The Jew possesses the largest share of all wealth, movable and immovable. . . . The credit of States is in the hands of a few Jews. One finds Jews in the ministries, the civil service, the armies and the navies, the universities and in control of the press. . . If there is one nation that more than any other has the right to turn to antisemitism, it is France, which first gave their political rights to the Jews, and which was thus the first to prepare the way for its own servitude to them." The daily also noted a turning of the tide that year. "Masonry and Judaism, sprung up together to combat and destroy Christianity in the world, must now together defend themselves against the Christian awakening and against the people's wrath."[173]

In a bizarre twist of logic, *L'Osservatore* developed another theme that would appear regularly in the first few decades of the twentieth century, that there is a good kind and a bad kind of antisemitism: "Antisemitism ought to be the natural, sober, thoughtful, Christian reaction against Jewish predominance." The writer of the article goes on to explain that unfortunately there is another kind of antisemitism, a non-Christian form that was attracting much attention. The new form of antisemitism was "nothing but an artificial form of Judaism itself, which has introduced and maintained it so that it will be impossible for the true antisemitism to be organized, to be put into action, and to succeed." *L'Osservatore* was not content with absurdly accusing Judaism of creating the new form of antisemitism. The Vatican paper then proceeded to claim that this other form of antisemitism was not desirable, as according to the paper true antisemitism "is and can be in substance nothing other than Christianity, completed and perfected in Catholicism."[174]

The next day the journalist, addressing himself directly to the Jews, issued a warning: "As we have said on other occasions, take care what you are doing. Don't play with fire. The people's ire, although at the moment somewhat dampened by sentiments of Christian charity and by the tender influence of the Catholic clergy, may at any moment erupt like a volcano and strike like a thunderbolt." Given what happened in Europe half a century later, this warning curdles the blood.[175]

On the eve of the promulgation of the Italian anti-Jewish laws in June 1938, Jesuit Father Enrico Rosa condemned violence and brutality against Jews, but at the same time maintained that the Jews "usurp the best positions in every field, and not always by legitimate means," cause "the suffering of the immense majority of the native populations," hate and struggle against the Christian religion, and favor Freemasons and other subversive groups. He called for "an equable and lasting solution to the formidable Jewish problem," but counseled to do so through legal means.[176]

In a homily published in January 1939, the same month in which Hitler promised to annihilate the Jewish race in Europe if war broke out, Bishop Giovanni Cezzani of Cremona suggested approval of some aspects of the Fascist anti-Jewish measures of 1938. As was typically the case of articles written by low level prelates like this one, Vatican officials, if not the Pope himself, had to approve them. The tenor of the homily encouraged Italian Catholics to be at ease with the Fascist anti-Jewish laws. The homily evoked "the horrendous deicide, the odious Jewish persecution against the Messiah, his apostles and disciples, and the nascent Church." Cezzani went on to say, among much else:

> "The Church has always regarded living side by side with Jews, as long as they remain Jews, as dangerous to the faith and tranquility of Christian people. It is for this reason that you find an old and long tradition of ecclesiastical legislation and discipline, intended to brake and limit the action and influence of the Jews in the midst of Christians, and the contact of Christians with them, isolating the Jews and not allowing them the exercise of those offices and professions in which they could dominate or influence the spirit, the education, the customs of Christians."

He then provided his readers with the reassurance that the Church "has always done everything, and continues to do everything, to prevent mixed marriages" and "Also, Catholics obedient to the directives of the Church at present do not take on or accept Jewish domestic servants, or put themselves in the service of Jews when they must live with the family; and still less do they entrust their babies to Jewish wet nurses, or their children to be instructed or educated by Jewish teachers. If in our schools, until recently, Jewish teachers were not few, it was not because of work of the Church."[177]

In France the situation was not much better. *La Croix* (The Cross) was the authoritative voice of Catholic antisemitism and was published as a daily newspaper in Paris. The Assumptionists, an Augustinian order of priests, published it. At the time of the Dreyfus Affair at the turn of the nineteenth century, *La Croix* was the most widely read Catholic publication in France including in its readership more than twenty-five thousand Catholic clergy and hundreds of thousands of people. During the Dreyfus Affair, an editor wrote in response to Zola's *"J'Accuse...!"* published five days before: "Help! Help! Are we going to leave our beloved France in the hands of the Jews and the Dreyfusards?"

Again raising the specter of revolution, *La Croix* published, "The first revolution was by France on behalf of the Jews. The Jews against the French wage the revolution that is in the making. This is how Jews show their gratitude."[178] A few days later, in January 19, 1898, *La Croix* published:

> "We know well that the Jew was the inventor of our anti-Christian laws, that he put them on stage like the puppet master, concealed behind a curtain, pulls the string which makes the devil appear before the unsuspecting audience.
>
> The proof that the man hidden behind the curtain was the Jew emerges in the first battle engaged by Judaism – that engaged by the Syndicate [trade unions] . . .
>
> You don't have to be a great scholar to understand that law which . . . removes the Crucifix from hospitals and schools come from the same Pharisees who underhandedly persuaded people to free Barabbas and to vote for the death of the innocent Jesus.
>
> The parents, the children of France have only benefited from the parochial schools just as the people of Judea only received healing from the Savior, while universal suffrage cried on all sides 'Death! Death!'
>
> Who is whispering this cry today as they whispered it to Pilate?
>
> The Savior died saying of the poor crew of opportunists, 'They know not what they do.'
>
> But the organizers of the Jewish plan know well what they are doing . . . This is how the Israelite financiers, so adroit at ruining France . . . with clever phrases, are trying to persuade a naïve people that Jesus was condemned according to the law of the people . . .
>
> The subtle alliance of all the makers of the anti-Christian laws, with the powerful Dreyfus syndicate, leaves no room for doubt. They are all of a piece. Destroy the army, destroy the religious orders and let the Jew reign! That is the goal."[179]

This diatribe shows how Jews could illogically be portrayed as both revolutionaries *and* financiers, as a syndicate member *and* an owner, as a solitary betrayer *and* an international conspirator. Jews are still portrayed as "the deicide people," manipulating Pilate, fooling the crowds, and crucifying Jesus.[180] For a population steeped in Catholic teachings about Jews having murdered Christ, the judicial charge of murder against Jews was all it took to ignite an old, latent fire.

When the guilty verdict in Dreyfus' first trial was read, Dreyfus, standing at attention looking straight ahead at the crucifix placed in front of the French courtroom, cried out *"Vive la France!"* The next day, in an editorial *La Croix* called this act the "last kiss of Judas."

This and similar publications, while creating a strong animosity toward Jews, were also intended to re-christianize the masses of people that had become somewhat indifferent toward the Church. This was the reason the bishops, who may have been appalled by the vulgarity of the antisemitism disseminated in those publications, did not make any attempt to silence them.[181]

In the United States Father Charles Coughlin was one of the most vocal and popular antisemitic radio priests. His reach and tone eventually made him an embarrassment to the Catholic Church. He had an enormous following in the U.S. in the 1930s, and he published a newspaper called *Social Justice*.

In 1938 he published *The Protocols of the Elders of Zion*. He used that to fight the gold standard, which he believed came from the Jews who in his mind worshipped gold, as he said in one of his broadcast sermons: "gold is sacred, gold is wealth, gold is more precious than men and the homes in which they live." To Father Coughlin, that was "the theory of the European Jew." The influence at home was visible with the bankers of Wall Street, who were "modern Shylocks . . . grown fat and wealthy." At the same time, he tended to refer to Jews as "communistic Jews." In one *Social Justice* editorial in 1938 the priest wrote, "Almost without exception, the intellectual leaders—if not the foot and hand leaders—of

Marxist atheism in Germany were Jews." What makes this editorial and other libel he published especially interesting was that they were in fact plagiarized from a speech given by Joseph Goebbels, the Nazi Minister of Propaganda.[182] Father Coughlin often ranted against Jews, whom he called "Christ-killers and Christ-rejecters." At a rally in the Bronx in 1938, he gave a Nazi salute and ominously said, "When we get through with the Jews in America, they'll think the treatment they received in Germany was nothing."[183]

During the Nazi era both the Catholic and Protestant churches issued many pastoral letters to the clergy or laity of the bishop's dioceses containing either general admonition, instruction, consolation, or directions for behavior in particular circumstances. Two weeks after Hitler's January 1939 promise to annihilate the Jews if war broke out, Archbishop Gröber, one of the most esteemed and influential Catholic leaders in Germany, published a pastoral letter in which he again libeled the Jews by telling his flock that Jews hated Jesus and so crucified him, and that their lethality continued to threaten the world. He claimed that "their murderous hatred has continued in later centuries." For a population susceptible to believe what their bishop told them, the Jewish threat meant that the fight against Judaism was one of self-defense, and together with Hitler's threat prepared them to take violent action if necessary. Archbishop Gröber's comments could have likely and reasonably been understood as supporting that intent.[184]

In a pastoral letter in March 1941, by which time the Germans had already greatly harmed the Jews, Archbishop Gröber once again placed the blame for Jesus' death on the Jews and implied that that justified what was happening to them: "The self-imposed curse of the Jews, 'His blood be upon us and upon our children,' has come true terribly until the present time, until today."[185]

Just like Archbishop Gröber, who admitted that Jesus could not be made into an Aryan but had been fundamentally different from the Jews of his time, Bishop Hilfrich of Limburg said in his pastoral letter for the Christian practice of Lent in 1939 that Jesus had been a Jew, but "the Christian religion has not grown out of the nature of this people, that is, is not influenced by their racial characteristics. Rather it has had to make its way against this people." The bishop added that the Jewish people were guilty of the murder of God and had been under a divine curse since the day of the crucifixion.[186]

This pattern was repeated everywhere during the war. Nazi collaborator Bishop Gregory Rožman from Slovenia wrote a pastoral letter urging his flock to join the Nazi cause to "assure our existence and better future, in the fight against [the] Jewish conspiracy."[187]

# 7

# Antisemitism in Sermons, Liturgy, and the Christian Bible

To diminish the image of Jesus as a human being and fill the picture of him as a deity, as well as portray Jews as his enemies and Romans as innocent and unwilling participants in the historical events unfolding at the time of the crucifixion, facts had to be manipulated and history rewritten. The authors of the Gospels felt compelled to alter the roles and functions of the various institutions and leaders in Judea at the time of Jesus. The evangelists had to do this so that neither themselves nor Christianity would be perceived as a threat or challenge to the Roman authorities.

St. Paul's religious teachings had political significance because of the strife they were creating between Jews and their gentile neighbors throughout the Roman Empire. The evangelist Luke felt it necessary to hide the details of Paul's execution in Rome. Luke had to do this because to have ended the story of the Christian hero by narrating how he was executed as an enemy of the Roman state would have alienated Roman readers and defeated the purpose of trying to establish Christianity in the Roman world. The result of what was said in the Gospels, and how it was said, had the long lasting effect of continuous enmity toward Jews.[188]

Anti-Jewish references are so pervasive in the Christian Bible that inventorying them all would take volumes.[189] However, we can take a cursory look in this book. In the Christian Bible, just the Gospels and the Acts of the Apostles combined have approximately four hundred and fifty explicit antisemitic verses, averaging more than two per page. The Gospel according to Mark has approximately forty, the Gospel according to Luke has approximately sixty, the Gospel according to Matthew has approximately eighty, the Gospel according to John has approximately one hundred and thirty and Acts of the Apostles has approximately one hundred and forty. Only eight of its twenty-eight chapters are free of antisemitism.

We can see the supersessionistic tenor of the Gospels by taking a brief look at the Gospel according to John. John's account of the Passion may very well be the most powerful of the four Gospels, and this narrative encompasses the essential beliefs of Christianity. In this book the evangelist clearly blames "the Jews," whom he characterizes as bloodthirsty and hateful, for the crucifixion. He repeatedly portrays Jesus, the disciples and subsequent followers as distinct from the Jews, initiating a long history of divisiveness in which there is a clear demarcation between "us" and "them." This can be seen in a number of places along the narrative, such as in a couple of instances in which he refers to the "Passover of the Jews" as if Jesus and his followers were not part of the Jewish national festivity.[190] John makes repeated libelous references to the evil nature of the Jews as a whole, always referring to them as "the Jews." In chapter eight he completes the identification of "the Jews" and Satan himself, and reinforces the notion that Jews were no longer the children of God in statements that helped pave the roads to the death camps:

"Jesus said to them [the Jews], 'If God were your Father, you would love me, for I came from God and now am here. I have not come on my own; but he sent me. Why is my language not clear to you? Because you are unable to hear what I say. You belong to your father, the devil, and you want to carry out your father's desire. He was a murderer from the beginning, not holding to the truth, for there is no truth in him. When he lies, he speaks his native language, for he is a liar and the father of lies. Yet because I tell the truth, you do not believe me! He who belongs to God hears what God says. The reason you do not hear is that you do not belong to God.'"[191]

*The Nazi propaganda machine spoke to the German people in familiar language they understood. A sign in the countryside in Eschenbach in central Franconia (Germany) in July 1935 reads, "The father of the Jews is the devil." In smaller type below it reads, "Jesus Christ."*

In this way the Jews become the negative "other," the ontological enemy instead of just the historical enemy, and they are portrayed in sharp relief against every positive aspect of Christianity.[192]

Until the nineteenth century, common people, usually untutored or even illiterate, had no capacity to read or understand scholarly theological treatises. Instead, they took the readymade negative image of the Jews and assigned to them blame for their own misfortunes, failures and omissions. For the common folk, the Jew simply symbolized the dark mythical forces that threatened the social order.[193]

The masses learned the simple and suitably popular negative message about the Jews from popular literature disseminated in Germany in the nineteenth century. However, reading that literature required some intellectual effort and leisure time. A more effective method of dissemination of these ideas was through the oral transmission of messages, and no preacher was more popular than the ecclesiastical preacher. Through their sermons, preachers were able to revive the preexisting emotional revulsion from Judaism that had been latent on the popular mind for centuries. To the masses of unlearned Christians, what mattered was the spoken word of the priest and not the written Scriptures.[194] Among populations with a majority of still devout peasantry, the influence of Christian anti-Jewish rhetoric was particularly effective and prevalent. As Nietzsche wrote, "But in Germany . . . there was but one type of public and artistic address: that delivered from the pulpit."[195]

Antisemitism had been a staple of priestly sermons for centuries. For the purpose of this study it may be useful to very briefly look at some sermons in nineteenth century Germany. These sermons formed the backbone of the religious indoctrination of the grandparents and parents of the mass murderers of the Second World War.

Catholic catechism and liturgy shaped the outlook of priests who discussed the Jews, their beliefs, their writings and the role Jesus had assigned to them in their sermons in crude, clear and simple ways.[196] These sermons were delivered in unambiguous language as dogmatic, absolute truths, as by definition sermons were meant to explain to people what is written in Scriptures as if they were hearing the divine message directly. These sermons (and things like the Good Friday prayer, which referred to Jews as "Perfidious Jews" and contained the accusation of the Jews as killers of Jesus) left an image of the Jews imprinted on the naïve Christian mind that was the only thing Christians knew about Jews as they met them as neighbors. This is because early Christian theology had created an image of a mythical Jew that had completely replaced the real Jew in the Christian medieval mind, so much so that the actual Jew ceased to exist. For the average medieval Christian, the only Jew they knew only existed in their imagination.[197]

The myth of the wandering Jew and the theme of exile were often used in sermons and literature as evidence that the dispersed Jews were agitating elements in their midst. In the nineteenth century, as theological antisemitism turned into social antisemitism, the traditional religious conflict served to mark the class gap between the Jew and the Christian. This was reflected in sermons as well: "In places where the Jews dwell among the Christian population, the Christians are poverty stricken, while the Jews suck their blood like vampires."[198]

Echoing the teachings of St. Augustine, German priest Joseph Deharbe explained to his flock in a sermon in 1869 why the Jews were permitted to live: "God did not wish this people—which deserved to be annihilated more than any other people—to be totally destroyed, in order that we should have living testimony of the truth of our holy religion."[199] And echoing the teachings and language of the Christian Bible, Georg Patiss preached in 1882 in Germany that "They [the Jews] were truly revealed to be cunning serpents, who, from their place of concealment, stung with their fatal venom; the descendants of their forefathers are a nest of vipers."[200]

Another way to reach often-illiterate masses was by using derogatory iconography. A very common antisemitic motif frequently found in carvings on church or cathedral walls everywhere in

Europe is the *Judensau* (German for "Jewish swine"). This was an image or a sculpture of a female pig—the filthy, impure taboo that biblical Jews were meant to loathe—surrounded by Jews violating it, sucking at its teats, and eating its excrement.[201] These images portray Jews doing incomprehensible things, rather closer to what the devil would do rather than Christians. In fact, in *Judensau* illustrations the devil himself appears not just next to the Jews, which he seems to be influencing, but rather as a Jew himself. The obscene nature of these supposed acts brought into question whether Jews were human at all, a conception that would be reflected by many Germans during the Holocaust.

*A form of particularly offensive slander was the depiction of the purported ritual murder and that of Jews performing obscene acts with a pig, as seen in this Frankfurt* Judensau *from the early seventeenth century. In this illustration a horned devil—himself wearing the medieval Jewish badge—encourages Jewish men also wearing Jewish clothes and insignia to pleasure themselves with a sow and eat its excrement while a Jewish child sucks its teats. Also, a Jewish woman rides a goat, another symbol of the devil.*

## Similarities Between Nazi and Christian Thought

The antisemitism espoused by the Nazis was different from traditional Christian antisemitism as it was racial and secular, but it did not germinate in a vacuum. As we have seen earlier in this book, antipathy toward Jews and Judaism originated in the early days of the Christian movement and evolved over time into full-blown distrust and hatred. In the Middle Ages demonic and racial aspects were introduced in which for the first time the Church defined people by their blood. After the Enlightenment Jews were emancipated in most of Europe and the Church began to loose its grip on the people. As it was no longer acceptable to hate Jews due to just theological reasons as before, a secular aversion toward Jews took hold of Europe. In this new enmity Jews *as Jews* were abhorred as an ethnically inferior race bent on the destruction of Christian civilization and world domination. The foundation laid out by almost two thousand years of systematic and relentless Christian contempt and execration toward Jews prepared the soil for decades of accusing Jews of having caused all the social and economic chaos of the nineteenth century.

When Germany lost the Great War, the political, economic and social upheavals that ensued set the stage for Hitler to preach to the German masses in language they were familiar with, and about things they had heard about all their lives from their parents, their schools, and their priests.

Nazi theory employed methodology similar to that of the German Catholic catechism to prove that Jews were inherently corrupt. Hitler referred to the destructive character of the Jew, and this description was common in nineteenth century sermons as well. The idea of the "chosen people" was central to both ideologies: Both Christianity and Nazism saw Judaism as superfluous, debased and accursed, and coincided on the idea of the invalidation of the status of the Jewish people as the chosen people.[202]

Both sermons and catechistic literature propounded the theme of the demonic nature of the Jews. While Christian teachings confronted Satan and Jesus, Hitler confronted the Jew with everything that was human in contrast with the Aryan. This association of the Jew with demonic forces and the Devil is an expression of a latent desire to cause the death of the Jew since, as the proverb says, "in the battle against Satan, all means are justified." Ever since the Middle Ages the Church disseminated propaganda focusing on the demonic nature of the Jews and their association with the Devil, and his struggle against Jesus. Christianity was summoned to a holy war to exterminate Satan. Hitler adapted the teachings from a sermon into action: "This satanic generation was not destroyed when the Old Testament was forced to yield place to the New Testament; this hells-spawn still lives. . . . It sneaked from the Old Testament into the New, and spreads within the Christian community like poisonous weeds which cannot be eradicated."[203]

*A roadside warning sign in Germany during the Third Reich: "Jews in the Blossersberg community are not welcome! To know the Jew is to know the devil!"*

Catholic catechism charged the Jews with materialism. Over the centuries, this evolved into an image of the Jew characterized by his covetous nature, worship of worldly things, and greedy exploitation of others. Hitler absorbed this message and turned it into an anti-Jewish diatribe, referring to "moneyed Jewry" as possessing solely capitalistic thoughts only interested in "the deification of money," "Jewish profit" and "Jewish materialism."[204]

Preachers declared that "the Jew has little interest in artistic and scientific aspirations." The Nazis declared that the Jews had no aesthetic sense and disregarded the work of many prominent Jewish scientists as "Jewish science." As Hitler wrote in *Mein Kampf,* "The Jews lack those qualities which mark the creative and the cultural elements in gifted races."[205]

The terminology used by Catholic preachers and writers was permeated with images taken from death, from the demonic world and from the insect kingdom, doomed to extermination. Hitler readily embraced this terminology. As he said, "for fifteen hundred years the Catholic church considered the Jews to be pests." Poisonous serpents, vipers, hells-spawn and rats were transformed in Hitler's lexicon into vampires, germs, bloodsuckers and parasites.[206]

Christian teachings often portrayed the fight against the Jews as one of self defense, as expressed by a German Catholic periodical published in mid nineteenth century: "Both the Book of the *Zohar* and the *Shulkhan Arukh* exhort the Jew explicitly to destroy Christians and they perceive the advent of the Messiah as dependent on the extermination of the Christians." SS Chief Heinrich Himmler learned the lesson well. As he instructed Rudolf Höss, commandant of the Auschwitz death camp, "All Jews who are now in our grasp, without exception, must be exterminated in this war. If we do not now succeed in destroying the biological foundations of Judaism, the Jews will some day arise and destroy the German people."[207]

To demonstrate Christian superiority Christianity negated, debased and oppressed Judaism. To bring about the salvation of the Nordic race Hitler sought to destroy Judaism. For Christians, the degradation of the Jews was the substitute for their extermination, which ultimately was the logical outcome of the principles laid out in Christian teaching.[208]

## Canonical Anti-Jewish Laws, and Parallel to Nazi Laws.

When the Nazis came to power in 1933 and began to implement their war against the Jews, they did not have to invent anything. They inherited an environment whose soil was already permeated with Jew-hatred and they found that they simply had to update the language of laws against Jews that had been implemented for centuries by the Church.

The following table shows some of the canonical anti-Jewish laws that had been promulgated by the Catholic Church and put in place in Christian Europe since the time of Emperor Constantine, when Christianity became the official religion of the Roman Empire. For each of these laws, there was an equivalent law promulgated by the Nazis during the Third Reich:

| | | |
|---|---|---|
| Prohibition of intermarriage and of sexual intercourse between Christians and Jews. | Synod of Elvira | 306 CE |
| Jews and Christians not permitted to eat together. | Synod of Elvira | 306 CE |
| Jews not allowed to hold public office. | Synod of Clermont | 535 CE |
| Jews not allowed to employ Christian servants or posses Christian slaves. | 3rd Synod of Orléans | 538 CE |
| Jews not allowed to show themselves in the streets during Passion Week. | 3rd Synod of Orléans | 538 CE |
| Burning of the Talmud and other books. | 12th Synod of Toledo | 681 CE |
| Christians not permitted to patronize Jewish doctors. | Trulanic Synod | 692 CE |
| Christians not permitted to live in Jewish homes. | Synod of Narbonne | 1050 CE |

| | | |
|---|---|---|
| Jews obliged to pay taxes for support of the Church to the same extent as Christians. | Synod of Gerona | 1078 CE |
| Jews not permitted to be plaintiffs, or witnesses against Christians in the courts. | 3rd Lateran Council, Canon 26 | 1179 CE |
| Jews not permitted to withhold inheritance from descendants who had accepted Christianity. | 3rd Lateran Council, Canon 26 | 1179 CE |
| Jews forced to mark their clothes with a badge. | 4th Lateran Council, Canon 68 | 1215 CE |
| Construction of new synagogues prohibited. | Council of Oxford | 1222 CE |
| Christians not permitted to attend Jewish ceremonies. | Synod of Vienna | 1267 CE |
| Jews forced to live in compulsory ghettos. | Synod of Breslau | 1267 CE |
| Christians not permitted to sell or rent real estate to Jews. | Synod of Ofen | 1279 CE |
| Adoption by a Christian of the Jewish religion or return by a baptized Jew to the Jewish religion defined as a heresy. | Synod of Mainz | 1310 CE |
| Jews not permitted to act as agents in the conclusion of contracts, especially marriage contracts, between Christians | Council of Basel | 1434 CE |
| Jews not permitted to obtain academic degrees | Council of Basel | 1434 CE |

Table 1: Canonical Anti-Jewish Laws[209]

# Part III:
# The Role of the Churches During the Nazi Era

*"The hottest places in hell are reserved for those who, in time of great moral crisis, maintain their neutrality."*

*Dante Alighieri*

# 8

## Dealing with the Enemy

The Church professes to be the guardian of morals and Christian values, and is the self-avowed protector and shepherd of Christian souls. For this reason, it is important to examine the role the Church played during the years leading to, and during, the extermination of about two-thirds of the Jewish population of Europe during the Second World War by a largely Christian population.

### Religious Statistics

The Catholic Church prospered greatly under the Weimar Republic, increasing the number of priests to over twenty-thousand for twenty-million Catholics, as opposed to sixteen thousand pastors for forty-million Protestants. Catholic organizations of every kind multiplied; new monasteries were built, new religious orders were founded, new schools were established. As the historian Karl Bachem said in 1931, "Never yet has a Catholic country possessed such a developed system of all conceivable Catholic associations as today's Catholic Germany."[210]

Religious statistics in prewar Germany show Christian preeminence despite neo-pagan claims and Nazi efforts to eliminate Christianity from Germany; in 1943 in Thuringia, a region in central Germany, there were 1427 Nazi rituals and 35,853 traditional rituals conducted in churches. According to the Nazis' own survey, a mere 3.5% of the German population described themselves as *Gottläubige* (neo-pagan) as late as 1944.[211]

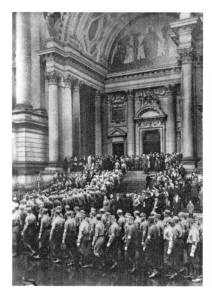

*SA Brown Shirt troopers attending church. Hitler's birthday, April 20, 1933.*

Catholics comprised a little less than half of the population of the Greater German Reich (43.1% in 1939) and, despite all pressures to leave the Church, even among the SS almost a fourth (22.7% in December 1938) remained in the Catholic faith. By 1940 over 95% of the German population were still tax-paying members of their respective Protestant or Catholic churches.[212] In other words, indisputably Christianity was—before and during the war—the powerful common denominator that permeated German society at all levels and the indelible identity that anchored the ordinary German.

Catholic Austria had a higher percentage of Nazi party members than Germany and a disproportionately large role in the execution of the "Final Solution," even when compared to the overwhelmingly more populous Germany, which was predominately

Protestant, It may be possible to establish a similar correlation between the efficiency of the slaughter of millions of Jews in Poland, a deeply Catholic country steeped in the antisemitism inculcated by the Church, and those antisemitic beliefs. The Poles, like Ukrainians, Lithuanians, French, Slovaks and Croats who willfully collaborated with the Nazis in their genocidal rampage, shared the same heritage of Catholic antisemitic tradition and teachings. In a survey commissioned during the Second Vatican Council in the mid 1960s, it was found that "the respondents' antisemitism varies in direct relation to their position on this measure [of orthodoxy]... the more the religious beliefs are subscribed to, the greater the antisemitism." Orthodox beliefs are in fact "a powerful predictor of secular antisemitism." The degree of secular antisemitism is often linked to specifically theological positions—e.g., that the Jews are a cursed race, guilty of rejecting their own Messiah, responsible for killing Christ.[213]

## Hitler's Antisemitic Foundation

One of the most important confluences of world-views of the Church and Nazism was in the simultaneous identification of the Jew as financier and as Communist. Even though the Church as such did not adhere to Nazi racial theories, and did not participate directly in mass murder, racial antisemitism and anti-Jewish incitement were linked, as the Nazi anti-Jewish viewpoint is impossible to be understood outside of the Christian context.[214]

Many citizens of France, Italy and Germany during the 1920s, 1930s and 1940s when fascist governments promulgated decrees restricting the Jewish population's freedom to choose what to wear, where to live, what jobs they could have, what they could read, who they could marry and so on were alive in 1870 when equivalent restrictions were enforced on Jews. The main difference was that in 1870 those restrictions were imposed not in the name of Hitler or Mussolini, but in the name of Jesus Christ. Active participation or passive acquiescence in the assault on European Jewry during the 1930s and during the war came naturally to a population prepared for that by the Church. Nazi concentration camps were the natural successors to the concentration camps the Church established and maintained for hundreds of years, that is, the ghettos. As Cardinal Edward Cassidy said, "the ghetto, which came into being in 1555 with a papal bull, became in Nazi Germany the antechamber of the extermination."[215]

One of the reasons why France (who had gone through the Dreyfus affair only a few decades before) fell so quickly and easily to the German onslaught is because Hitler's propaganda spoke a very familiar language that was never quite forgotten there.

In Germany, Christian teachings about the Jews were highly influential on the popular view toward them. During the second half of the nineteenth century these teachings prepared the ground for rapid assimilation of modern anti-Jewish views by a wide spectrum of the population, which set the stage for Nazism on the first half of the twentieth century. Nazi antisemitism, despite its racial nature, adopted and used common and familiar language from Christianity that triggered hostility toward Jews, therefore establishing a link between Christian anti-Jewish elements and Nazi crimes.[216] For instance, during the 1930s the Nazis employed a little pamphlet for the education of young Germans in schools called *Deutscher National-Katechismus* ("German National Catechism"). Even though the content was secular, the title clearly uses a religious metaphor.[217]

The general populations most everywhere in Europe and America, together with active and passive collaborators, and of course Nazi murderers, were all steeped in Christian antisemitism. Christian supersessionism and prejudice had the effect of setting the Jew apart and poisoning the minds and hearts of millions of Germans and other European Christians. This is a central element that explains the general indifference and lack of surprise of the people when the Nazis translated the previously known theory into practice. Moreover, this doctrinarian brainwashing was instrumental in allowing Hitler to easily and quickly gain support, as he was already speaking to his listeners in well-known language.[218]

In 1939, Roberto Farinacci, a member of Mussolini's Fascist Grand Council, while speaking on "The Church and the Jews" said: "We fascist Catholics consider the Jewish problem from a strictly political point of view. . . . But it comforts our souls to know that if, as Catholics, we became antisemites, we owe it to the teachings that the Church has promulgated over the past twenty centuries."[219]

## *Reichskonkordat*: Opening the Floodgates to Nazism

Before Hitler came to power in 1933, Catholics were banned from becoming members of the Nazi Party. In the German town of Kirschhausen, the parish priest gave his flock very clear guidance:

"1. No Catholic may be a card-carrying member of the Hitler Party.

2. No member of the Hitler Party may participate in [parish gatherings], at funerals or any other events.

3. So long as a Catholic is a card-carrying member of the Hitler Party he may not be admitted to the sacraments."[220]

Even though this was not official Church policy, the episcopate agreed that this was in line with what the Church thought was proper.

In 1931 several German bishops provided a more subdued and unified stance when they said, "As guardians of the true teaching of faith and morals, the bishops must warn against National Socialism, so long and so far as it proclaims cultural and political opinions that are incompatible with Catholic teaching." Those who persisted in becoming members of the party even after warning them were to be denied admission to the sacraments.[221]

During the period the Nazis were trying to take over power in Germany between 1919 and 1933 there were two other political parties more powerful than the Nazis, the leading Social Democrats and the Catholic Center Party. During that period five Catholic Center Party members became chancellors in ten cabinets. The only thing Catholics would have had to do to prevent Hitler from coming to power was to make a coalition with the Social Democrats. However, to avoid Catholic German opposition to absolute papal power, Cardinal Pacelli (the papal nuncio in Germany at the time) agreed to Hitler's demands to disband the Catholic Center Party.[222] This was a big political gain for Hitler, and he saw it as a big gain for religion: "Imbued with the desire to secure for the German people the great religious, moral, and cultural values rooted in the two Christian Confessions, we have abolished the political organizations but strengthened the religious institutions."[223]

The Church, however, continued to see Nazism as evil and sustained their efforts to keep its flock far from it. The bishops, meeting at Fulda in August 1932, declared:

> "All the bishoprics have forbidden membership of the Party because parts of its official program contain false teachings. . . . Considerable numbers of people join the Party solely because of their support for the Party in the secular sphere, for its economic policies and political aims. But this cannot be justified. Support for the Party necessarily involves, whether one wants this or not, furthering its aims as a whole."[224]

Yet a little over six months later the bishops came to believe that Nazism was not as bad as they had initially thought, and therefore acceptable to Catholics:

> "Without therefore departing from the condemnation of certain religious and moral errors voiced in our earlier measures, the episcopate believes it has ground for confidence that the general

prohibitions and admonitions mentioned above need no longer be regarded as necessary."[225]

The Church revoked the ban on membership to the Nazi party shortly after Hitler became chancellor in March 1933 and after then Vatican Secretary of State Pacelli offered an overture to Hitler. The negotiations between the Vatican and Nazi Germany culminated in a concordat between the two states—the *Reichskonkordat.* Cardinal Eugenio Pacelli and Franz von Papen signed the Concordat between the Holy See and Germany on July 20, 1933, on behalf of Pope Pius XI and President Paul von Hindenburg, respectively.

*Cardinal Secretary of State, Eugenio Pacelli (later to become Pope Pius XII) signs the Concordat between Nazi Germany and the Vatican at a formal ceremony in Rome on 20 July 1933. Nazi Vice-Chancellor Franz von Papen sits at the left, Pacelli in the middle, and Rudolf Buttmann sits at the right. Bundesarchiv, Bild 183-R70353.*

The revocation of the ban was very significant because that was something the German bishops would not have done if they had thought that National Socialist and Catholic ideas and principles were in conflict. The bishops expressed, as they put it, "a certain confidence in the new government, subject to reservations concerning some religious and moral lapses."[226] It is also noteworthy that the Church never saw fit to lift the ban of membership in the Communist party.

Beginning in the 1920s, the Church unsuccessfully lobbied the Weimar Republic. Later, it pursued the Nazi state in an effort that culminated with the signing of the Reich Concordat in 1933. To understand the German people's rapid acceptance of Hitler and his policies one needs to understand that long process, Pacelli's crucial role in it, and Hitler's reasons for signing the Concordat.[227] German Catholics had reasons to believe that the Concordat between Catholic Hitler and the Catholic Church meant their days as second-class citizens, dating to the days of the *Kulturkampf,* were over.

In 1937, Father Muckermann wrote in amazement in the Dutch weekly *Der Deutsche Weg* about the warm attitude the German bishops showed toward Nazism. He said that "despite the inhuman brutalities perpetrated in the concentration camps, despite the currency and defamation trials, despite the personal insults against individual princes of the Church, against the Holy Father and the entire Church, and in spite of all hostile measures amounting to another *Kulturkampf,* . . . the bishops find words of appreciation for what (next to Bolshevism) is their worst enemy."[228]

The first and main beneficiary of the *Reichskonkordat* was Hitler himself as the agreement was his first bilateral treaty with a foreign power, which gave him much needed international prestige. At home, the treaty meant that Hitler got his way with his demand that in Germany Catholics, as *Catholics,* should cease to be a political force and thus cease to be a potential obstacle to Nazism. As a Catholic, Hitler would have been very aware of the Catholic resistance to Bismarck's *Kulturkampf* just a few decades before, and he made sure that instead of Catholics being called by the Pope to "passive resistance," they were called instead to look for common ground between Catholicism and Nazism, which they did. As Hitler told his cabinet, the Concordat established the context that would be "especially significant in the urgent struggle against international Jewry."[229] As the Nazi newspaper *Völkischer Beobachter* wrote, "The long drive against the alleged atheistic tendencies of our Party is now silenced by Church authority. This represents an enormous strengthening of the National Socialism government."[230]

Although *L'Osservatore Romano* had declared that the Concordat was not an endorsement of Nazism, both Hitler and the German bishops certainly saw it that way. As Hitler declared, "The fact that the Vatican is concluding a treaty with the new Germany means the acknowledgement of the National Socialist state by the Catholic Church. This treaty shows the whole world clearly and unequivocally that the assertion that National Socialism is hostile to religion is a lie."[231] The Catholic German population perceived the Concordat as a validation of Nazi policies. In the November 1933 congressional elections and plebiscite on the withdrawal from the League of Nations, the Nazis received an overwhelming percentage of "yes" votes from the Catholic segments of the electorate. The bishops reminded Hitler in 1935 that Pius XI had "exchanged the handshake of trust with you through the Concordat—the first foreign sovereign to do so . . . Pope Pius XI spoke high praise of you . . . Millions in foreign countries, Catholics and non-Catholics alike, have overcome their original mistrust because of this expression of papal trust, and have placed their trust in your regime."[232] Their message ended with "We pray to Almighty God that he take under his protection the life of our Führer and Reich Chancellor, and that he grant his blessing to your statesmanly goals."

When the Nuremberg Laws (meant to legalize German racial discrimination against the Jewish people) were passed a month later, the bishops kept quiet.[233] Cardinal Faulhaber declared in a sermon in 1937,

> "At a time when the heads of the major nations in the world faced the new Germany with reserve and considerable suspicion, the Catholic Church, the greatest moral power on Earth,

through the Concordat, expressed its confidence in the new German government. This was a deed of immeasurable significance for the reputation of the new government abroad."[234]

After the treaty had been ratified by both governments, the *Te Deum* was sung in Catholic churches across Germany, and a pontifical Mass was celebrated by the papal nuncio in the Berlin Cathedral, overflowing with worshippers and with Vatican and Nazi flags everywhere, hung side by side. The nuncio praised Hitler at the Berlin Cathedral as "a man marked by his devotion to God, and sincerely concerned for the well-being of the German people."

*Thanksgiving service celebrating the signing of the* Reichskonkordat *at the cathedral of St. Hedwig, Berlin, 1933, with Vatican and Nazi flags hung side by side.*

Even after the true nature of Nazism was clearly exposed, and even after the Nazis had violated numerous provisions of the treaty, the Vatican never saw fit to repudiate the Concordat. German Catholic bishops and priests interpreted the still valid treaty with the Vatican during the war as an indication of the Reich's ongoing legitimacy, and thus of the requirement of its Catholic citizens to continue to carry out its orders.[235]

## The German Catholic Church's Use of Antisemitism

The Catholic Church used antisemitism from a racial perspective whenever it was convenient and useful. During the years 1933-1939 many journals published by priests or in books bearing the *Imprimatur* (official declaration from the Catholic Church that a published work is free from error in matters of Roman Catholic doctrine) published that the Jews had had a "demoralizing influence on religiosity and national character"[236] and that the Jews, as a spiritual community, had brought the German people "more damage than benefit."[237] Again they promoted the old canards that the Jews had displayed a mortal hatred toward Jesus while the "Aryan" Pontius Pilate would have gladly let him go free, and that the Jews had been "the first and most cruel persecutors of the young Church."[238] As always, as the *coup de grâce*, they invoked the deicide accusation: the Jews had not only killed Jesus but were also at the forefront of those that still wanted to destroy the Church.[239] In this kind of environment it is not surprising then that the veteran Nazi priest, Father Senn, hailed Hitler in 1934 as "the tool of God, called upon to overcome Judaism."[240] Repeating anew old Christian teachings, Cardinal Faulhaber declared in his Advent sermons of 1933 "that with the coming of Christ, Jews and Judaism have lost their place in the world."[241]

## Belief that the Jews were the Driving Force Behind Bolshevism

With the arrival of Communism in the Soviet Union, with its atheistic outlook, the Church became convinced it was a "Satanic" force bent on destroying Christianity and European civilization. This line of thinking permeated the Church at all levels, and steered it in directions that could effectively counter the Communist menace, irrespective of the moral failings this may have led to.

For Cardinal Pacelli, later to become Pope Pius XII, this was no different. His first close experience with Communism was negative and dated to the time when he was papal nuncio in Munich after the First World War, when Germany had become the Weimar Republic. This was a chaotic time in which revolutionary groups tried to gain power in the vacuum left by the abdicating Kaiser. Among them were socialist groups who had recently gained power installing the Munich Soviet Republic. At the Munich nunciature where Pacelli was stationed, there was a meeting of the diplomatic corps in which it was decided to talk to a man named Levien, head of the Munich Soviet, to ensure an understanding that the Communist government should recognize the immunity of diplomatic representatives and the extraterritoriality of their residences. Pacelli, thinking that it would be undignified for him to appear personally, sent Monsignor Schioppa. When Schioppa returned, he gave the nuncio sufficient eyewitness information to recreate the circumstances of the meeting. Pacelli then wrote a letter to the Vatican Secretary of State. In this letter Pacelli relayed the information he had heard and endorsed, or that he added himself, including occasional personal annotations:

"The scene that presented itself at the palace was indescribable. The confusion totally chaotic, the filth completely nauseating; soldiers and armed workers coming and going; the building, once the home of a king, resounding with screams, vile language, profanities. Absolute hell. An army of employees were dashing to and fro, giving out orders, waving bits of paper, and in the midst of all this, a gang of young women, of dubious appearance, Jews like the rest of them, hanging around in all the offices with lecherous demeanor and suggestive smiles. The boss of this female rabble was Levien's mistress, a young Russian woman, a Jew and a divorcée, who was in charge. And it was to her that the nunciature was obliged to pay homage in order to proceed.

This Levien is a young man, of about thirty or thirty-five, also

Russian and a Jew. Pale, dirty, with drugged eyes, hoarse voice, vulgar, repulsive, with a face that is both intelligent and sly. He deigned to receive the Monsignor Uditore in the corridor, surrounded by an armed escort, one of whom was an armed hunchback, his faithful bodyguard. With a hat on his head and smoking a cigarette, he listened to what Monsignor Schioppa told him, whining repeatedly that he was in a hurry and had more important things to do."

It is important to point out that Pacelli's constant reference to the Jewishness of this group of power usurpers was consistent with Germany's growing belief that the Jews were the instigators of the Bolshevik revolution, and that they had as their aim the destruction of Christian civilization. Also, the use of a catalog of epithets describing their moral and physical repulsiveness was consistent with old Christian stereotypical antisemitic contempt.

*Vatican nuncio in Bavaria Eugenio Pacelli visits a group of bishops, 1922.*

A week later, an incident with the Red mob profoundly marked Pacelli, instilling in him a lifelong hatred of Communism. Members of the Red Brigade of the South showed up at the nunciature demanding the nuncio gave up the official limousine. When Pacelli refused, one of the armed men "pressed his rifle against my breast and the commander, a horrible type of delinquent, having given the order to his satellites to hold ready their hand grenades, told me insolently that talk was pointless and he must have the car immediately." Thanks to the intervention of Monsignor Schioppa they desisted, but the next day they came again. Pacelli was out, supposedly ill at the doctor. Again Schioppa managed to defuse the situation, but not, according to Pacelli's account, without the sound of gunfire, signaling "the fratricidal battle between the Red Brigade and the White Brigade struggling for the liberation of the capital of Bavaria, which is suffering under a harsh Jewish-Russian revolutionary tyranny."[242]

Like his successor Pius XII, Achille Ratti, before he became Pius XI, subscribed to the belief that Jews were behind Bolshevism. After his trip to Poland, where he was sent by Pope Benedict XV to help the Jews who were being persecuted by Catholic Poles, he reported back to the Vatican that "the Jews form the principal force [of Bolshevism] in Poland" instead. Relating his experience in Warsaw, Ratti reported, "I saw that the [Bolshevik] Commissioners . . . were all Jews."[243]

Hitler understood Christianity's hatred and fear of Communism, and forcefully used the argument that Communism was Christianity's greatest foe in discussions with princes of the Church. According to the eyewitness account of Sister Pascalina (the personal aide and devout admirer of Eugenio Pacelli while he was Papal Nuncio in Munich), Hitler came to visit Pacelli in Munich and told him he was out to fight the spread of atheistic Communism. Pacelli then presented Hitler with a large cache of Church money to aide him and his struggling band of anti-Communists in their fight against the Communists.[244]

In a conversation with Cardinal Faulhaber before the war, Hitler said:

"The Catholic Church should not deceive herself: if National Socialism does not succeed in defeating Bolshevism, then Church and Christianity in Europe too are finished. Bolshevism is the mortal enemy of the Church as much as of Fascism." He then said "Think about all this, Cardinal, and consult with the other leaders of the Church how you can support the great undertaking of National Socialism to prevent the victory of Bolshevism and how you can achieve a peaceful relationship to the state. Either National Socialism and the Church are both victorious or they perish together."

*Propaganda slide entitled "Jewry, Freemasonry and Bolshevism" featuring a poisonous snake with bared fangs, circa 1936. The thinking that permeated the German worldview in the first half of the twentieth century, in which Jews were behind all the modern evils of the world—including Freemasonry and Bolshevism, was a direct offspring of that of the nineteenth century in which the Church had considered the "Freemasons, Protestants, and Jews" as their most bitter enemies.*

A pastoral letter read from the pulpits a few months later, in January 1937, assured the *Führer* that the bishops "support with all available moral resources his world-historical struggle aimed at re-pelling Bolshevism."[245]

The Church communicated to the flock in every conceivable way that Bolshevism was evil and was not only to be avoided, but also fought against. They also missed no opportunity to reinforce the libelous putative connexion between Bolshevism and the Jews. Archbishop Konrad Gröber defined Bolshevism in the *German Handbook of Contemporary Religious Questions*, a book widely circulated in Germany in the 1930s, as "an Asiatic state despotism, in point of fact in the service of a group of terrorists led by Jews" and defined Marxism as "the materialistic socialism founded primarily by the Jew Karl Marx." In the same article Gröber explained how the *Führer* warned that "No people can avoid this clash between its national tradition and Marxism, which is opposed to national ties and led mostly by Jewish agitators and revolutionaries." Even the article on "Art" in the *Handbook* warned that most of the pernicious manifestations of art since the nineteenth century had been produced either by or under the influence of Jews.[246]

As always, members of the Church could draw new meaning out of the old anti-Jewish venom in the Christian Bible and later writings. Bishop Ivan Šarić of Sarajevo could thus explain in 1941 how inherently evil political systems like Socialism and Communism came about:

> "The descendants of those who hated the Son of God, persecuted him to death, crucified him and persecuted his disciples are guilty of greater sins than their forebears. . . . Satan aided them in the creation of socialism and communism. . . . The movement of liberation of the world from the Jews is a movement for the renewal of human dignity."[247]

# 9

# The Church's Positive Attitudes Toward the War

The Catholic Church in Germany was instrumental in encouraging the German flock to follow the authorities' orders and fight for what was perceived to be Germany's just war. The Church's four criteria to consider a war a just one were: it had to be declared by the legitimate authority; there had to be a just cause; recourse to war was permitted only as a last recourse; and it had to be conducted according to natural and international law.[248]

The German bishops taught the faithful to blindly follow their leaders and serve the fatherland. Archbishop Gröber added that Catholic theologians had "never left it to the judgment of the individual [Catholic], with all his shortsightedness and emotionalism, in the event of war to decide its permissibility or lack of permissibility. Instead, the final decision has always been in the province of the lawful authority."[249]

A few days after the start of the war, the German bishops issued a joint pastoral letter in which they urged Catholic soldiers to do their duty:

> "In this decisive hour we encourage and admonish our Catholic soldiers, in obedience to the *Führer*, to do their duty and to be ready to sacrifice their whole person. We appeal to the faithful to

join in ardent prayers that God's providence may lead this war to blessed success and peace for fatherland and people."[250]

The bishop of Berlin, Bishop Preysing, only expressed his feeling of paternal concern for those called to arms.

*Priests giving the Nazi salute at a Catholic youth rally in the Berlin-Neukolln stadium in August 1933.*

The Church used its many publications to exhort the faithful to comply with the Nazi authorities and to fight in Hitler's wars. The voice of the Bavarian Priests' Association, the *Klerusblatt*, urged Catholics to serve their country and to support the German armies that were fighting a war "to defend the homeland." The paper of Cardinal Bertram's diocese called the conflict a struggle of the German people for their self-preservation" and "for a just distribution of necessary *Lebensraum* [German for 'living space']." Germany was participating in "a holy struggle not for the mere reconquest and repossession of stolen territories, but for the highest on earth: life in accordance to God's commands." Clearly any Catholic possibly doubting the justice of the German cause would end up concluding they were indeed noble and just based on the blessing of their bishops and their papers.[251]

The German Catholic bishops believed they had to assuage the Nazis' suspicions that Catholics felt a stronger allegiance to Rome than to Germany and were thus compelled to openly and repeatedly support Hitler's cause. The leading representatives of the Catholic Church in Germany during WWII, deeply imbued with the myths of *Volk* (German for "our people") and Fatherland and determined to prove that Catholics were good and loyal Germans, urged the faithful to obey the Nazi government as the holders of the legitimate authority or by persuading them to do so in defense of *Volk* and Fatherland as a Christian duty.[252] Orders were given in all dioceses so that no teaching on the issue of war was detrimental to the war effort: ". . . carefully to avoid everything that could have an injurious effect upon Germany's war situation."[253] The pastoral letter issued in January 1941 by Bishop Kaller of Ermland elicited praise even of the brutal Chief of Police Heydrich:

> "In this staunchly Christian spirit we also now participate wholeheartedly in the great struggle of our people for the protection of their life and importance in the world. With admiration we look upon our army, which in courageous fighting under extraordinary leadership has achieved and continues to achieve unparalleled success. We thank God for his support. Especially as Christians we are determined to rally all our strength so that the final victory will be secured for our fatherland. Especially as believing Christians, inspired by God's love, we faithfully stand behind our *Führer* who with firm hands guides the fortunes of our people."[254]

The Catholic bishops felt they needed to show a stronger support for the German cause against Bolshevism. Bishop Rackl of Eichstätt, in a pastoral letter issued in September 1941, three months after the invasion of the Soviet Union, termed the campaign "a crusade, a holy war for homeland and people, for faith and church, for Christ and His most holy cross."[255] The Archbishop of Paderborn spoke of a struggle "for the protection of Christianity in our fatherland, for the rescue of the Church from the threat of anti-Christian Bolshevism." This pattern repeated itself numerous times from numerous bishops across Germany.[256]

There is overwhelming evidence to show that the episcopate, at least during the first three years of the war and probably later as well, truly believed the justice of the German cause in fighting a war for the attainment of *Lebensraum* and for the defense against plutocracy and Bolshevism, and thus had no qualms in sending their followers to serve and die fighting what they believed to be a just war.[257]

*Nazi officials and Catholic clergy raise their hands in the Nazi salute at a ceremony in the Saarbrucken city hall marking the reincorporation of the Saarland into the German Reich. Pictured left to right are Bishop Franz Rudolf Bornewasser of Trier, Bishop Ludwig Sebastian of Speyer, Reichskommissar for the Reunification of the Saarland with the German Reich Josef Burckel, Minister of the Interior Willhem Frick, and Minister of Propaganda Joseph Goebbels.*

Obviously there were some German Catholics who opposed Hitler's military effort. However, only seven Catholics in the entire Greater German Reich were conscientious objectors to the war and refused military service. In almost all cases the Church tried to persuade these conscientious objectors to induce them to conform to the official line. Also, Catholic soldiers did not desert in disproportionate numbers, a fact that shows that there was nothing in the teachings of their church that made these soldiers particularly prone to be conscientious objectors. The Church had the obligation to elucidate moral questions to their flock, to teach and to provide moral leadership. The way they taught the faithful to conduct themselves in the war and when confronted with the criminality and immorality of mass murder was to place them deeper and irrevocably under the moral obligation to support the war effort. Catholic bishops called for martyrdom of German Catholics, but it was martyrdom for the *Volk* and Fatherland, not for the values represented by the traditional Catholic morality of war.[258]

## Positive Attitudes Toward Nazism Shown by German Catholic Prelates

Bishop Berning of Osnabrück and Archbishop Gröber were the two members of the German episcopate most openly supportive of a partnership between German Catholics and the new state. As we saw earlier, Archbishop Gröber was the editor of the popular *Handbook of Contemporary Religious Questions*. Addressing a meeting of Catholic organizations in Karlsruhe, Gröber declared to an enthusiastic audience that he gave "his complete and wholehearted support to the new government and the new Reich."[259]

As the German Ambassador Bergen reported after Bishop Berning's visit to Rome in 1933, the "Bishop of Osnabrück, during his recent stay in Rome, showed a gratifying understanding of the wishes of the government and of the needs of our times."[260] Bishop Berning declared that German Bishops not only accepted and recognized the new state but served it "with ardent love and with all our strength."[261] When he was informed in February 1942 of the massacre of eighteen thousand Jews that had taken place in Kovno, which included five thousand children, and the horrific conditions in which twenty thousand Jews from Berlin, Vienna and several other large cities lived and died in the Łódź ghetto in Poland, Bishop Berning wrote in his diary that "it appears likely that a plan exists to murder the Jews."[262] By this time most of the ecclesiastical authorities in Germany must have learned of the exterminatory campaign to eliminate the Jews, either from internal communication from the Church or through informal reports or confessions from the soldiers and police units in the eastern front, or their families.

Cardinal Bertram wrote in a letter to Catholic students of theology that no one should doubt the sincerity of the Church in accepting and standing up for the new order. Bertram addressed thirty-thousand German Catholics in his diocese of Breslau in 1938, invoking Scriptures to support the Nazi regime: "There is no need to urge you to give respect and obedience to the new authorities of the German state. You all know the words of the apostle: 'Everyone must submit himself to the governing authorities.'"[263] When he sent Hitler birthday greetings in 1939 in the name of all German Catholic bishops, Bishop Preysing of Berlin reacted furiously.[264]

After Hitler's rise to power, Bishop Bornewasser of Trier exhibited the Seamless Robe as an exceptional show of support. The tunic had not been exhibited to the faithful since 1891. He declared to a congregation of Catholic youth in Tier Cathedral that "with raised heads and firm step we have entered the new Reich and we are prepared to serve it with all the might of our body and soul."[265]

## Examples of Antisemitic Remarks from the Protestant Church

The Protestant leadership had considered Jews to be Germany's bitter enemies long before Hitler came to power. Bishop Otto Dibelius declared in a letter written in April 1933 that he had been "always an antisemite. One cannot fail to appreciate that in all of the corrosive manifestations of modern civilization Jewry plays a leading role." As a possible "solution" to the "Jewish Problem" he suggested all Jewish immigration from Eastern Europe should be prohibited as that would bring a quick decline of the Jewish population. "The number of children of the Jewish families is small. The process of dying out occurs surprisingly rapidly." Bishop Dibelius' views were representative of German Christendom in the beginning of 1933. Bishop Dibelius' hopeful thoughts about a Jewish bloodless extinction was a prelude to the open endorsement of the Nazis' eliminationist policies that German Church leaders gave the regime during their most violent and radical actions against the Jews.[266]

*Reich Bishop Ludwig Muller, Wittenberg, 1933. Bundesarchiv, Bild 183-H25547.*

Even Protestant minister Niemöller, one of the most celebrated German opponents of Nazism, could not detach himself from his Christian heritage when he spoke to his flock during the early years of Nazi rule. In a sermon to them, he said:

"We speak of the 'eternal Jew' and conjure up the picture of the restless wanderer who has no home and who cannot find peace. We see a highly gifted people which produces idea after idea for the benefit of the world, but whatever it takes up becomes poisoned, and all that it ever reaps is contempt and hatred because ever and anon the world notices the deception and avenges itself in its own way."

Despite Niemöller's hatred of the Nazi regime, he concurred on the Nazi worldview in one fundamental point, and that was that the Jews were eternally evil.[267]

Dietrich Bonhoeffer from the Confessing Church also displayed Christian ambivalence and theological anti-Judaism toward Jews: "The state's measures against the Jewish people are connected . . . in a very special way with the Church," he declared regarding the April boycott. "In the church of Christ, we have never lost sight of the idea that the 'Chosen People,' who nailed the Savior of the world to the cross, must bear the curse of the action through a long history of suffering."[268]

## What the Pope and Churches Knew

In order for someone to act in defense of someone else, the former needs to know the latter needs help. Therefore, it is important to establish what the Catholic and Protestant Churches knew of the exterminatory campaign against the Jews during the Second World War. We will cover what the Churches could and should have done to help elsewhere.

As early as January 1941, if not earlier, the Pope must have learned of the assault on European Jews. In a letter to the Pope that January, Bishop Preysing, one of the very few Catholic prelates that opposed the Nazis and their antisemitism, wrote to the Pope, "Your Holiness is certainly informed about the situation of the Jews in Germany and the neighboring countries. I wish to mention that I have been asked both from the Catholic and Protestant side if the Holy See could not do something on this subject . . . in favor of these unfortunates." The Pope did not respond.

The systematic murder of Europe's Jews had begun in earnest after the June 1941 invasion of the Soviet Union. By the end of the year the widespread massacres had become well known among German colonizers and the millions of German soldiers serving on the eastern front, as well as among the German population back home. As Stewart Herman, the Minister of the American Church in Berlin who remained in Germany until December 1941, corroborated: "It became definitely known through the soldiers returning from the front that in occupied Russia, especially at Kiev [the site of the Babi Yar massacre of more than thirty-three thousand Jews at the end of September], Jewish civilians—men, women, and babies—were being lined up and machine-gunned by the thousands."[269]

*German policeman killing a Jewish mother and child. The photograph was sent home by the policeman in 1942. The original inscription on its back reads: "Ukraine 1942, Jewish Action, Ivangorod." Thousands of murderers kept photographic albums of their deeds and shared them with pride amongst themselves and with their loved ones back home.*

These kind of stories met with some understandable incredulity. A religious German Protestant called Kurt Gerstein joined the *Waffen-SS* to investigate rumors of atrocities against the mentally handicapped. When he was sent to the East as an expert in disinfection, he managed to personally witness a mass gassing of Jews at Bełżec in August 1942. When he attempted to inform Papal Nuncio Orsenigo in Berlin of the atrocity, the nuncio refused to receive him. Gerstein then asked the legal advisor to Bishop von Preysing, the Pope's good friend, to deliver the report to the Vatican.[270]

Throughout 1942 and in subsequent years there were a flurry of reports that flowed into the Vatican. Although most of the clergy around Europe was not informed of the details of what was happening to Europe's Jews, there is no question that the Pope, the Secretariat of State, and some nuncios had a good understanding of the situation starting at least in 1942. They may not have understood precisely the nature of the deportations, the selection process, the precise manner of death, or had complete statistics. It is also immaterial that they could not verify all the information received, but the repetition of similar reports over time, by widely different sources including many trusted Italian businessmen or Italian priests should have constituted adequate confirmation. Given the information available to them, and the magnitude and horror of the disaster unfolding in front of their very eyes, the Pope and his diplomatic officials should have acted more vigorously.[271]

On September 18, 1942, Monsignor Giovanni Battista Montini, the Vatican Undersecretary of State and future Pope Paul VI, wrote, "The massacres of the Jews reach frightening proportions and forms." However, when later that month the U.S. representative to the Vatican told the Pope his silence was endangering his moral prestige, the Secretary of State answered on his behalf that it was "impossible to verify rumors about crimes committed against the Jews."[272]

The Vatican could have played a role in slowing down the ongoing genocide, but chose not to disseminate the information they had about the exterminatory campaign. They did not share the information with other diplomats or within their extensive diplomatic and ecclesiastic network around Europe. Not making the information public had lethal consequences because most of the victims were fooled into thinking they were being resettled to work in the East and thus did not escape or go into hiding.[273]

Within the Church, however, ecclesiastical authorities *did* disseminate the information. A memo prepared by the Vatican Secretary of State Maglione in May 1943, summarizing the situation of Jews in Poland, said in part:

> "In Poland, there were, before the war, 4,500,000 Jews; it is calculated now that there remain (including all those who came there from other countries occupied by the Germans) only 100,000.

> In Warsaw a ghetto containing about 650,000 was created: now there are only 20-25,000 Jews there.

> Naturally many Jews have gotten away; but *there is no doubt that the majority have been killed.* After months and months of transport of thousands and thousands of people, they have made nothing known of themselves: something that can only be explained by their deaths. . .

> Special death camps at Lublin (Treblinka) and near Brest Litovsk. It is said that several hundred at a time are jammed into large rooms, where they die by gassing."

The author of this report got the geographical locations of the camps wrong, and knew nothing of Auschwitz, but otherwise the information is quite accurate.[274]

Two months later Monsignor Angelo Roncalli, apostolic delegate in Turkey and Greece and later to become Pope John XXIII, met with Franz von Papen, the German ambassador to Turkey. In the conversation, as reported by Roncalli to Monsignor Montini, they discussed among other things the Katyn Forest massacre in which the bodies of several thousand Polish officers, supposedly murdered by the Russians, were found.[275] Papen told Roncalli that this showed it was better for the Poles to side with the Germans rather than the Russians. Roncalli reported that he "answered with a sad smile that first it would be necessary to make them forget the millions of Jews sent to and executed in Poland." Neither Roncalli nor Vatican officials ignored by then the nature and magnitude of the genocide.[276]

## The Deportation of the Jews of Rome

The roundup and deportation of the Jews of Rome, just like the ghetto of Rome of prior centuries, is a special case due to the physical proximity to the Vatican and thus to the place where the Pope had the greatest influence.

Despite German concerns that the Pope may have objected to the deportation, the roundup of Rome's eight thousand Jews began in October 1943. Bishop Hudal, the openly pro-Nazi head of the German church in Rome, sent a letter to General Stahel, the German military commander in Rome, in which he asked the General to stop the arrests as "I fear that otherwise the Pope will have to make an open stand, which will serve the anti-German propaganda as a weapon against us."[277]

The next day Ernst von Weizsäcker, the new German ambassador at the Holy See, was driven to an audience with the Pope in the papal limousine with the papal and Nazi flags side by side in "peaceful harmony." He then reported to his superiors that the Vatican was upset as the arrests had been made, as it were, from right under the Pope's windows:

> "The people hostile to us in Rome are taking advantage of this affair to force the Vatican from its reserve. People say that the bishops of French cities, where similar incidents occurred, have taken a firm stand. The Pope, as supreme head of the Church and Bishop of Rome, cannot be more reticent than they. They

are also drawing a parallel between the stronger character of Pius XI and that of the present Pope."[278]

Contrary to both men's misgivings, the Pope remained silent. As Weizsäcker reported, "Although under pressure from all sides, the Pope has not let himself be drawn into any demonstrative censure of the deportation of the Jews of Rome." Over one thousand Roman Jews—more than two-thirds of them women and children—were arrested and deported to their deaths in Auschwitz. As opposed to what was the case of most of the deportations that were taking place in Europe, the majority of the Jews in Rome were aware of the imminent roundup. Thanks to this, about seven thousand managed to hide, about half of them in the numerous monasteries and houses of religious orders in Rome. A few dozen were sheltered in the Vatican itself. Even though these Christian acts of charity were performed with the knowledge and approval of the Pope, there is no evidence to show that they were performed under his command. Even though some Jews found refuge in the Pope's summer residence at Castel Gandolfo, no Jews were hidden or sheltered in the Pope's fourteen-hundred-room palace in the Vatican.[279]

The fate of those Jews from Rome that were indeed deported is known. An entry in the Auschwitz logs tersely reads: "Transport, Jews from Rome. After the selection 149 men (registered with numbers 158451-158639) and 47 women (registered with numbers 66172-66218) have been admitted to the detention camp. The rest have been gassed." Only fourteen men and one woman returned alive; by any measure an abysmal survival rate.[280]

The Vatican heard of Auschwitz at the latest in 1944 through a report called "The Auschwitz Protocol," written by two Jews who escaped from the camp in April of that year and wrote a detailed thirty page report describing the selection and killing process as well as giving thorough statistics of those killed.

## The Church's Plausible Deniability Strategy

In April 1943 the Vatican articulated a strategy of plausible deniability of the extent of the Church's defense of the Jews. This was communicated in an internal Vatican memo written by Pope Pius XII's long time aide Monsignor Domenico Tardini, in which Tardini wrote a summary of the state of the Vatican's measures regarding Jews.

*Pope Pius XII and Monsignor Domenico Tardini.*

Tardini was concerned about the potential embarrassment due to the Slovakian Church's involvement in the deportation of the Slovakian Jews. To protect the Church's political standing, he recommended that the Vatican protest to Slovakian President Tiso, and do so with the express purpose of then leaking the admonishment to the world. He explained in the memo that "it would not be out of place to discreetly make known to the public this diplomatic note of the Holy See (the fact of its being sent and the content of the document rather than the text). This will make known to the world that the Holy See fulfills its duty of charity." He then went on to say that issuing a protest that could be leaked would not "attract the sympathy of the Jews in case they are among the victors given the fact that the Jews will never be too friendly to the Holy See and to the Catholic Church." It appears that for Monsignor Tardini, the fact that the Jews would never be friendly to the Church was not to be lamented since the Church's apparent gesture of aid was being made to people allegedly already hostile to it, which "will render more meritorious any charitable efforts" by the Church. Apart from the transparently antisemitic view that the Jews, who were being exterminated, had no country and no army yet could be counted among the "victors," this level of cynicism from such high official in the Vatican is astonishing.[281]

It seems that for Pope Pius XII keeping up appearances was sufficient. He wrote a letter to his good friend Bishop Preysing of Berlin (who had been strongly urging his German colleagues and the Pope to make strong pronouncements in defense of the Jews), stating he would not issue any further statements against the annihilation of the Jews. The Pope believed this was not necessary because what the German bishops had done by urging humane treatment of "other races" in a previous statement was enough to secure "the respect of world opinion" for them after the war.[282]

After the deportation of the Jews of Rome in October 1943, Vatican officials made polite inquiries about the whereabouts of the Jews intended to make it look like the Vatican was working to help them. Most of these inquiries were about specific "baptized non-Aryan" individuals, however. Two days after most of the deportees from Rome had already perished in Auschwitz and under pressure from Jewish relatives, Jesuit Father Tacchi Venturi made a symbolic inquiry about the fate of those Jews. He then informed the Vatican Secretary of State Maglione that "A step like this by the Holy See, even if it does not obtain the desired effect, will without doubt help increase the veneration and gratitude toward the August Person of the Holy Father." It must be remembered, when considering the cynicism of these words, that the Jews in question here were those abandoned by the Pope to be exterminated by allowing the Germans to deport them from Rome.[283]

In internal correspondence within the Vatican Secretariat of State, an official reported in December 1943 that the archbishop of Ferrara had asked the Holy See to intervene on behalf of "non-Aryans," especially those in mixed families. The official went on to mention some potential actions the Holy See could take, knowing that they would be totally ineffective and they would fail. That request for help, however, was aimed at Jews in mixed marriages, and not Jews in general. With undisguised cynicism he showed no intention of intervening on behalf of the Jews, but rather was simply trying to preserve appearances by taking some token action he could report to the archbishop of Ferrara as well as future critics. He concluded: "if nothing else, it will always be possible to say that the Holy See has done everything possible to help these unhappy people."[284]

In Slovakia, the Church found itself with a big problem toward the end of the war. Slovakia's mass-murdering president-priest Tiso and many other politician-priests had willingly handed over to the Nazis most of their country's Jews, and neither the Pope nor the Vatican had done much to stop them. These politicians were the political heirs to Father Hlinka, who had established the Slovak People's Party in 1905 and who, sharing the views of many Catholics of the time, but in violation of official Church doctrine, said, "A Jew remains a Jew even if he is baptized by a hundred Bishops." In October 1944, to control the predicament created by Father Tiso now that the Allied victory was imminent and the Church felt it had to position itself politically for the new realities on the ground, the Church tried to dissociate itself from the Slovakian clergy's deeds by continuing with their strategy of disinformation and keeping appearances. At the Vatican, the authoritative Monsignor Tardini expressed concern that the mass murder of Slovakia's Jews produced "the danger that the responsibility can be shifted to the Catholic Church itself." They sent an emissary to Father Tiso who warned him for the record that the mass annihilation "is harmful to the prestige of this country and enemies will exploit it to discredit clergy and the Church the world over."[285] The Church did not use this or any other opportunity to say that the annihilation of the Jews was criminal and immoral.

# 10

## What the Churches Said.
## What the Churches Failed to Say.

The Church was never reticent to criticize, render judgment and condemn certain aspects of society or politics it objected to whenever and wherever they may have been found. However, concerning the genocidal assault on European Jews during the Second World War the Church kept silent. With such silence in the face of the enormity of the events, it is reasonable to conclude that there was no disapproval.[286] For the Church, as well as to its head, Pope Pius XII, the desire to fight Bolshevism was enough for them not to do anything that could weaken the German power of resistance to the Soviet Union, as they saw atheistic Bolshevism as the Church's mortal enemy and Nazism as the only possible protection against it.

### The Church in Action: the *Kulturkampf*

One of the arguments usually wielded in defense of a silent Catholic Church during WWII is that it was impotent against an all-powerful state. After all, the Vatican had no army and Germany had Europe's most powerful and well-equipped military and repression apparatus. However, there are precedents to the Catholic Church standing up for its rights when it felt threatened, even against a powerful state. One such case was the very important cultural struggle that took place in Germany between the German government and the Catholic Church in 1871.

After Chancellor Otto von Bismarck's victory over the French in 1870 in the Franco-Prussian War, Bismarck thought he had achieved enough to enable him to establish a new German empire. To achieve this, he believed he needed to keep Catholic Austria outside the empire to keep Catholics a decided minority, given that Prussia was predominantly Protestant. To control the empire, Bismarck felt he had to control the one-third of the population that was Catholic. By defining Catholics as the enemy, he managed to get the liberals on his side (who Pope Pius IX had so resolutely defined as the enemy himself when he declared the Church's opposition to modernism). Since Bismarck was a conservative and part of his appeal was as defender of the old order against liberalism, he managed to make both conservatives and liberals in the new Germany join forces to fight Catholics. What followed was a sustained and systematic anti-Catholic campaign involving banishing priests and nuns from the country, removing bishops from their positions, closing of Catholic schools, confiscation of Church property, disbanding of Catholic associations, and an open rift with the Vatican. This campaign was called the *Kulturkampf,* meaning "cultural struggle," and raged between 1871 until about 1887.

This campaign is significant because it shows what a resolute Church could do, and did, when it found itself on the receiving end of a ruthless and calculated campaign to destroy it. In 1875 Pius IX issued an encyclical to counterattack the *Kulturkampf.* In it, he used direct and clear language that declared laws that authorized the government to oversee the training and assignment of priests invalid, "since they are completely contrary to the God-given institutions of the church." He also urged the Catholic population of Germany to engage in a strategy of "passive resistance," and he immediately excommunicated all priests who cooperated with the German government's implementation of the anti-Catholic policies. As the policies of the *Kulturkampf* escalated, millions of German Catholics complied with the Pope's request and made passive resistance the prevalent response to the government's assault.[287]

Anticipating Bismarck's campaign, German Catholics formed the Center Party, which was to become very powerful in the years to come. During those early years they became defenders of minorities, including Jews, although the Center Party still exploited old Jewish stereotypes when it was politically convenient. As the *Kulturkampf* continued over the years, it became clear to Germans that not only were Catholics not capitulating, they were actually becoming even more closely devoted to the Pope. As the conflict proceeded, Catholic voices critical of the Vatican ceased to be heard. As Pope Leo XIII succeeded the unyielding Pius IX, he joined the German Catholic Church on the demand of the full restoration of its rights and property. When Bismarck realized he needed the support of the (by then increasingly more powerful) Center Party on a number of legislative and budget matters, he yielded. The Church had shown that, when it wanted to, it could successfully resist.[288]

Even though German Catholics of this pre-fascist period were not free of antisemitism, they would prove to be less antisemitic than their Protestant coreligionists in Germany, and Catholics in Austria and France. As the Prussian government continued its attack on German Catholics, a pro-Jewish trend developed among German Catholics, reinstating the positive side of Christian ambivalence toward Jews introduced by Augustine in reaction to Ambrose, and in the papal tradition *Sicut Judaeis*.[289]

For the sake of comparison between the period of the *Kulturkampf* and the Nazi era, it is worth pointing out that just in Prussia nine of twelve bishops had been exiled during the *Kulturkampf*, while the total number of Catholic bishops removed from their seats during the twelve years of Nazi rule was three, despite the Nazis' intentions and efforts to eradicate Christianity from German life.

## The Bishop's Duty

Throughout the Nazi period the German bishops expressed themselves in favor of supporting traditional Christian values of love and morality, and strongly pledged to uphold their pastoral duties. The Bavarian bishops declared in 1936, "We would rather go to jail or face death, than become unfaithful to our pastoral duty."[290] At a time when Hitler was becoming a godlike figure to so many Germans, Cardinal Faulhaber felt he had to counteract that trend when he stressed that the bishop's first duty was toward God: "The bishop no longer would be the servant of God if he were to please men or remain silent out of fear of men."[291] Bishop Galen, famous for his energetic and successful campaign to stop the Nazi Euthanasia Program, declared in a sermon delivered in July 1941: "I am aware that as a bishop, as harbinger and defender of the legal and moral order desired by God, which grants everyone basic rights and liberties not to be invaded by human demands, I am called upon . . . courageously to represent the authority of the law and to brand as an injustice crying to heaven the condemnation of defenseless innocents."[292]

These noble sentiments of course proved to be empty formulas, as the bishops did not speak up against the persecution and then extermination of the Jews, and thus did not provide moral guidance to their flocks, therefore becoming unfaithful to their pastoral duties. Thus, and according to Christian theology, the souls of millions of Christians were forsaken as their eternal salvation was put in jeopardy. The Christian churches, who as a shepherd has as its principal duty and reason for being to tend to the moral and spiritual safety of their flock, failed to do just that by not telling their congregants that with every act of omission and of commission, particularly in their participation in the extermination of the Jews, they committed a crime against humanity and a sin against God. According to Church doctrine, the failure to have warned Christians is a sin because we incur the "responsibility for the sins committed by others" by "not disclosing or not hindering them when we have an obligation to do so."[293] As the Church made clear in the encyclical *Mit brennender Sorge* published before the war erupted, the Church was responsible for securing for Germany "the salva-tion of the souls in her care." The inescapable conclusion, then, is that the Church did not believe that the participation of Catholics in the annihilation of the Jews was a sin and therefore was endangering "the salvation of the souls in her care" by not admonishing them to stop the genocide.[294]

Pope Pius XI continued his recrimination of the German racial policies, as he had expressed in *Mit brennender Sorge*. In a letter sent to rectors of Catholic educational institutions in April 1938, at a time when the anti-Jewish racial laws in Italy were about to be passed, the Vatican clearly opposed what they perceived to be eight errors of Nazi doctrine involving race. This letter was later published in *La Civiltà Cattolica*. It never mentioned Jews or antisemitism.

### *Res, non verba*: The Bishops in Action

It is easy to see how the masses of people in Germany, Poland, France and other Christian countries became immune to the horror of the exterminatory campaign against the Jews once we understand that these peoples had heard, all their lives, that Jews were evil, killers of God, an enemy of Christianity and deservers of the fate that had befallen them. Throughout Europe Christian prelates and priests of all levels insistently promoted these ideas to a flock ready to listen.

Cardinal Augustyn Hlond, primate of Poland, said in a pastoral letter in 1936:

"I warn against that moral stance, imported from abroad, that is basically and ruthlessly anti-Jewish. It is contrary to Catholic ethics. One may not hate anyone. It is forbidden to assault, beat up, maim or slander Jews. One should honor Jews as human beings and neighbors. . . Beware of those who are inciting anti-Jewish violence. They serve an evil cause."

As good as this statement was, he felt compelled to precede it with:

"There will be the Jewish problem as long as Jews remain. It is a fact that the Jews are fighting against the Catholic Church, persisting in freethinking, and are the vanguard of godlessness, Bolshevism and subversion. It is a fact that the Jewish influence on morality is pernicious and that their publishing houses disseminate pornography. It is a fact that the Jews deceive, levy interest, and are pimps. It is a fact that the religious and ethical influence of the Jewish young people on the Polish young people is a negative one."[295]

This letter was part of an official Catholic endorsement of the Nazi boycott of Jewish business in Poland and was read from the pulpits of all churches in the country. It clearly shows the centuries-old ambivalence high prelates of the Church showed toward Judaism. This dichotomy found expression in a Church that tried to protect Jews while at the same time instilling on the faithful the hatred that later developed into indifference at best and active collaboration in the genocide at worst.

In January 1940 Pius XII instructed Vatican Radio to broadcast a complaint about how the Germans were treating the Poles: "Conditions of religious, political, and economic life have thrown the Polish people, especially in those areas occupied by Germany, into a state of terror, of degradation, and, we dare say, of barbarism. . . . The Germans employ the same methods, perhaps even worse, as those used by the Soviets." Any mention of the suffering of the Jewish people in the same place and time is conspicuously absent from this message, even though the German treatment of the Jews was much worse than that meted out to the Poles. And there is no doubt that "Poles" referred to "Catholic Poles" as it was customary at the time, and did not include "Jewish Poles" which would have been referred to as simply "Jews." This message is also interesting as it was rare for the Pope to say that the Nazis were worse than the Communists.[296]

Leaders of the Protestant Evangelical Church of seven regions of Germany issued an official pronouncement in December 1941 declaring the Jews as incapable of being saved by baptism due to their racial constitution, to be responsible for the war, and to be "born enemies of the world and Germany." Having completely assimilated the logic of racial, demonological antisemitism, and in complete contravention of Christian doctrine, those church leaders gave their explicit ecclesiastical authorization for the implementation of the "severest measures" against the Jews. The superlative "severest measures" could only mean one thing in the context of the ongoing titanic struggle raging in the Russian front and the ongoing extermination of Soviet Jewry.[297]

*SA Storm Troopers attend church.*

During WWII, the German episcopate repeatedly issued orders to exclude from the sacraments Catholics who engaged in dueling or who agreed to have their bodies cremated. They did not object to the crematoria in the extermination camps, of which they knew. That the episcopate never saw fit to issue orders prohibiting the faithful, on pain of excommunication, from participating in the massacre of the Jews, meant that Catholics, along with the rest of the German population, went on conscientiously participating in the mass murder.

In August of 1941, despite the ongoing slaughter of Lithuania's Jews, the leaders of the Lithuanian Catholic Church "forbade the priests to help Jews in any way whatsoever." Those church leaders did this even after representatives of the Jewish community had approached them begging for help. As a whole, the Lithuanian Church collaborated with the Germans until the tide of the war turned against Germany.[298]

In April 1942 the Slovak bishops issued a collective pastoral letter that justified the deportation of the Jews as Christ-killers: "The greatest tragedy of the Jewish nation lies in the fact of not having recognized the Redeemer and of having prepared a terrible and ignominious death for Him on the cross." This was complemented by further antisemitic charges and support for the deportations:

> "The influence of the Jews [has] been pernicious. In a short time they have taken control of almost all the economic and financial life of the country to the detriment of our people. Not only economically, but also in the cultural and moral spheres, they have harmed our people. The Church cannot be opposed, therefore, if the state with legal regulations hinders the dangerous influence of the Jews."[299]

Sometimes the sermons were quite explicit. On a Sunday sermon in May 1942 in Kowel, Poland, the priest gave clear guidance to his flock: "No trace of a Jew is to remain. We should erase them from the face of the earth."[300]

Whenever anyone appealed on behalf of the Jews, Vatican Secretary of State Cardinal Maglione would consistently reply that the Vatican had done, was doing, and would continue to do everything possible for the Jews. He instructed his nuncios and apostolic delegates to use this or a similar response when receiving entreaties for the Jews.[301]

At the height of the German genocidal campaign Cardinal Faulhaber approached his colleague Cardinal Bertram and proposed they compose a manifesto protesting the murder of Jews. Bertram's response reflected the typical Catholic attitude toward the subject, namely that the Church should limit its influence to matters "of greater importance in the long term."[302]

There was not a single time in which German Catholic or Protestant bishops spoke out nationally on behalf of the Jews during the Nazi era. This is particularly significant because if any bishop in Italy, France or elsewhere had spoken out against the extermination of the Jews, it would have only had local repercussions, whereas if the German bishops had spoken out publicly and nationally, it may have had a chance of morally preventing Christians from executing the "Final Solution." Moreover, after Germany had suppressed freedom of speech and political parties, only the churches remained as a possible force to influence public opinion.[303] This acquiescence with Nazi policies during the years of the Third Reich was due to the widespread complicity of the German Churches and the Nazi regime. The Churches may have disagreed with the ultimate exterminatory measures, but they were certainly in agreement with the eliminationist policies of the Nazis. The reason for this was because these were in essence an extension of the policies vis-à-vis the Jews the Churches held on to for centuries, and that the Catholic Church had been eager to restore everywhere in Europe ever since the French Revolution had initiated the movement to emancipate them (and indeed succeeded in restoring in the Papal States).

In 1941, when the "Final Solution of the Jewish Question" was already underway, it is possible that some bishops might have wanted to speak out against the extermination of the Jews. However, they found themselves prisoners of their own antisemitic teachings, as they had to conform to the indifference of the surrounding population. Thus, an important reason why the German episcopate did not act against the genocide was because of their fear that they could not count on the support of their faithful, if they did act. In other words, the failure of the episcopate mirrored the failure of the Christian flock, and the Christian flock's attitude stemmed from the teachings of the episcopate.

The single use of the word "Jew" by a Vatican organ was in two articles published in December 1943 by *L'Osservatore Romano* in which they protested an Italian measure ordering Italian police to arrest Jews and intern them within the country, neglecting to make any mention whatsoever of the deportation and destruction of European Jewry.

In June of 1944, as the Jews of Hungary were being deported to Auschwitz and the end of the war was imminent, the Allies intensified their pressure on the Horthy régime in Hungary to put a stop to the deportations. Only after Horthy received a deluge of protests from many countries (including an ultimatum by President Roosevelt in which he said that "Hungary's fate will not be like any other civilized nation . . . unless the deportations are stopped"), followed by an unusually heavy bombing raid on Budapest, were the deportations halted. The Vatican waited until that time to make a protest to halt the deportations, but by then most of the four hundred and thirty-thousand Jews the Germans would eventually deport had already been deported. However, the papal nuncio in Budapest, on conveying the message to Horthy, took advantage of the opportunity to clarify that the Vatican's protest was not at all due to a "false sense of compassion" for the Jews.[304]

### The Role of the Military Chaplains

There was considerable variation in the attitude of chaplains to the Holocaust, from rabid endorsement of Nazi ideology and policies, to protest against genocide and brutality. One priest recalled how another priest explained the extermination of the Jews in theological terms, saying, "There is a curse on this people ever since the crucifixion of Jesus when they cried: 'Let his blood be on our heads and on the heads of our children.'" However, the priest also explained that "most of the other" clergy did not share this position, which leads to the logical conclusion that a minority of the clergy did approve of it.[305] There is one well-documented case of military chaplains that tried to obstruct the machinery of destruction, albeit unsuccessfully. Catholic Father Tewes and Protestant Minister Wilczek tried to save a group of Jewish children whose parents had already been shot in the Ukrainian town of Belaya Tserkov. They did not express surprise at the fact that special units in the Army and the *Einsatzgruppen* had already murdered thousands of adult Jews, including the children's families. However, their act of dismay at the torture and murder of the children was atypical and perhaps unique. It shows that the men who asked for the chaplains' help with the children, and the chaplains' act of resistance itself, did not result in punishment of any kind for the soldiers or the chaplains. If other chaplains tried to save Jews or admonished the killers to refrain from committing mass murder, no such acts of resistance came to light after the war despite the incentive the chaplains had to show their putative opposition to the genocidal drive of their compatriots.[306]

Catholic military Bishop Franz Justus Rarkowski was the spiritual leader of the priests assigned to the German armed forces, the *Wehrmacht*. He provided group absolution and succor to soldiers and was deeply Nazified. In his 1940 Christmas message, sent to all Catholic soldiers, he blamed Jews for the war and all of Germany's misfortunes:

> "The German people . . . has a good conscience and knows which people it is that before God and history bears the responsibility for this presently raging, gigantic struggle. The German people knows who lightheartedly unleashed the dogs of war. . . . Our opponents . . . believed in the power of their money bags and the repressive force of that shameful and un-Christian Treaty of Versailles."[307]

In a pastoral letter in August 1942 he advised the faithful in the armed forces, who by then were drenched in the blood of many hundreds of thousands of Jewish victims murdered at point-blank range:

> "Whatever the times demand in efforts, blood and tears, whatever the *Führer* and Supreme Commander commands you soldiers to do and whatever your country expects from you: behind all this stands God himself with his will and command." The German soldier "remains staunchly loyal to his military oath, to his country, his people and to his *Führer*, not out of expectation of reward, not out of fear of punishment, but out of holiest conviction of conscience."[308]

*Belt buckle issued to Wehrmacht soldiers with the "God With Us" inscription.*

To the German soldiers, members of police units or the SS, all of them guilty of terrible atrocities, the oath of allegiance to Hitler was binding. Members of the *Wehrmacht* swore this loyalty oath: "I swear by God this holy oath that I shall render unconditional obedience to the *Führer* of the German Reich and the German people, Adolf Hitler." For the members of the elite SS, it was: "I pledge to you, Adolf Hitler, my obedience unto death, so help me God." Many of these soldiers took their religion very seriously and the association of God, Hitler, duty, and *Volk* was a powerful, indissoluble one. Every German army soldier's belt buckle had the inscription *Gott mit uns* (German for "God with us") stamped on it.[309]

According to Catholic teachings, an oath cannot make lawful what is otherwise morally illicit. The German bishops allowed their flock to take this and similar oaths by explaining to them that no oath could obligate a Christian to do that which violated God's laws. The waiver thus obtained allowed Catholics to take these oaths without pangs of conscience and therefore eliminated the possibility of conflicts of loyalties. Moreover, this also gave *carte blanche* to Christians to perpetrate the heinous acts they did as they were morally bound to fulfill their duty to *Volk* and fatherland through the spirit of blind obedience instilled in them and sealed by this oath, a feeling strongly reinforced by Army Bishop Rarkowski.[310] Additionally, the admonition to continue to do whatever was asked of them and that God was behind those commands gave the perpetrators clear conscience as they were in essence being told that mass murder of Jews was not a violation of God's laws.

The incessant exhortations to obey the *Führer* proved to be more powerful than the scriptural injunction to obey God instead of men. The bishops at home occasionally referred to that dictum, but not the Army Catholic Bishop, Rarkowski. As one former Catholic recruit recalled, there was constant advise on how to avoid sexual adventures and relentless talk of the Bolshevik threat, but "no word about Hitler, no word about antisemitism, about possible conflicts between command and conscience."[311] After the war at least some German veterans complained bitterly that the military chaplains tasked with tending to their souls in that time of distress had not complained against the murder of civilians. The theologian Hans Richard Nevermann wrote long after his experience in the war that never in the entire conflict an officer, comrade, or chaplain ever had anything to say about German atrocities other than complain that the war was terrible.

The clergy who ministered to mass murderers certainly faced different challenges compared to regular chaplains who ministered to regular soldiers in all the world's armed forces. As a German Catholic priest stationed in the Crimea reported of his conversation with a wounded soldier who had been part of a machine gun commando in Sevastopol, "The guy was completely ruined by this experience. Line up the Jews, clothes off, naked before his eyes, women, children, men, and then the machine guns. He had to man one of the guns himself. 'I can say I did not hit any of them. I always shot in the air.' But the experience, how the people fell backwards, earth over them, and then the next row, until the anti-tank trench was full . . . forty-thousand people. 'What should I have done?' the man wanted to know. He had a wife and family. Should he have refused?" The priest did not have an answer. "And I am expected to respond as a priest?" he wondered. Echoing the rationalizations and self-exonerating line of thinking of the postwar reckoning with the wartime actions, the priest continued, "I do not know how I would have reacted in that situation. Am I supposed to tell the soldier that he was a coward and should have stood up against it? He would immediately have been put in the same row and shot along with them. Is that what God wants? For us that was the first time that we heard anything about the shooting of Jews. The commanders of the *Wehrmacht* who were in charge should have refused to have anything to do with it."[312]

We know today that these type of statements may be self-serving half-truths, as most clergy, especially those attached to units in the East, knew very well what those units were actually doing besides fighting Soviet soldiers and partisans. This would be especially true of chaplains attached to *Waffen*-SS, *Ordnungspolizei* battalions (Order Police) and the *Einsatzgruppen* mobile killing squads, whose only function was to go behind the army and exterminate all Jews in their wake. We also know that it is a myth repeatedly promoted after the war that soldiers were coerced into killing against their will, and that those that opposed the mass murder operations, or who refused to participate in them, were punished in any significant way. Even though it might be true that the soldier above shot in the air it is doubtful he did so as these machine gun units were not a firing squad in which a shooter could aim to miss without anyone noticing. These machine gun killing operations typically had just one man shooting at a time.

*German Police Battalion in a field worship service on the Eastern Front (Autumn 1943, Dorogobush, Soviet Union).*

Ultimately, the clergy's presence among the killers was predicated upon their view that Christianity was compatible with Nazi principles: both were opposed to liberalism, Bolshevism, atheism, relativism, and public immorality. Also, both had in common the approval of corporatist ideology, the importance of faith as something grand and heroic, and both supported the return to the Germanic sources of the Germanic people.[313]

## Open Protests with no Consequences

Even though the vast majority of the clergy on both the Protestant and Catholic churches were—at best—indifferent to the plight of the Jews during the war, there were some cases in which the Church *did* oppose Hitler. Some church leaders, prelates and low level clergy showed true concern and acted both in words and deeds to defend Jews, even at their own personal risk sometimes. Everywhere in Europe a few individual priests and nuns—out of true Christian *caritas*—provided shelter to hounded Jews. In this section we will examine the behavior of some national churches as well as that of some individual priests and prelates from those churches. Also, to establish whether official inaction on the part of the Church was due to fear of personal or institutional retribution, we will examine acts of opposition to Nazi policies and the consequences, if any, they triggered.

Perhaps one of the most remarkable—and successful—acts of Catholic opposition to Hitler's policies was the fight against the Euthanasia Program. The Nazis had set up a program in the 1930s to eliminate undesirables like the mentally insane or terminally ill. They managed to kill seventy-thousand people under the Euthanasia Program before an energetic and expressly Catholic resistance led by Bishop Clement August von Galen of Münster, as well as Cardinal Faulhaber and Cardinal Adolf Bertram finally got it to stop. Bishop Galen did not mince words, as he actually used the word "murder" when referring to the program. In a sermon preached in August 1941 Galen said that "If they start out by killing the insane, it can well be extended to the old, the infirm, sick, seriously crippled soldiers. What do you do to a machine that no longer runs, to an old horse that is incurably lame, a cow that does not give milk? They now want to treat humans the same way." This language and line of thinking is particularly striking when one compares it to that used to discuss the "Final Solution" program.[314]

German bishops and the Vatican rallied behind Galen. The Nazis wanted to punish him, but they did not because as Nazi Minister of Propaganda Joseph Goebbels said, "The population of Münster could be regarded as lost during the war if anything was done against the Bishop . . . [indeed] the whole of Westphalia" would be lost to the cause. Three weeks after Galen's sermon, Hitler halted the Euthanasia Program.[315]

Also, when the Nazis attempted to remove crucifixes in schools in Bavaria there was a popular protest that effectively made the Nazis stop. These two examples are particularly significant as they show Church determination to fight the Nazis on something it believed was wrong, and it shows it could do so without consequences to itself, its institutions, or its flock. The Church did not do anything remotely comparable to this on behalf of the Jews. Christian victims of the Euthanasia Program and removal of crucifixes from school walls qualified as matters of Church prerogatives, power and doctrine. The Jews did not. It is likely that if the Nazi hierarchy had encountered massive and sustained protest against their antisemitic policies, if the would-be perpetrators, camp guards, train engineers and the millions of Christians actively or passively involved in the genocide had received unambiguous and sustained instruction from their church leaders to fight against Nazi antisemitic policies, there probably would have been no Final Solution.[316]

In 1942 the Nazis decided to forcibly annul marriages between Aryans and non-Aryans (i.e., Jews). Since according to Catholic doctrine marriage is indissoluble, Cardinal Bertram wrote a letter in the name of the episcopate to the Ministry of the Interior requesting that the ministry withdraw the planned divorce ordinance. While this was taking place, the Gestapo seized six thousand Christian non-Aryans in mixed marriages in Berlin. What followed was unprecedented, as the Aryan wives of these men followed them to the Rosenstrasse Jewish Community Center where they were detained and waited for hours yelling and wailing for their men. The Gestapo, concerned about the secrecy of their policy of extermination being exposed by the scandal and about similar outbursts of popular discontent erupting in the future, released the men. This is an example of what determined, ordinary Christian Germans unwilling to be part of the execution of the Jews, could do. It is important to note that none of these regular citizens, who defied the all-powerful Gestapo, were punished in any way.[317]

There were a few courageous cases of national churches that chose to defend the Jewish population of their countries. Most notably among them were the cases of Norway and Denmark.

When the Germans were about to deport the Jews from Norway, the Norwegian Protestant churches protested to Vidkun Quisling, the nation's collaborationist leader. The letter was read from the pulpits twice in 1942, published as the New Year's message for 1943 and broadcast to Norway and Sweden:

> "For ninety-one years Jews have had a legal right to reside and to earn a livelihood in our country. Now they are being deprived of their property without warning. . . . Jews have not been charged with transgression of the country's laws much less convicted of such transgressions by judicial procedure. Nevertheless, they are being punished as severely as the worst criminals are punished. They are being punished because of their racial background, wholly and solely because they are Jews. . . . According to God's Word, all people have, in the first instance, the same human worth and thereby the same human rights. Our state authorities are by law obligated to respect this basic view. To remain silent about this legalized injustice against the Jews would render ourselves co-guilty in this injustice."[318]

Through the help of the Norwegian Protestant churches fifty percent of Norway's Jews made it safely to neutral Sweden. The Catholic Church, on the other hand, chose not to participate in the protest, limiting their concern to five families that had converts from Judaism.[319]

As opposed to the Catholic Church or the Evangelical Church in Germany, the Danish Lutheran Church did speak in strong, unambiguous language on behalf of the Danish Jews, thereby helping mobilize ordinary Danes to help Jews. In a letter of protest sent to the German authorities before the deportations began in October 1943, which was read from the pulpit in churches in Denmark, Bishop Hans Fuglsang-Damgaard, with the support of all the Church's bishops, said:

> "Whenever persecutions are undertaken for racial or religious reasons against the Jews, it is the duty of the Christian Church to raise a protest against it for the following reasons:
>
> . . . Because the persecution of the Jews is irreconcilable with the humanitarian concept of love of neighbors which follows from the message which the Church of Jesus Christ is commissioned to proclaim. With Christ there is no respect of persons, and he has taught us that every man is precious in the eyes of God. . . .
>
> . . . race and religion can never be in themselves a reason to deprive a man of his rights, freedom or property. . . . We shall therefore struggle to ensure the continued guarantee to our Jewish brothers and sisters [of] the same freedom which we ourselves treasure more than life.
>
> . . . We are obliged by our conscience to maintain the law and to protest against any violation of human rights. Therefore we desire to declare unambiguously our allegiance to the word, we must obey God rather than man."[320]

Bishop Fuglsang-Damgaard was not intimidated by the Nazis, and was determined to act: "We shall pray and kindle the spirit. There was never any use for cowardly clergymen, least of all today."[321] The Germans did not do anything to either the Danish Lutheran Church for all their activities on behalf of the Jews or to the Danes for their collective efforts to thwart the German's exterminationist attempt. Pope Pius XII must have been aware of this, which happened two weeks before the deportation of the Jews of Rome. He chose to reject this model of action against the German's annihilation of the Jews.

When Danish officials, including the Danish Lutheran State Church, heard of a possible roundup of Denmark's Jews, only a few weeks before the roundup of the Jews of Rome, they inundated the offices of the German authorities with questions and objections. Most Jews escaped to neutral Sweden with the help of Danish civilians, and the four hundred and seventy-four that were caught were not sent to Auschwitz, but rather to Theresienstadt where representatives of the Danish and International Red Cross visited them, and of which four hundred and twenty-two survived. One hundred percent of the seven thousand Danish Jews rescued survived the war, while less than one percent of the nineteen hundred Jews deported from Rome to Auschwitz survived.

The extraordinary case of the Danish Lutheran Church represents a perfect example of successful action against German policies the Catholic and other national Protestant Churches could (and should) have taken, but chose not to.[322]

At about the same time there were other righteous Christian church leaders making open protests against the eliminationist policies toward the Jews besides the Danes and Norwegians, including some of the French Catholic bishops, the Orthodox Bulgarian Synod of Bishops and the Greek Orthodox archbishop of Athens.

In Germany, Bishop Konrad von Preysing was a stern opponent of the Nazi regime who said, "We have fallen into the hands of criminals and fools" when the party came to power.[323] Preysing tried repeatedly but futilely to get other German bishops to protest against the deportations and extermination of the Jews. When he tried to persuade the papal nuncio to Berlin Cesare Orsenigo, the nuncio evaded the issue. This led Preysing, who was one of the main correspondents with the Pope, to complain to him that the nuncio had told him that "charity is well and good but the greatest charity is not to make problems for the church."[324] Preysing wanted Pope Pius to recall his nuncio to Germany, break off diplomatic relations with the murderous Nazi regime and condemn the systematic murder of European Jews, however, Pius declined to do any of it. He rejected Bishop Preysing's advice to break off diplomatic relations with Germany in order not to jeopardize his

Concordat with Germany.[325] After the war, on the anniversary of *Kristallnacht*, Bishop Preysing always publicly remembered the millions of murdered Jews: "It was a crime that has no parallel," he said.[326]

One notable case of a member of the clergy that dared to speak out on behalf of the Jews that did have a negative consequence was that of the Provost of St. Hedwig Cathedral in Berlin, Bernhard Lichtenberg. Lichtenberg prayed daily for the persecuted non-Aryans and Jews. The day after the *Kristallnacht* pogrom, after his daily prayer, he added, "What took place yesterday, we know; what will be tomorrow, we do not know; but what happens today that we have witnessed; outside [this church] the synagogue is burning, and that also is the house of God."[327] Lichtenberg was eventually arrested in October 1941, a week after the first mass deportation of Jews had begun, and sentenced to two years imprisonment for abuse of the pulpit. In case the nuncio inquired about the priest, German officials had prepared a reply. However, it was not necessary, as the nuncio did not inquire until later, when it was a question of the priest's health.[328] After his release in October 1943 he was seized by the Gestapo and sent to the Dachau concentration camp. He died in transit.

Angelo Giuseppe Roncalli, who referred to the extermination of the Jews in Europe as "six million crucifixions," was the Vatican's legate and apostolic vicar to Istanbul's small Catholic population.[329] He made the most of his post outside the circle of prime locations in the Vatican orbit by strenuous efforts to help Jews. While in Istanbul he worked with Chaim Barlas, an emissary of the Jewish Agency in Palestine sent to Europe to save Jews in the 1940s. In correspondence with Barlas Roncalli expressed criticism of the Vatican's silence during the war. In June 1944 Barlas sent Roncalli a copy of the *Auschwitz Protocol*, which he forwarded to the Vatican. The Holy See later unbelievably claimed they did not know about Auschwitz until October of that year. He also forwarded a request to the Vatican to inquire whether other neutral countries could grant asylum to Jews, to inform the German government that the Palestine Jewish Agency had five thousand immigration certificates available and to ask Vatican Radio to broadcast that helping Jews was an act of mercy approved by the Church, but the Vatican declined to do any of it as they thought that Jewish presence in Palestine might interfere with the Holy Places.

Roncalli wrote a letter to the Catholic priest president of Slovakia at the behest of Barlas to ask him to stop the deportations of Jews. Roncalli also appealed to personal colleagues in other occupied countries. He asked Bulgaria's King Boris, who was his old friend, to let Jews emigrate, and forwarded messages to the Vatican.[330]

Roncalli and Barlas also worked together to establish a network of escape routes and tactics to rescue thousands of endangered Jews from Eastern Europe. According to the American delegate of the War Refugee Board in Istanbul Ira Hirschmann, Roncalli used diplomatic couriers, papal representatives and the Sisters of Our Lady of Zion in Hungary to transport and issue baptismal certificates, immigration certificates and visas—many of them forged—to Hungarian Jews in what was called "Operation Baptism," which saved thousands of Hungarian Jews.[331]

As Barlas wrote in his memoirs, Roncalli had told him privately that he was filled with resentment toward his superiors, "whose power and influence are great, but who refrain from action and resourcefulness in extending concrete help."[332] Publicly however, as was to be expected, he defended the Pope's actions and claimed he had acted at his behest.

Despite widespread antisemitism in France, a few members of the Catholic Church stood up in defense of the Jews. For instance, Monsignor F. W. Theas, Bishop of Montauban, read from the pulpits of churches in his jurisdiction:

> "Scenes of indescribable suffering and horror are occurring in our land. In Paris, tens of thousands of Jews are being subjected to the most barbaric treatment. In our diocese we are witnesses to the most heartbreaking happenings of similar uprooting of men and women being treated like beasts.

In the name of Christian conscience, I am protesting and I proclaim that all men are brothers created by one God.

The current antisemitic measures constitute a violation of human dignity and of the sacred rights of the individual and the family. May God comfort those who are persecuted and may He give them strength."[333]

In Toulouse, French Catholic Archbishop Jules-Gérard Saliège read a pastoral letter in all the churches of his diocese in August 1942, which had a tremendous positive influence in the years to come:

"It has been reserved to our time to witness the sad spectacle of children, of women, of fathers and mothers, being treated like a herd of beasts; to see members of the same family separated one from another and shipped away to an unknown destination. . . . Jews are men. Jewesses are women. . . . They cannot be maltreated at will. . . . They are part of the human race. They are our brethren as much as are so many others. A Christian cannot forget that."[334]

Echoing Roncalli's feelings Cardinal Tisserant wrote to Archbishop of Paris Cardinal Suhard, that "our superiors do not want to understand the real nature of this conflict." Tisserant had futilely pleaded with Pius XII to issue an encyclical clearly stating that Catholic individuals have an obligation to follow the dictates of their conscience rather than blindly executing all orders, no matter how powerful the source. He added, "I fear that history will reproach the Holy See with having practiced a policy of selfish convenience and not much else."[335]

Protests by these French bishops did not lead to more Jews dying, as Pope Pius XII was afraid would happen if he spoke on behalf of the Jews. On the contrary, not only was there an absence of consequence to these prelates, their protests spurred Catholic clergy and lay people to save Jews.[336]

In Great Britain, the Archbishop of Canterbury, head of the Anglican Church, in conjunction with the Anglican archbishop of York and of Wales proclaimed in December 1942:

> "The bishops of the Church of England state that the number of victims of the cold blooded policy go into the hundreds of thousands, that Hitler himself revealed that he plans to annihilate the Jews which means the end of six million Jewish humans. The bishops of England declare that the suffering of these millions of Jews and the announced plan to kill them place upon humanity an obligation which nobody can shirk.
>
> There must be no delay in saving them. The bishops believe that it is the duty of the civilized nations, whether Allied or neutral, to provide havens to these victims. Therefore they appeal to the British government to take the leadership for the whole world by declaring its readiness together with the dominions and all Allied and neutral governments to provide havens within the British empire and elsewhere for all those who are threatened with annihilation and can escape from the Axis countries, as well as for those who already have escaped so as to provide space to those who so far could not escape."[337]

The American bishop Joseph P. Hurley was unique in that he worked for years in the Vatican under popes Pius XI and XII, and overcame his inculcated antisemitism when confronted with the tragedy of the Jewish people during the war to become and out-spoken critic of the Vatican and a defender of the Jews. Hurley understood clearly that Nazism was "a rapacious, murderous, power which has loosed a torrent of injustice, violence and religious persecution upon almost the whole of Europe and which will destroy our Christian civilization the world over unless we oppose it with all our strength."[338] He began to drift apart from Cardinal Pacelli due to his dissatisfaction with Pacelli's inability to recognize Nazism as the primary enemy to Catholicism, and wrote in 1940 concerning Pius XII's reluctance to explicitly condemn Germany by name after the invasion of Poland that "Any man who is not moved by a profound moral indignation is thereby disqualified as a moral force."[339] Pius XII chose a path of subdued diplomacy, but Hurley disagreed with this policy and wrote that this was "no time to be devious, subtle, or diplomatic."[340] Hurley lost respect for the Vatican princes of the Church. Dispensing with Old World diplomatic subtleties, and showing what is perhaps a characteristic American forwardness, he called the Roman cardinals "Old men in dresses." He wrote about Pius XII, "Here the weakness which many of us feared has come to light with the first appearance of danger."[341]

At a time in which the pontiff instructed the faithful to limit their actions during the war to just prayer and mortification, a time in which the Pope refrained from open, clear denouncements of the extermination of the Jews and even mentioning by name the Jews and the Germans as victims and murderers, respectively, Hurley published an editorial in a St. Augustine, Florida newspaper explicitly confirming the extermination of the Jews.[342] He made it compulsory for Catholics to specifically condemn the Jewish genocide as a matter of religious conscience and used clear, unambiguous terms such as "slaughter" and "orgies of extermination." He believed the extermination of the Jews was a profound moral evil and a downright Catholic emergency. He said that "the very basis of our faith is challenged by the orgies of extermination that are going on among the Jews of Europe" and "All Christians, and especially those who have the fullness of the Christian faith," should "deem it an honor to take up the defense of the Jews." Unfortunately, what is perhaps the first and only moral reckoning of the Nazi genocide by an American Catholic bishop was consigned to the pages of an obscure Catholic newspaper with no real influence.[343]

There was no German retribution for these efforts to save Jews. There is every reason to believe these ecclesiastical activities helped to save Jewish lives, and no reason to believe that they caused the deaths of more Jews.

## Reaction of the Holy See to
## Anti-Jewish Laws in Italy and France

Even though during the 1930s Pius XI generally expressed his negative opinion about racism, he never mentioned Jews or antisemitism. His anti-racist stance created some friction with the Italian government, bent on pursuing their racist agenda. The Pope, already eighty-one years old and ill for some months, was starting to lose some influence on those within the Vatican who wanted to avoid a break with the Italian government. Pius XI, never strongly opposed to anti-Jewish measures anyway, quietly ceased his opposition to racism, an attitude reflected in the Vatican newspapers that published a number of articles in which they showed some approval for the racial laws. In one of these articles in *L'Osservatore Romano* they went as far as grossly distorting the historical record regarding the treatment the Jews got under the reign of Pius IX and how ungrateful the Jews had been in response to the Pope's purported extraordinary benevolence. The message behind all these articles was always the same, that is, that the Jews were usurping the best jobs, manipulating the economy in their favor, destabilizing governments through revolutionary action, poisoning the minds of the Christian population and were ungrateful for everything Christians did for them. The implication was that the Jews had to be separated from the rest of society and their influence severely curtailed, which of course was precisely what the racial laws, heirs to the Christian Blood Purity Statute of XVI century Spain, were meant to do.

Mussolini, discussing future anti-Jewish measures, approved of a private note sent by the government to the Vatican in which it said "The Jews, in a word, can be sure that they will not be subject to worse treatment than that applied to them for centuries by the popes who hosted them in the Eternal City and in the lands of [the Church's] temporal domain."[344]

In Italy, Pope Pius XI objected to the marriage law, but Mussolini did not alter it. The Pope failed to oppose the racial antisemitic laws of 1938. By acting that way, the Pope missed a chance to impart moral guidance on the issue of anti-Judaism to Catholics in Italy and around the world. The papal silence did not go unnoticed by Hitler, who was quick to realize that the Pope would remain silent on Jewish issues as long as the rights of Catholics were not affected directly. The Vatican's policy, and the silence that made it possible, was to preserve the institutional obligations for Catholics, the safety and inviolability of the Holy See in German-occupied Italy, and to protect and retain the loyalties of German Catholics. Pius XI denounced racialism as contrary to the laws of God, to the dictates of good reason and the welfare of civilization. However, when it came to protesting against cruel laws imposed on Jews in Italy and elsewhere, he remained silent.[345] The main reason why the Vatican and the Catholic prelates failed to express any objection to Mussolini's anti-Jewish policies was simply because they agreed with them. During that time, both *L'Osservatore Romano* and *La Civiltà Cattolica* published numerous articles expressing Christian desire to be segregated from Jews.

The collaborationist government of Vichy France also passed its own anti-Jewish legislation, the *Statut des Juifs*. Regarding these anti-Jewish laws, the Vichy ambassador to the Vatican reported back to the French leader Marshal Pétain that "there is nothing in these measures that can give rise to criticism, from the viewpoint of the Holy See." He also said that Vatican officials "have no intention of quarreling with us over the Jewish statute." He went on to explain that "It would be unreasonable, in a Christian state, to permit them [Jews] to exercise the functions of government and thus to submit the Catholics to their authority. Consequently it is legitimate to bar them from public functions." Even though this report is not evidence of Vatican approval of the entire anti-Jewish statute, it is significant and telling that there was no public expression of disapproval or dissatisfaction.[346]

Vichy felt confident on the legitimacy of their anti-Jewish measures in France as shortly afterwards they issued a press release invoking the Church's blessing: "From information obtained at the most authorized sources it results that nothing in the legislation designed to protect France from the Jewish influence is opposed to the doctrine of the Church." No Church official contested this and thus provided implicit endorsement of Vichy's criminal anti-Jewish measures.[347]

Even though the Church may have objected to some provisions of the anti-Jewish laws, clearly they thought that as a body they should be "confirmed" as, according to the Church's highest authority, they were an expression of the Church's own antisemitic "principles." That the entire upper echelons of the Vatican, who had the power to oppose these laws in Germany, Italy and France did not do so is irrefutable evidence that for Pope Pius XII and those around him these criminal laws were appropriate and not immoral.

By 1943, after the fall of Mussolini's government, the Vatican knew without any doubt the extent and nature of the persecution and extermination that these laws led to, yet they continued to believe they ought to be "confirmed." Father Tacchi Venturi reported to the Vatican Secretary of State Cardinal Luigi Maglione that he had met with the new antifascist Minister of the Interior and only asked him to rescind the two provisions of the laws that dealt with Catholics that had converted from Judaism. He wrote: "I took care not to call for the total abrogation of a law [i.e. the race laws] which, according to the principles and traditions of the Catholic Church, certainly has some clauses that should be abolished, but which clearly contains others that have merit and should be confirmed." This must have been the Pope's wish. It must be noted that these laws were grave human rights violations that revoked the Jews' social, personal, economic, political and civil rights in draconian, severe ways: prohibiting the possession of assets, including businesses over a certain value; from marrying non-Jews; from working in government, from becoming soldiers, or working in various professions such as medicine, law, agronomy, and others; from having a public life by appearing in telephone directories or having death notices in newspapers; from hiring non-Jews to work in their homes; even from contact with non-Jewish Italians on vacation. It is also important to point out that this was the position of the Church, while by this time the Allied military government in liberated Sicily had already abrogated all the antisemitic legislation in that part of Italy.[348]

## Did the Pope Have Anything to Say?

Pope Pius XII claimed that one of the reasons for his silence in the face of mass murder was to maintain the Vatican's neutrality. However, the Pope broke his policy of strict neutrality when he expressed concern over the German violation of Holland's neutrality. After some German Catholics criticized him for that, he wrote to the German bishops that neutrality was not synonymous "with indifference and apathy where moral and humane considerations demanded a candid word."[349] It seems that for Pius the ongoing extermination of millions of Jews did not offend his principles of morality, or that morality and humane considerations were involved in this issue at all. The Vatican defended their position of "neutrality" in a broadcast in English in September 1940, but again assured the listeners that "where morality is involved, no neutrality was possible."[350] This implies that to the Vatican, mass murder, or at least mass murder of Jews, was not a moral issue.

Also showing the Vatican had no compunctions about speaking about atrocities, even if doing so would violate their neutrality, is a report compiled by Monsignor Giovanni Battista Montini, Pope Pius XII's Undersecretary of State, in which he detailed and denounced in stark contrast several abuses committed by the Soviet Army against German inhabitants of the Soviet Union. After the war, Montini provided detailed reports to the Western powers about the living conditions in the Soviet zone in Berlin. In these reports, he provided stories of proliferation of abortions as a result of widespread rape by Soviet troops, deportations, confiscations, deprivation, disease and deliberate starvation.[351]

In summary, by September 1942 Pius XII believed that:

- He had already spoken generally, and the Germans understood what he meant (as their suppression of what he said proved);

- He could not speak particularly because it would hurt the people he was trying to help;

- He could not get much through the barriers of censorship; and

- In private he was doing real work for some of the victims and he did not want to block that chance of helping.[352]

The Allied powers would not accept this position, and exerted a considerable amount of pressure on the Pope to act more decisively as they believed he had the power to make a difference in influencing at least Catholic perpetrators.

The British ambassador to the Vatican, Sir Francis D'Arcy Osborne, wrote to the Pope in a démarche in September 1942 about "the merciless persecution of the Jews throughout Europe." He added "that His Holiness has already publicly denounced moral crimes arising out of the war. But such occasional declarations in general terms do not have the lasting force and validity that, in the timeless atmosphere of the Vatican, they might perhaps be expected to retain . . . A policy of silence in regard to such offenses against the conscience of the world must necessarily involve a renunciation of moral leadership and a consequent atrophy of the influence and assertion of such authority that must depend any prospect of a Papal contribution to the reestablishment of world peace."[353]

Also in September 1942 Myron Taylor, Roosevelt's personal representative, arrived in Rome to meet with the Pope. His main mission was to persuade the Pope that the Americans would win the war but, he also took advantage of the opportunity to give the Pope American information about the maltreatment of the populations of occupied Europe. The information included a memorandum of the Jewish Agency for Palestine in which it reported mass executions of Jews in Poland and Russia and deportations to death camps from France, Germany, Belgium, Holland, Slovakia, etc. He inquired if the Vatican could confirm these reports, and if so, asked "whether the Holy Father has any suggestion as to any practical manner in which the forces of civilized public opinion could be utilized in order to prevent a continuation of these barbarities." He also made a suggestion of a papal utterance. He then met with the pope's long-time aide in the Secretariat of State Cardinal Tardini, who wrote in his notes: "Mr. Taylor talked of the opportunity and the necessity of a word from the Pope against such huge atrocities by the Germans. He said that from all sides people are calling for such a word. I assented with a sigh, as one who knows the truth of this too well! I said in reply that the Pope had already spoken several times to condemn crimes by whomsoever they are committed. I added that some people want the Pope to condemn by name Hitler and Germany, which is an impossibility. Taylor said to me 'I don't ask this. I have not asked that he speak out against Hitler, just about the atrocities.' I said again, 'The Pope has already spoken.' Taylor said, 'He can repeat.' And I could not but agree."[354]

Three days later Taylor met with the Vatican's Secretary of State Cardinal Maglione. In this meeting Mr. Taylor said that there was a general impression both in America and Europe—and he said that he could not be wrong in reporting this impression—that it was necessary now for the Pope again to denounce the inhuman treatment of refugees, hostages, and above all the Jews in the occupied countries. Maglione said the Holy See was continually trying to help the victims, and spoke as strong as it could without descending into the particulars, which would involve the Pope in political questions. He then said Mr Taylor showed he agreed with this, but insisted that it was time for another appeal of a high character. Cardinal Maglione assured Mr. Taylor that at the first possible opportunity the Pope would not fail to express anew this thought with clarity. The result of this was the Pope's 1942 Christmas message in which he vaguely referred to the atrocities taking place and did not mention the Jews, the Germans, or the specific exterminationist persecutions of the Jews.[355]

High-placed officials of the Curia told the Assistant Chief of the U.S. delegation to the Vatican that the Pope's silence was due to the following reasons: the understanding that papal pronouncements had to stand the test of time and that the environment during a time of global war would induce errors in the formulation of these declarations; the Holy See's determination to maintain its absolute neutrality in the world war; and the concern that the Nazis would further harm Catholics in the occupied territories if the Vatican would protest. Also, the Pope was concerned that the German people would later reproach the Catholic Church if through its condemnation of German atrocities it contributed in any way to Germany's defeat.[356]

Given the general Christian attitude toward Jews, as we have seen earlier in this book, and all these *realpolitik* constraints, it is not surprising that the Pope remained silent about the destruction of the Jews, even when confronted with the enormity of the tragedy unfolding. Pope Pius XII only gave two public speeches in which he referenced the persecution and extermination of European Jews. He did so in an indirect, oblique way, never mentioning the words Jew, antisemitism or race. Neither did he denounce the "exterminatory measures" he mentioned in the 1943 speech, nor did he name the perpetrators.

The British minister to the Vatican, Francis D'Arcy Osborne, recorded that he virtually intimated to the Vatican Secretary of State that the Vatican "should consider their duties in respect to the unprecedented crime against humanity of Hitler's campaign of extermination of the Jews."[357] Two weeks later, after the Allies had pressured him intensively to condemn the mass murder, and after millions of Jews had already been exterminated, the Pope delivered his Christmas message of 1942 on Vatican Radio. After having been speaking for about forty-five minutes on other topics he said,

> "We owe it to the innumerable dead . . . to the suffering groups of mothers, widows and orphans . . . to the innumerable exiles . . . to the hundreds of thousands who, without personal guilt, are doomed to death or to a progressive deterioration of their condition, sometimes for no other reason than their nationality or descent . . . to the many thousands of non-combatants whom the air war has [harmed]."[358]

In his speech he chose not to mention Jews, Germans, or the mass murder explicitly.

Regarding how he saw his work on behalf of the Jews, in April 1943 he wrote to Msgr. Preysing, Archbishop of Berlin:

> "In Our Christmas message We said a word about the things that are presently being done to non-Aryans in the territories under German authority. It was short, but it was well understood. It is superfluous to say that Our paternal love and solicitude are greater today toward non-Aryans or semi-Aryan Catholics, children of the Church like the others, when their outward existence is collapsing and they are going through moral distress. We cannot offer them effective help other than through Our prayers. We are, however, determined to raise Our voice anew on their behalf as circumstances indicate and permit."[359]

The second and last time he referenced the genocidal nightmare then engulfing Europe was in his address to the Sacred College of Cardinals of June 1943. He spoke of his compassion for "those who have turned an anxiously imploring eye to Us, tormented as they are, for reasons of their nationality or descent, by major misfortunes and by more acute and grave suffering, and destined sometimes, even without guilt on their part, to exterminatory measures."[360] He then attempted to explain the reasons for his extreme restraint by adding:

"Every word We address to the competent authority on this subject, and all Our public utterances, have to be carefully weighed and measured by Us in the interests of the victims themselves, lest, contrary to Our intentions, We make their situation worse and harder to bear. To put the matter at its lowest, the ameliorations apparently obtained do not match the scope of the Church's maternal solicitude on behalf of particular groups that are suffering the most appalling fate. The Vicar of Christ, who asked no more than pity and a sincere return to elementary standards of justice and humanity, then found himself facing a door that no key could open."[361]

These claims are unsubstantiated because there is not a single instance where the intervention of Christian churches led to the deaths of more Jews than the Germans were already planning to kill anyway. On the contrary, there are many cases in which interventions on behalf of Jews saved many lives. Besides, we must point out that by this time the Holy See was perfectly aware of the roundups, the brutal deportations in cattle cars, the death by starvation and disease in overcrowded ghettos, the burning alive of masses of Jews locked inside of barns or synagogues, the mass executions by machine gun fire, the gas vans, and of the death camps. By the time of this address more than three million Jews had been murdered. Auschwitz, the largest of several death camps, was extinguishing the lives of close to ten thousand people *every day*. In 1963, shortly before his election as Pope Paul VI, the close wartime confidant of Pius XII, Cardinal Giovanni Battista Montini, who had been second only to Secretary of State Maglione at the Secretariat of State, stated, "An attitude of protest and condemnation [of the persecutions of the Jews] . . . would have been not only futile but harmful."[362] One has to ask the uncomfortable question of how the Pope could be "harmful" or "make their situation worse and harder to bear" if he made a loud and clear protest in their defense.

*Just a few centuries after the Holy Inquisition's tradition of burning Jews alive at the stake during the Middle Ages the SS burned Jewish prisoners alive during WWII.*

Moreover, his belief that by not confronting the Germans he was protecting himself, the Church and the Eternal City was a convenient fiction. This is demonstrated by his absolute silence during the deportation of the Jews of the northern Italian city of Trieste after the Allied liberation of Rome in June 1944, when he and the Vatican were beyond the reach of the Germans.

In his address to the Sacred College the Pope gave the impression he had approached the Germans but was unable to achieve any positive results. However, apart from three interventions by Nuncio Orsenigo in which he appeared "somewhat embarrassed and without pressing the point," the Wilhelmstrasse (German Foreign Ministry) archives do not contain any document recording a discussion between the Pope and one of the Reich ambassadors or between the Secretary of State and the German diplomats in which they discussed the Jewish problem.[363]

There were two other indirect references, neither of which mentioned that the victims were being murdered, nor that the victims were Jews. The first one was ten days after the deportation of the Jews of Rome in October 1943, when the Vatican newspaper *L'Osservatore Romano* mentioned the Pope's compassion and charity, which did not "pause before boundaries of nationality, religion, or descent."[364] Then again in June 1944, toward the end of the war, when speaking to a group of assembled cardinals, when he reiterated that his compassion and charity extended to all "without distinction of nationality or descent." This is the extent of what the Pope said publicly.[365]

Considering the ambivalence of the German Church toward antisemitism and the indifference of the German population toward the fate of the Jews, it is not surprising that the Pope feared that if he spoke out against the extermination of the Jews the Church may loose the allegiance of Germany's Catholics. This apprehension is manifest in the answer he gave a correspondent for *L'Osservatore Romano* when he asked the Pope whether he was not going to protest the extermination of the Jews: "Dear friend, do not forget that millions of Catholics serve in the German armies. Shall I bring them into conflicts of conscience?"[366]

# 11

## Smuggling Nazis Out of Europe

As the Allied armies liberated Europe from the Nazi yoke they captured thousands of German prisoners of war. The Allied powers intended to try most of the captured Nazi leaders in Nuremberg for initiating a war of aggression and for crimes against humanity. However, when the Nazi hierarchy realized the war was lost they began plotting their escape and looking for ways to get the plundered treasure they had collected from the national treasuries of occupied countries and from millions of murdered Jews into safe havens. Paradoxically, even though some among the Allies were chasing these Nazi perpetrators, some others were helping them escape. Their hope was to recruit these Nazis as so-called "freedom fighters" to use them in the forthcoming fight against Communism. Organizing and managing the escape routes, known as the "Ratlines," was the Vatican.

### The Church's Role in Aiding Nazis Escape Europe

The Ratlines were established by the Vatican to allow fugitive Nazi war criminals abscond Europe to avoid Allied Justice. When we use the term "Vatican" here we only refer to the small cabal of prelates, priests and diplomats at all levels in the Vatican who were active participants in the Ratlines. The Ratlines were originally organized by Bishop Alois Hudal, the rector of the Santa Maria dell'Anima college in Rome and Spiritual Director of the German community in Italy. He was an enthusiastic supporter of Hitler who held religious services for the Nazi occupiers in Italy. He was given a Golden Nazi party membership badge and until liberation drove around the Vatican with a Greater Germany flag flying on his official car. He was an unapologetic supporter of the Nazi cause and an ardent defender of Nazi murderers, who he believed were being unjustly chased:

> "After 1945 all my charitable work was primarily devoted to the former members of National Socialism and Fascism, particularly the so-called 'war criminals' . . . who were being persecuted" [and whom he considered to be] "frequently personally completely without guilt." [He boasted that he] "by means of false personal documents, rescued not a few of them so that they could flee their tormentors to happier lands."[367]

Hudal's pro-Nazi views were well known. He was rather notorious in Rome for being openly philo-Nazi. He believed that it was his divine call to settle relations between the Catholic Church and the Nazis. By the early 1930s he traveled widely through Italy and Germany to address large gatherings of German-speaking Catholics and openly supported Hitler in speeches to these groups. He was an ardent anti-Communist convinced that the real enemy of the Church was "atheistic Bolshevism."[368] In April 1933, during the negotiations for the *Reichskonkordat,* he believed that "in this hour of destiny all German Catholics living abroad welcome the new German Reich, whose philosophies accord both with Christian and National values."[369] In 1936 he published a "philosophical" treatise called "The Foundations of National Socialism" and sent a copy to Hitler with the handwritten dedication: "To the architect of German greatness."[370] Hudal had a very close, personal relationship with Pope Pius XII who years before, as papal nuncio, had officiated at his episcopal ordination in Germany. They were friends. Hudal communicated with the Vatican during the war, and also corresponded with the Jesuit confidant of the Pope, Robert Leiber.[371]

Hudal began to put together his escape network in 1944 when the Pope's Pontifical Commission of Assistance was divided into regional subcommittees and he was put in charge of the Austrian section. He issued false papers including identity documents issued by the Pontifical Commission of Assistance, which would start a paper trail that could be later used to obtain a displaced person passport from the International Committee of the Red Cross.

Hudal operated his smuggling network under the full authority of the Vatican. Without Vatican diplomatic pressure, he would have never been able to obtain the Allied travel pass, which enabled him to travel around Europe and get into internment camps to reach so many Nazi war criminals.

He worked with Monsignor Karl Bayer in Rome, with whom he shared space next door to the German embassy. Bayer was well loved by the Nazis. He remarked that he and Hudal had helped Nazis with the Vatican's support: "The Pope did provide money for this; in driblets sometimes, but it did come."[372] As Gertrude Depuis from the Red Cross in Rome recalled, at the Red Cross they assumed that Vatican funds were being used to help refugees, including fugitives from justice.

Franz Stangl, commandant of the Treblinka death camp, where about nine hundred thousand Jews were exterminated, declared that the Nazis knew of the Vatican escape route. "During the time we were in the interment camps we knew that we should go to Rome. . . . Catholics should go to Bishop Hudal [who would] give us an International Red Cross Identity card and then a visa." He said that the bishop arranged "quarters in Rome where I was to stay till my papers came through. And he gave me a bit more money—I had almost nothing left."[373]

Some of the worst and most wanted Nazi war criminals passed through the network that included Walter Rauff in Milan, on to Bishop Hudal at the Anima in Rome, and then to Pius XII's good friend Archbishop Siri in Genoa where they boarded ships headed for South America:

- Adolf Eichmann, who coordinated the annihilation of millions of Jews and was responsible for their transportation to the death camps;
- Franz Stangl, the commander successively of two extermination camps, Sobibór and Treblinka, where more than a million Jews were murdered;
- Kurt Christmann, the commander of Sonderkommando 10a, which slaughtered tens of thousands of Jews in the Soviet Union;
- Walter Rauff, in charge of developing the gas vans used in the mass murder of hundreds of thousands of Jews before the gas chambers were used;
- Klaus Barbie, the cruel Gestapo "Butcher of Lyon" who was responsible for the torture and death of countless people;
- Gustav Wagner, commanding officer of Sobibór, where over two hundred thousand Jews were murdered;
- Alois Brunner, a brutal official in the Jewish deportation program in France and Slovakia, responsible for deporting hundreds of thousands of Jews to their deaths;
- Ante Pavelić, the head of the mass-murdering Croatian Ustasha regime, responsible for hundreds of thousands of gruesome murders or Orthodox Serbs and Jews;
- Perhaps most infamous of all, Auschwitz's "Angel of Death," Dr. Josef Mengele, responsible for unspeakable medical experiments and deciding who was to live and who to die in Auschwitz.[374]

Eichmann, in appreciation for the help given him by the Catholic Church, wrote in his new Argentinean passport that he was Catholic, even though he was Protestant. "I recall with deep gratitude the aid given to me by Catholic priests in my flight from Europe and decided to honor the Catholic faith by becoming an honorary member."[375]

Correspondence between Hudal and other Nazis underscored the preoccupations shared between the bishop, the Nazis and Argentina's ruling military class: Communism, "Jewish Capitalism," the perceived negative aspects of democracy, and the conviction that a third world war was unavoidable.[376]

As Hudal continued to send fugitives down the Ratlines, eventually a series of articles appeared in the Italian press in August 1947 questioning the motives of Pius XII, who by then was widely labeled the "German Pope." Facing the potential exposure of the entire operation and how that would greatly damage their international reputation, the Vatican pressured Hudal to leave, and some time afterwards he did. He remained a convinced antisemite until his death, believing that the Germans should be excused of their crimes in the name of Christian charity, however he believed that justice when applied to the killers of Jews was vengeance.[377]

Even before Hudal left the scene, the Vatican already had new recruits ready to take his place. The Vatican selected fascist priests from Central and Eastern Europe to assist the tens of thousands of non-German Nazi collaborators who perpetrated atrocities in the eastern theater of war.[378] Most of the personnel in the smuggling operation came out of the ranks of the Ustasha, the terrorist organization installed by Hitler in Croatia as a puppet state of the Nazis after the takeover of Yugoslavia. The methods used by the Ustasha henchmen were barbaric. The *Poglavnik* (leader) of the "Independent" state of Croatia was the founder and leader of the Croatian national socialist/fascist Ustasha movement in the 1930s, Ante Pavelić.

Pavelić was aware that Pius XII and his senior advisers thought highly of his militant Catholicism.[379] During the war he had converted tens of thousands Serbian Orthodox under penalty of death. In April 1941 he was received by the Pope, creating an uproar at the British Foreign Office who was dismayed that the Pope would even consider meeting with such a notorious mass murderer and thus described the Pope as "the greatest moral coward of our age." As the Foreign Office later told the British ambassador to the Holy See, the Pope's reception of Pavelić "has done more to damage his reputation in this country than any other act since the war began." This of course was hypocritical, as British Intelligence had used Pavelić before the war. In defense of British Intelligence, however, that was before the bloody massacres Pavelić perpetrated during the war and before the audience with the Pope who already knew about them. Montini was definitely well informed of the situation as he admonished Croatia's representatives to the Holy See on a number of occasions; however, he always reassured them that the Pope would assist Catholic Croatia.[380]

Special Agent Gowen, from the U.S. Army Counter Intelligence Corps in Rome, wrote in a report:

> "Thus, today, in the eyes of the Vatican, Pavelić is a militant Catholic, a man who erred, but who erred fighting for Catholicism. It is for this reason that [Pavelić] now enjoys Vatican protection . . . Pavelić is known to be in contact with the Vatican which sees in him the militant Catholic who yesterday fought the Orthodox Church and today is fighting Communist atheism. . .

> For the reasons given above he is receiving the protection of the Vatican whose view of the 'Pavelić question' is that, since the Croat state does not exist and, since the Tito regime cannot be expected to give anyone a fair trial, [Pavelić] should not be turned over to the present Yugoslav regime with the excuse of bringing him to justice. The extradition of Pavelić would only weaken the forces fighting atheism and aid Communism in its fight against the church."[381]

The most important member of the Vatican escape network was Croat Father Krunoslav Draganović. The center of the clandestine smuggling operation was the San Girolamo monastery in Rome, which was the national Catholic Church of Croatia in Rome and a seminary for Croat priests. Through the Pontifical Commission, the Croatian Committee in San Girolamo, ostensibly there to help refugees, also maintained close connections with the International Red Cross and the Allied authorities in Italy. According to Monsignor Petranović, who was Draganović's Genoa contact, Draganović was "reserved, distant and very serious," not someone who often shared a joke or engaged in lighthearted conversation. According to Monsignor Simcić, who was the closest to

Draganović and a member of the Ratline in Rome, he was "an amazing person, a great activist and a superb organizer, a man of great ideas." Draganović was "one of the most important men in Europe, a great scholar with an excellent knowledge of history." Among British and American intelligence operatives he was widely known as the "Balkan gray eminence."[382]

Draganović was a wanted war criminal who had been a senior official of the committee responsible for the forced conversion of Orthodox Serbs to Catholicism as well as the forced requisition of food during the brutal Nazi anti-partisan offensive in western Bosnia in 1942. He fully embraced Ante Pavelić's puppet state and cooperated with it "as a citizen according to the laws of the Lord." Toward the end of the war he was entrusted with all valuables plundered by the Ustashi government and smuggled to the Vatican, and he initially used these funds to build his escape Ratline.[383]

He was the personal secretary and confidant of Bishop Ivan Šarić, the worst supporter of the *Poglavnik*, Ante Pavelić. During the Ustasha assault on Croatia's Jews, Bishop Šarić appropriated Jewish property for his own use. His diocesan paper published that "there is limit to love. The movement of liberation of the world from the Jews is a movement for the renewal of human dignity. Omniscient and omnipotent God stands behind this movement." After the war he was sheltered at the Oriental Institute, a Catholic institution in Rome.[384]

The Pope had established an official organization to aid genuine refugees called the "Pontifical Welfare Commission." Draganović's access and use of the organization could not have gone unnoticed by the Pope and in senior Vatican circles, as the false identity cards issued to fugitive war criminals were printed at the Franciscan printing press, and this had been arranged by the Vatican's official representative at San Girolamo, Father Dominik Mandić. Through his connections with the Italian secret police, Draganović got the Franciscan's false identity papers accepted as official documents on which Italian identity cards and residence permits were issued.[385]

Using American travel papers obtained though intercession of
the Vatican, Draganović travelled freely to the camps where his
fellow countrymen were interned. During his travels through Italy
and Austria he established contacts with fellow Ustashi and other
Fascist priests with whom he later worked on the Ratline. The escape network Draganović established handled as many as thirty-
thousand people who were channeled from Austria to Rome, and
then to Genoa where they boarded ships that took them to new
lives in North and South America and Australia. Most of the personnel running the Ratlines were not members of some fanatic
German SS brotherhood, but rather nearly all were Croatian
Catholic priests.[386]

Draganović established contacts with Pope Pius XII, as well as
senior officials of the Vatican Secretariat of State and Italian Intelligence. His most critical contact was with Monsignor Montini,
Undersecretary of State for Ordinary Affairs and the man in charge
of the Pope's charitable work for refugees, who helped him gain
access to the Pontifical Assistance Commission that provided him
with large quantities of identity papers.[387] Monsignor Montini,
Pope Pius' favorite and right hand man, reported at length twice
daily to the Pope on the activities at the Vatican's Secretariat of
State. It is inconceivable Pope Pius XII was unaware or did not approve of the activities of Draganović's Ratline. Draganović met
with Montini many times to discuss San Girolamo's work, and he
often asked Montini for advice and assistance in specific cases related to his activities there. Often he would ask Montini to obtain
more visas from countries that were not issuing enough, and the
Vatican bureaucrat would intercede with the relevant diplomats to
obtain them. Draganović boasted that he was the Holy See's
official representative for the emigration of all Nazi groups, not just
Croatians.[388]

*Monsignor Montini next to Pius XII during his years of service in the Secretariat of State.*

The smuggling operation began in Austria, with Croat Catholic Father Cecelja. During the war, when the Ustasha were perpetrating horrific atrocities, Cecelja had been the Deputy Military Vicar to the Ustasha militia. He was appointed by Pavelić and later confirmed by Archbishop Stepinac. He was part of the delegation that visited the Vatican in 1941, which was blessed by Pius XII. By then the genocide in Croatia was underway.

In 1944 Cecelja moved to Austria, ostensibly to care for wounded Croatian troops. Actually, his job was to prepare the Austrian end of the escape network. During this time he founded the Croatian Red Cross, which proved invaluable in providing him with cover to hide his illegal activities. Just like Draganović, Cecelja was provided with American and International Red Cross papers that allowed him to travel freely between prisoner camps where he contacted other fellow Ustashi. As he proudly declared, "As I travelled in the American zone, I used to leave these small Red Cross identity papers in all the camps," which wanted war criminals then used to change their names and personal histories. As he later declared, he provided the fugitives "with food and accommodation, registering them and providing them with immigrant papers, giving them the opportunity to move around the world to Argentina, Australia and South America. I got the papers from the Red Cross."[389] As he said, "Draganović was fully empowered by the Holy See and was in charge not only for Croatians, but for everybody." Cecelja arranged for the fugitives to travel from Austria to Rome, where Draganović provided them with international travel papers and through his high level contacts with South American consulates, particularly Argentina, he secured entry visas. Once a week Draganović spoke to Cecelja and told him how many places he had available, and Cecelja sent that number to Rome.[390]

Special Agent Robert Clayton Mudd from the American Army's Counter Intelligence Corps. (CIC) had infiltrated the San Girolamo monastery with an agent in February 1947 who reported that ten members of Pavelić's Ustashi cabinet were living either there or in the Vatican itself. He also reported that San Girolamo "was honeycombed with cells of Ustashi operatives." He had achieved a position of trust, as he knew the identities of those taking part in Draganović's regular clandestine meetings, which were attended by the most wanted and notorious Croatian war criminals. To obtain further proof American intelligence agents arranged for a daring burglary at San Girolamo in which they bugged its code room and that allowed them to photograph many of Draganović's top-secret documents. Among them was a list of all the Croatians supported by the monastery, many of whom were on the American's lists of wanted war criminals. The list disclosed not only their true identities, but also the false names Draganović had given them. Other documents showed detailed information of Draganović's system of procurement of Central and South American visas.[391] It was further established that:

"These Croats travel back and forth from the Vatican several times a week in a car with a chauffeur whose license plate bears the two initials CD, 'Corpo Diplomatico.' It issues forth from the Vatican and discharges its passengers inside the Monastery of San Girolamo. Subject to diplomatic immunity it is impossible to stop the car and discover who are its passengers."

And concluded: "Draganović's sponsorship of these Croat Quislings definitely links him up with the plan of the Vatican to shield these ex-Ustashi nationalists until such time as they are able to procure for them the proper documents to enable them to go to South America. The Vatican, undoubtedly banking on the strong anti-Communist feelings of these men, is endeavoring to infiltrate them into South America in any way possible to counteract the spread of Red doctrine."

Draganović supposedly negotiated these operations through his connections in the Vatican.[392]

The other key station in the Vatican's Ratline was in Genoa, where Monsignor Karlo Petranović assumed responsibility for the passengers Draganović sent from Rome. Petranović had been a chaplain in the Ustashi army and he was an important factor in the policies that led to the slaughter of thousands of innocent Serbs. His role in the Ratline was quite simple: he had to visit the local shipping offices in Genoa and secure a number of guaranteed berths. He would then call Draganović and he would send the required number of passengers a couple of days before embarkation. Since Draganović had already secured documentation for them, Petranović simply had to find them lodging for a few days and then transport them to the ship. Bishop Siri, the other senior prelate in Genoa part of the Ratline, assisted Petranović. Siri had been Walter Rauff's contact when they set up the network to smuggle fugitive German Nazis who were sent to Genoa from Rome by Bishop Hudal.[393]

The Ratline was funded with money plundered from Jewish and Serb victims of the Ustasha regime. When the regime collapsed in 1944, the fleeing Ustashi took the treasure—most of it in gold coins—to Rome where it was used to feed, clothe, shelter and provide travel passage to wanted war criminals. It is not known whether the looted gold was held at the Vatican Bank, but there is no question that had it been placed there the Vatican would have recognized the origins of the gold as coming from murdered victims of the Ustasha regime. Vatican Bank officials would have known this given who brought the treasure and when, and the fact that they were gold coins and jewelry and not gold ingots (which would have indicated it came from a national treasury).[394]

Franciscan Father Dominik Mandić was the representative of the Vatican at San Girolamo and the treasurer of the Croatian section of the Pope's Assistance Commission for Refugees, and in that role was responsible for handling the valuables of Pavelić's murdered victims stolen by the Ustashi. Mandić put the Franciscan order's printing press at the disposal of San Girolamo so that false identity cards could be provided to the refugees.

The highest Vatican officials were indisputably behind Draganović's activities, who was additionally helped by American and British intelligence agents. All of them were motivated to protect fugitive Nazis because they wanted to recruit them as "freedom fighters" in the Cold War battle against Communism. Their first order of battle was as regrouped militant Catholic warriors that Pavelić dubbed the "Krizari"—Crusaders—who were to infiltrate Communist Yugoslavia to gather intelligence and conduct attacks against Communist personnel and strategic targets.[395]

Perhaps the last major Nazi war criminal to pass through the Catholic Church's escape network was SS mass murderer Klaus Barbie, the "Butcher of Lyon," responsible for the death of thousands of Jews in occupied France. He had been in the hands of the Americans to whom he had provided with anti-Communist assistance, and the Americans repaid the favor by handing him over to Draganović so he could be swiftly taken to safety in South America. When he asked Draganović why he was helping him, Draganović answered, "We've got to keep a sort of reserve on which we can draw in the future."[396]

Based on information from the files of the International Red Cross and other sources it is certain beyond any doubt that Undersecretary of State Cardinal Montini, anti-Communist French Cardinal Tisserant and like-minded Argentinean Cardinal Antonio Caggiano masterminded the escape of Nazis to Argentina, while bishops and archbishops like Hudal, Siri and Barrére implemented the necessary logistics, and priests such as Draganović, Heinemann and Dömöter signed their passport applications and organized the details of the operations.[397] Even though it cannot be established conclusively, given the frequency and nature of the relationship between the Pope and Montini, it is almost certain that the Pope knew and approved of the Ratlines. He had every reason to suspect what was really going on with Hudal as his agent. The Vatican knew full well it was helping war criminals. Just days after Pius XII's death, the Vatican ordered Draganović to leave San Girolamo.[398]

## Argentina's Role

After the war wanted war criminals escaped to several countries, however Argentina stands out as it was one of the principal providers of visas and shelter to fascist and Nazi war criminals looking for asylum. At the time General Juan Perón and a military elite who shared and admired the Nazi ideology ruled Argentina. They were complicit with Nazi Germany during the war despite claims of neutrality. According to Walter Schellenberg, the head of Himmler's foreign secret service (SD), Nazi military chiefs already considered Argentina's wartime military regime as being "based upon a similar world view to ours."[399]

Until 1994 Argentina constitutionally required the president to be Roman Catholic. The leaders of this country during the 1940s were all ultra-nationalist, Catholic, largely antisemitic, and strongly allied with the Catholic Church.[400]

Perón sent a priest to open an office in Rome with the intent of bringing to Argentina four million European immigrants. The organization was called Delegation for Argentine Immigration in Europe (DAIE). The DAIE enjoyed a highly favorable reputation among fugitive Nazis in Italy. From the start, the DAIE worked closely with the Catholic Church in Italy, helping real refugees (very few of which were Jewish) as well as war criminals.[401] Perón issued thirty-four visas to Croatians: both the Nazi collaborators and the anti-Communists that fled from the new Communist government led by Josip Broz Tito.

Argentine Cardinal Antonio Caggiano flew with Bishop Agustín Barrére to Rome where they passed on a message to French Cardinal Eugène Tisserant that "the Government of the Argentine Republic was willing to receive French persons, whose political attitude during the recent war would expose them, should they return to France, to harsh measures and private revenge."[402]

Adolf Eichmann was one of the main architects of the Holocaust and was directly responsible for coordinating the deportation and transport of millions of Jews to their deaths. In 1960, when Eichmann was going to be tried in Jerusalem, Caggiano showed where his allegiances still were when he said, "Our obligation as Christians is to forgive him for what he's done."[403]


## American & British Roles

As the Second World War was coming to a close and the collapse of Nazi Germany was almost certain, a rift among the Allies began to taint the relationship between the American and British on the one hand, and the Soviets on the other. A sense of conviction that Communism was evil and that the Soviets were determined to spread the ideology everywhere they could, made the Americans and the British look for ways to counter the red menace. Toward this goal, they turned a blind eye to the background of anyone who professed to be an anti-Communist and was wiling to fight them in any way possible.

The "La Vista Report," circulated secretly in U.S. government circles on May 15, 1947 and not declassified until 1984, showed how members of the Vatican were involved in the Ratlines. In it, State Department official Vincent La Vista listed nearly two dozen "Vatican relief and welfare organizations engaged in or suspected of engaging in illegal immigration." At the top of the list was Bishop Hudal. La Vista also told about how he obtained false International Red Cross (IRC) documents for two bogus Hungarian refugees with the help of a letter from Hungarian Father Joseph Gallov. Father Gallov ran a Vatican sponsored charity for Hungarian refugees and he wrote a letter to his personal contact in the IRC who without asking questions then issued the passports.[404]

La Vista even discovered that the Vatican was pressuring the governments of Catholic states in Latin America to accept the Nazis, which resulted "in the foreign missions of those countries taking an attitude almost favoring the entry into their country of former Nazis and former Fascists or other political groups, so long as they are anti-Communist."[405] Documents in the Argentinean embassy in Rome corroborate the report's conclusion by showing how cardinals Tisserant and Caggiano pressured Argentinean representatives to accept French war criminals.[406] In his report La Vista also referred to another Vatican representative who had good connections with "South American Consulates and business firms." This was the last link in the "German emigration chain which funnels all of its clients through the International Red Cross."[407]

The American agents in Rome were convinced that the Vatican was "the largest single organization involved in the illegal movement of emigrants" willing to help "people of all political beliefs as long as they are anti-Communist and pro-Catholic Church."[408]

After the war, the British were also more sympathetic to anyone who claimed to be anti-Communist, and thus decided to bring the eight thousand Ukrainian collaborators in the notorious Waffen SS "Galician Division" to safety in England and turn them into anti-Communist "freedom fighters." The British provided safe haven to these people without performing the minimal screening required for normal immigration to Britain and thus they included many people who had previously served with the SS mobile killing units responsible for the murder of hundreds of thousands of Jews in the Russian front, including the massacre at Babi Yar in the Ukraine where over thirty-thousand Jews were murdered in two days. In the U.S., the National Catholic Welfare Conference put a considerable amount of pressure on the State Department to support the "rescue" of the Ukrainians. The Vatican, with the help of Bishop Hudal, Bishop Bučko, and others, eventually accomplished this.[409]

The bulk of the blame for the Ratlines undoubtedly falls on the government of Great Britain. British intelligence sheltered Pavelić, smuggled Ustashi gold and arranged for the mass escape of prisoners interned in their camps. They also asked the Vatican for help in resettling "Gray" (collaborators) Nazis and asked their American allies to help by sabotaging the immigration screening process.[410] However, as much as the American State Department was willing to help their British colleagues, they stopped short of sending "Black" (war criminals) Nazis through the Vatican Ratline: "Such action should be confined to Whites and Grays only and Grays preferably before they have been formally labeled as such in order [to] facilitate their departure."[411]

# Part IV:
# The Quest for Justice

*"He who knows evil is being done, and does nothing to stop it, is guilty with the evildoer."*

*St. Ambrose*

# 12

## What the Pope and the Churches Should Have Done

Previous chapters of *Six Million Crucifixions* examined how the Protestant and Catholic churches prepared the soil in which hatred toward the Jewish people could grow. This enmity, when updated into modern language and actively promoted by a powerful state, eventually led Germany (and their helpers in the various European nations they invaded) to murder almost six million Jews during the Second World War. This figure accounts for two thirds of the Jewish population of Europe at that time. In this part of the book we will look at:

- Things the Churches could and should have done to if not prevent, at least minimize the effects of the murderous campaign against the Jews;

- What the Churches should say and do now and in the future and, lastly,

- The legal aspects of previous Church behavior, particularly during the Nazi Era, and make recommendations on how to proceed with members of the Churches who through acts of omission or commission may have been passively or actively responsible for the genocide.

The Pope could have done a number of things to prevent the Germans from continuing with the extermination of Europe's Jews, or at least the deportation of the Jews of Rome:

- He could have instructed all Catholic faithful, including Germans and their helpers, to immediately cease the deportations, as they were criminal and a sin;

- He could have confronted the Germans with a threat of an interdict or the excommunication of Hitler, Goebbels and other Nazis belonging to the Catholic faith; or

- He could have even used the very powerful weapon of a threat to the entire German Catholic population with excommunication.

At the very least, a public condemnation by the Pope clearly indicating the fate that awaited those people about to be deported, read from the pulpits by all his bishops and broadcast widely on Vatican Radio, would have alerted those people to go into hiding at all costs, as many of them truly believed they were being resettled to work in the East. Konrad Adenauer, the Catholic mayor of Cologne, who was persecuted for his anti-Nazi stance before the war, said in a private letter after the war when he had become chancellor of Germany, "I believe that if all the bishops had together made public statements from the pulpits on a particular day, they could have prevented a great deal."[412] If nothing else worked, the Pope could have stood in front of the train carrying Rome's Jews as it was departing Rome toward Auschwitz, as even if the Germans had forcibly removed him from the tracks the impression this symbolic gesture would have had would have been so powerful that it would have, if not halted the machinery of destruction, certainly saved many lives and firmly and honestly cemented the Church's moral standing.

The reaction and success the Church had against Bismarck's *Kulturkampf* and the effectiveness of the resolute reaction of the

German episcopate to the euthanasia program are two good examples of effective Church battles against those things it truly believed to be wrong. In addition, the determined intervention of the papal nuncios of countries like Slovakia, Hungary and Romania who threatened the quisling (i.e. collaborator) governments of those countries with a public condemnation by the Pope had the result of a halt, albeit temporarily, of the deportations.[413] Unquestionably, a combination of all potential actions, particularly if done simultaneously and in coordination with the Protestant Church, would have been most effective. The Churches chose to do none of them.

### Things Pius XII Did

Throughout the Nazi Era (1933-1945) and its aftermath, Eugenio Pacelli, first as Vatican Secretary of State and then as Pope Pius XII, did a number of things to oppose the Nazis on those areas he believed them to be wrong, or against the interests of the Catholic Church. He did these things despite claims of neutrality and risk to himself, Catholics or the Vatican:

- He intervened in Germany on behalf of Catholics who had converted from Judaism, but not on behalf of the Jews.

- He wrote or was involved in the writing of the strongly worded encyclical *Mit brennender Sorge* concerning the treatment of religion in Germany, and had it be read from pulpits across Germany, but did not similarly denounce the persecution and later extermination of the Jews.

- He violated the Vatican's neutrality by denouncing Germany's invasion of neutral Belgium, the Netherlands and Luxembourg by sending individual telegrams to the leaders of each country that were later printed on the front page of *L'Osservatore Romano*, but he did not do a similar thing about the Germans' extermination of the Jews.

- He spoke openly and clearly on behalf of the hardships of Catholic Poles, but not of Jewish Poles.

- He excommunicated all Communists of the world in 1949, but did not excommunicate any Catholic who served the German cause, including some of the world's greatest mass murderers who were born and raised Catholic, like Hitler, Himmler, Goebbels and Auschwitz commandant Rudolf Höss, to mention only a few.

- He sought clemency for war criminals that had been convicted after the war.[414]

## Things Pius XII Did Not Do

There are many things the Pope did not do but should have done:

- He did not direct all members of the Church to defend and help Jews.

- He did not protest or do anything to prevent the deportation of the Jews of Rome or other regions.

- He did not instruct all clergy to give the hunted Jews sanctuary in Church buildings.

- After the war he had ample opportunity to rethink Catholic-Jewish relations, but he did not do so.

- Also after the war he could have called for justice and spoken plainly about the guilt of the perpetrators and their deeds, but did not do so (instead he and the German bishops pled for clemency).

- He did not suspend or break diplomatic relations with those countries perpetrating the genocide of the Jewish people. Even by leaving the nuncios in their posts the Vatican was lending the prestige of their presence to the governments involved. There was a recent precedent of interruption of diplomatic relations with Czechoslovakia in 1925 as a protest against a government decision to which the Vatican objected.[415]

- He did not excommunicate any Catholics.

- By not preventing (and thus *at least* tacitly approving) Vatican prelates and clerics from becoming involved in, organizing and operating the Ratlines that whisked to safety outside of Europe thousands of Nazi mass murderers, Pius XII committed the greatest immorality of his pontificate.

- He did not return any profits the Vatican may have made from stolen treasure.

- He did not recognize the State of Israel.[416]

## Excommunication Issues

Excommunication is a religious condemnation used to deprive membership in a religious community. To believing Catholics, to whom there is no salvation outside of the Church, excommunication is a terrifying notion. It has been a formidable weapon wielded by the Catholic Church for centuries in multiple circumstances. Even in recent times, with the advent of the Enlightenment and modernity and a concomitant decline of religious fervor and fear of the Church, the Church used this powerful threat to the Christian soul whenever it felt it had to bring the faithful in line with its policy. For instance, Pius IX excommunicated all Italians who cooperated with Garibaldi's new unified Italian State in 1871 and, during the *Kulturkampf* in Germany in 1875, the Church excommunicated any priest that cooperated with Chancellor Bismarck against the Catholic Church.

More relevant to the period leading to the Holocaust is how Pius XII used—or neglected to use—this coercive and punitive tool. Pius XII did not excommunicate *any* Catholic Nazis, not even Minister of Propaganda Goebbels, SS Chief Himmler (whose godfather was bishop of Bamberg), the Head of the Party Chancellery and private secretary to Hitler, Martin Bormann, the commandant of the Auschwitz death camp, Rudolf Höss, Security Police Chief Kaltenbrunner, Chief of Gestapo Müller, or Hitler, all of whom died as Catholics. However, after the war Pius XII decreed that anyone who knowingly supported Communist teaching would be excluded from the sacraments and anyone who spread those teachings would be excommunicated. Eventually Pius had no compunction in excommunicating *all* Communists throughout the world *in one stroke.* He did this resolutely, despite any potential risks to Catholics or Church property or privileges behind the Iron Curtain. This provided a clear example of absolute moral and political clarity and delineated what he should have done in 1943 when the Jews of Rome were deported to their deaths and when he should have resisted the Nazis by acting strongly on their behalf. As opposed to his putative rejection of Nazi ideology and their abominable deeds, his hostility to Communists and Communism was never in doubt.

**What the Defenders of the Pope Say**

After the Second World War, once the death camps were liberated and the extent of the magnitude and nature of the horror of the German exterminatory campaign against the Jews became widely known, many people began asking what the Churches and Pope Pius XII knew and did to save the Jews. In this book we have provided a brief introduction to these matters, however, there are many voices that have began presenting an apologetic view of the Church's and the Pope's actions that contradict the views presented here. Among the people presenting this opposing view there were some Jews who may have felt it politically convenient to present a sympathetic view toward the Church at a time in which the Jews needed as much help from the Christian world as they could get. In the post-war years Jews not only needed help to rebuild their lives out of the ashes of the Holocaust, they also needed to secure as much support as possible to establish a national home for the Jewish people in Palestine/Israel. Some may have simply been ignorant of the facts. Many people project on to the pontiff the things they think he should have done, not being able to conceive he could not have done them. The evidence simply does not support this act of wishful thinking.

Despite the documentation available, including the multiple volumes of *Actes et Documents du Saint Siège relatifs à la Seconde Guerre Mondiale* (French for "Acts and Documents of the Holy See related to the Second World War"), published between 1965 and 1981 precisely to counter critics of Pope Pius XII after the controversy created by Rolf Hochhuth's *The Deputy*, the questions of what the Pope and the Church knew and especially what it did, remain contentious. It stands to reason that the Church would have released all documents clarifying this point among those documents released, but that might not be so. If the Secret Archives of the Vatican (the vast holdings of Vatican documents that remain inaccessible to outside researchers for many decades after the events covered) still contain documents exonerating or at least removing the cloud of doubt hovering over Pope Pius XII, it makes no sense the Vatican would have withheld them instead of releasing them together with the rest. It is therefore more likely that these documents do not exist. Unfortunately this issue will continue to be a matter of dispute until the Secret Archives of the Vatican covering this period are opened.

Defenders of the Pope usually point out that during the war he opened Church buildings in Rome to provide shelter, food and clothing to all those in need. Even though it is true many persecuted people, including some Jews, found refuge not only in Church property in Rome but also throughout Europe, there is no evidence to show that this was due to the Pope's influence. Many righteous local priests and nuns provided shelter and refuge on *motu proprio* out of true Christian charity, and not necessarily because they were ordered by the Pope to do so.

Papal apologists also stress how the Pope repeatedly and clearly spoke against the Nazis and in support of Jews, however the reality is that when the Pope spoke against the Nazis he did so generally and in opposition to their treatment of the Catholic Church in Germany, *not in defense of the Jews*. As examples of how the Pope spoke of brotherly love toward all peoples irrespective of race or religion they point to his first encyclical *Summi Pontificatus* where he urged solidarity to all who profess a belief in God, but in it the only mention of the word "Jew" is in a quote from *Colossians* from the Christian Bible. There is no complaint against the maltreatment meted out to Jews, and no urging to Catholics to treat Jews well.

Regarding how often the Pope spoke out publicly in defense of the Jews during the war, as we discussed above he did this only twice. His defenders also often cite the first of these two speeches, the Pope's 1942 Christmas message, as his strongest condemnation and as a clear example of how the Pope spoke out in defense of the Jews. In this radio address he spoke of "the hundreds of thousands who, without personal guilt, are doomed to death or to a progressive deterioration of their condition, sometimes for no other reason than their nationality or descent." As we have seen earlier, this vague, pusillanimous and ineffectual complaint about the greatest crime in history, uttered at the end of a very long speech on other matters and without even mentioning the victims or the perpetrators by name, seemed to be the best the infallible Vicar of Christ on Earth could say to defend the Jews. There is a vast chasm between the enormity of the extermination then taking place and this form of evasive language in which the Pope scaled down "millions" to "hundreds of thousands" and reduced human rights abuses like discrimination, physical assault and ill-treatment, segregation, deportation, widespread property plunder, ghettoization, forced starvation and systematic mass murder to "a progressive deterioration of their condition."

As the German ambassador to the Vatican Ernst von Weizsäcker reported after the deportation of the Jews of Rome, the Vatican issued a communiqué in its typical vague and complicated style declaring that "all men, without distinction of nationality, race or religion, benefit from the Pope's solicitude." Interestingly enough, the German ambassador understood the true effect of these pronouncements: "There is less reason to object to the terms of this message . . . as only a very small number of people will recognize in it a special allusion to the Jewish question."[417]

Again in 1943 the Pope explained in his encyclical *Mystici Corporis Christi*: "Our paternal love embraces all peoples, whatever their nationality or race," yet in the same encyclical he declared the Old Law—a term often used regarding Jews—to be void, buried and the "bearer of death." (See the section "Open Protests with no Consequences" for some contemporaneous examples of what other courageous Church leaders were saying in defense of the Jews to see the stark contrast between direct language that had effective positive influence and the Pope's vague language, which did not.)

The Pope's defenders often make reference to the pontiff's communications with the various collaborating governments commiserating with the hounded Jews, however this was not only very infrequent, it often happened too late to make a difference (as in the case of Hungary, where four hundred thousand Jews had already been slaughtered by the time the Pope complained to the Hungarian government) and as we saw earlier seemed to have been motivated mainly by the Vatican's need to protect their reputation and not because the Pope truly cared. As we covered in the previous section, "The Church's Plausible Deniability Strategy," Monsignor Montini, head of the foreign section of the Secretariat of State, said in an internal memo that the goal was to make "known to the world that the Holy See fulfills its duty of charity."

Another point used to defend the Pope's actions, or lack thereof, is the establishment of the Pontifical Commission of Assistance (*Commissione Pontificia d'Assistenza*) and the Vatican Information Office, which were meant to help individuals during the war without discrimination on the basis of race, religion or nationality. But this is no defense at all, as the point is not that the Pope did not help people, but rather that he did not make a special case of helping Jews. The point is that many people were victims of the war, but the Jews were the ones singled out for extermination and the Pope failed to single them out for help. Given that the perpetrators were *discriminating against* the Jews, the Pope should have also *discriminated in their favor*. Moreover, the Pontifical Commission of Assistance was used by Bishop Hudal and others in the Vatican to issue false identity papers that would be then used to help war criminals escape Europe (see the chapter "Smuggling Nazis out of Europe").

The Pope's defenders also make reference to the supposed repeated appeals in Vatican Radio in support of the Jews. This is misleading. There were no repeated appeals in support of the Jews, although there were some in support of Catholics who had converted from Judaism. Also, the Pope's apologists claim that the Pope's means of inspiring resistance was clearly understood during the war. Again, this is not true. Very few people understood the Pope's oblique references to the genocide as a call to resist and defend Jews. This is demonstrated by the passive acquiescence toward the deportation and extermination of the Jews shown by the vast majority of the general population and as the German ambassador to the Vatican pointed out in the quote above.

We must acknowledge that the Pope and Vatican clergy were under the very real fear of retaliation by Mussolini's fascists until 1943 and the Germans after that and until the Allies liberated Rome on June 4, 1944. There were historical precedents of abductions of popes by invading powers that must have weighed heavily on Pius XII. Italian and German censors consistently interrupted and read diplomatic communications of the Holy See and jammed Vatican Radio's signal.[418] However, given the depth of the abyss the world was sunk into, the Pope and his entourage might have found a way to move to a safer location in another neutral country or even moved to Great Britain or the U.S. where they would have been safe to perform their Christian duty to help the persecuted and provide moral guidance to the Catholic faithful, even if that meant sacrificing their chance to be neutral peace brokers after the conclusion of the war. There is historic precedent for moving the seat of the Papacy to a location outside of Rome.[419] In the end the Curia chose neither to move, nor to help the hounded Jews, nor to provide clear moral guidance to the Catholic flock. The Pope, at the time the sole remaining independent moral voice in Europe, could have defied the Germans by openly opposing them in defense of the Jews. In the highly unlikely case that he had been captured and imprisoned that would have sent such an electrifying shock across Christendom that it would have surely backfired on the Nazis, and in any case it would have reinforced the Church's moral authority. Regardless, even if they could not or did not want to move, their behavior did not change after the Allied liberation of Rome with its concomitant elimination of any potential threat to themselves or Church property in the Vatican.

It might be tempting to dismiss the assumption that had the Pope strongly and systematically urged Catholics everywhere to refrain from murdering Jews they would have indeed done so as naïve or unlikely, as Catholics might have feared the reprisals the Germans would have inflicted on them if they had shown opposition. The precedents of concerted popular and even clerical efforts against Nazi policies that had no consequences, however, do not support this. Even in the Police Battalions of the Order Police and the *Einsatzgruppen* killing squads, when and if a soldier objected to the extermination of Jews—an extremely rare occurrence—he was excused from this role without any consequences to himself or his career.[420] It may be tempting to defend the inactions of the Pope and the Church by claiming they could not *force* anyone to do anything. It is true that the Church could not compel the faithful to obey their commands, in the sense that the Pope could not enforce compliance with his orders, however this may be a disingenuous way of looking at this issue because it does not take into account the very real influence the Pope and clergy had on the faithful of a largely Catholic Europe, and does not take into account the very real capacity to threaten to excommunicate the faithful if they persevered in committing atrocities that were illegal and immoral. In the face of the magnitude of events, the Vatican should have repeatedly made strongly and clearly worded public appeals to Catholics and others everywhere to halt the exterminatory campaign against Jews.

Lastly, the Pope's apologists claim that the only way to save Jews was by secretly sheltering them and moving them to neutral countries, and that Pius XII did this in a scale unmatched by any state or organization. Again, unfortunately, the available evidence does not support this claim. As far as we know, neither the Pope nor the Catholic Church *as such* did anything of the sort. As we saw earlier in the section "Open Protests with no Consequences," many righteous Protestant and Catholic *individuals* and priests acting independently, as well as some Protestant Churches (most notably those in Scandinavia) saved many thousands of Jews in this way. In Italy the Catholic *population* gave warning and shelter to many of their Jewish neighbors, which allowed about eighty-five percent of the Jews living in Italy to survive the Holocaust. But even in places like Norway or Denmark, where the Protestant Churches were very successful in openly saving Jews, the Catholic Church remained silent except to protect a few Catholics that had converted from Judaism.[421]

## What a Repentant Church Should Say

The Church should be intellectually honest about their attitude past and present toward the Jews. Modern racial and secular antisemitism stands on a foundation laid out by centuries of Christian teachings. In the words of the Church's most favored theologian, Thomas Aquinas, the Church should stop using a "cultivated ignorance," *ignorantia affectata*, an ignorance so useful that one protects it in order to continue using it. It is a willed ignorance, though an unconfessed one.[422]

Shedding this "cultivated ignorance" and mustering the will to perform a true and thorough reckoning of the Church's actions and inactions, attitudes, sermons, liturgy and even the antisemitic passages in the Christian Bible, and remove any and all polemic involving the Jews, is of paramount importance to redeem the Church, request forgiveness, seek reconciliation with the Jewish people and reestablish the Church's moral standing. Toward this goal the Pope, every national Catholic and Protestant church, the official Christian Catechism and canon law, every doctrinal and theological statement and teaching medium that deals with Jewish matters should declare in the plainest and most direct language that the Jews are not responsible for the death of Jesus, who was killed by the Roman authorities of Judea.

They should also state unequivocally that Christianity has not superseded Judaism and that the Jews' way to God is as legitimate as the Christian's way. The salvation of the Jews remains solely the concern of the Jews, their religion, and their God, and the Catholic Church and Christianity are irrelevant to their salvation. Also, the ultimate salvation of Christians is in no way dependent upon the actions of the Jews and any claim that the Jews need to be converted, or that the Jews' actions in any way impede or hasten salvation for Christians, is wrong. Also, to avoid any possible misconceptions, the Church should also state clearly that all past positions or statements, doctrinal or theological, that contradict any of those just enunciated, whether they have emanated from the Church, any of its institutions or organs, or its clergy, are wrong, null and void.[423] The Church started to move in this direction after the Second Vatican Council in 1965. Much more remains to be done.

The Coordinating Committee for Christian-Jewish Cooperation had prepared a proposal that was forwarded to the Vatican for consideration in the preparation of what turned out to be the brief and often self-exculpatory 1998 Vatican document "*We Remember: a reflection on the Shoah.*" ("Shoah" is a Hebrew word connoting catastrophe, calamity, disaster, or destruction and is preferred by many Jews to the word "Holocaust.") Unfortunately, the Vatican only accepted very little of the proposal. Its first part, quoted below, was not used:

"The Catholic Church confesses to have become guilty because of theologically based enmity against Jews. She takes responsibility for the suffering the Jews had to endure throughout centuries. The Catholic Church thereby also shares responsibility for the genocide of the Shoah. To shoulder this responsibility means to

- admit the guilt;

- analyze the causes truthfully and free of prejudices;

- question exegetical and dogmatic teachings and to make aware of interpretations that are contemptuous of and hostile toward Jews in research, preaching and liturgy;

- search for a new identity in theological research, doctrine and practice, which understands itself as rooted in Judaism and which takes seriously and acknowledges present-day Judaism as an indispensable partner.

Any request to grant forgiveness or even reconciliation has to be preceded by an admittance of guilt and a repentant turning."[424]

# 13

## Legal Background

To evaluate whether there would have been any basis to a potential indictment of the Catholic or Protestant churches, and/or leaders and clergy of those churches, it will be useful to define some legal terms and discuss other legal issues. This legal background will be useful in the discussion that follows.

The London Charter, which provided the legal basis for the Nuremberg Trial of the Major War Criminals and subsequent war crimes trials, defined what constituted a crime against humanity. Many critics of the trial objected to the validity of the laws in the Charter (particularly those related to counts one and two on the indictment related to aggressive war) as they averred they were unknown when many of the crimes were committed. In legal terms it could be argued that those were retrospective laws, and thus in violation of the principles of prohibition of *ex post facto* (from the Latin for "after the fact") laws and the general principle of penal law *nullum crimen, nulla poena sine praevia lege poenali* (Latin for "No crime, no punishment without a previous penal law"). Simply put, this means that someone cannot be prosecuted for something that was not considered to be a crime when it was perpetrated. However, as Francis Biddle, one of the American judges in the International Military Tribunal at Nuremberg, wrote:

"The *ex post facto* argument . . . issued from a lack of understanding of the theory of *ex post facto* or of existing international law. The rubric *nullum crimen et nulla poena sine lege* did not mean that a crime had to be defined and its punishment fixed by statute before the offender could be tried. . . . Murder and treason were punished by courts in the middle ages long before they were incorporated into statute."[425]

Moreover, the legal systems of most European nations— understandably—prohibit *ex post facto* criminal laws, but subject to two exceptions:

- Acts illegal under international law at the time of their commission.
- Acts criminal according to "the general principles of law recognized by civilized nations."[426]

It could be argued that there was no comprehensive law dealing with all the crimes perpetrated against the Jewish people at the time many of the crimes were committed. However, as we will see, the crimes themselves, from defamation to murder and everything in between, were crimes either considered illegal under international law and/or were criminal according to "the general principles of law recognized by civilized nations." As Justice Robert Jackson, chief American prosecutor at the Nuremberg Trial of the Major War Criminals said in his opening statement:

"International Law is more than a scholarly collection on abstract and immutable principles. It is an outgrowth of treaties and agreements between nations and accepted customs. . . . The law, so far as International Law can be decreed, had been clearly pronounced when these acts took place."[427]

## Underlying Criminal Offenses

Defamation (also called calumny, libel, or slander) is the legal term used to describe an expressly stated or implied to be factual statement that may give a product, business, person, nation or people a negative image. It is used in those cases when it is unnecessary to distinguish between "slander" and "libel." Slander is a special case of defamation, which refers to a false, malicious and defamatory *spoken* statement, while libel refers to any other non-spoken form of communication such as images or written words.[428]

Even the Catholic Church's own rules, the Catechism of the Catholic Church, states: "every attitude and word likely to cause" a person "unjust injury" violates the "respect for the reputation of persons." This includes "calumny," which is therefore "forbidden" and brings with it "guilt."[429]

In this book we cannot make a thorough study of anti-defamation laws in every country in which the Christian Church had influence over the last few centuries. However, every country had different laws dealing with libel and slander and they would be applicable. A very relevant law to a potential count of defamation is the German Hate Speech law passed in 1998, the *Volksverhetzung*. This law seems to be an almost literal description of Christian acts toward Jews in the last two millennia:

A person commits a crime if he "incites hatred against parts of the population or instigates violence or arbitrary measures against them or . . . attacks the human dignity of others by insulting, maliciously disparaging or slandering parts of the population" in a manner capable of disturbing the public peace.[430]

The International Criminal Court is governed by the Rome Statute, which was enacted in 2002. This important document, the result of consensus between dozens of nations and the direct inheritor of the Nuremberg legacy, defines among others the laws covering crimes against humanity. It will be useful for the purpose of this discussion to review the parts of the law that may be relevant to the actions of the Church in the past.

A person commits a crime against humanity when he commits one of the following acts:

- Murder;
- Deportation or forced transfer of the population (forced displacement of the persons concerned by expulsion or other coercive acts from the area in which they are lawfully present);
- Imprisonment or other severe deprivation of physical liberty (Inquisition persecutions and imprisonment, and ghettoization);
- Torture (the intentional infliction of severe pain or suffering, whether physical or mental, upon a person in the custody or under the control of the accused);
- Persecution against any identifiable group or collectivity on racial, ethnic, cultural, or religious grounds (intentional and severe deprivation of fundamental rights contrary to international law by reason of the identity of the group or collectivity);
- The crime of apartheid (inhumane acts committed in the context of an institutionalized regime of systematic oppression and domination by one racial group over any other racial group or groups and committed with the intention of maintaining that regime)[431] and,
- Other inhumane acts of a similar character intentionally causing great suffering, or serious injury to body or to mental or physical health.[432]

Lastly, criminal law recognizes omissions as offenses whenever there is a determinate duty to act and that the suspected or accused party neglects to do so. If someone believes someone else is about to be killed, neglecting to warn the person would be considered in many countries a crime of failure to warn.[433] However, the laws in each country are different and this offense would be considered a civil wrong in some countries, where it would be handled as negligence in a civil court. This would be especially true of cases in which the defendant is shown to have had a moral obligation to act instead of a legal one. No one has a *legal* duty to warn others of impending harm, unless a "special relationship" exists with either the potentially dangerous person or the victim. Moreover, it should be "foreseeable" that the offender intends to cause harm to the victim.

Not preventing something that could be averted is equivalent to choosing to let it happen. Thus, *allowing* can be understood as *acting*, and usually intentionally. When someone sees that something they consider unjust or wrong is about to happen, they ordinarily oppose it, especially if such opposition, or at the very least warning, can be understood as that person's responsibility.

## Basis for Legal Liability

Substantive criminal common law has targeted for liability four basic categories of criminal actors. Liability can be extended to individuals involved before, during, and after the principal crime in question. The four basic categories in common law are:

*Principal in the First Degree*: This would be the main criminal perpetrator.

*Principal in the Second Degree*: This would be a person present at the time of the crime and who aids, counsels or otherwise encourages the main criminal actor. This category is traditionally conceived as synonymous to "aiding and abetting." If the actor actively participates in the commission of the offense then he is also complicit in the crime.

*Accessory before the Fact*: Refers to an actor who is not present at the time of the offense but otherwise aids, counsels or otherwise encourages the main criminal actor prior to the crime. Incitement to commit a crime falls in this category.

*Accessory after the Fact*: Is one who knows of the commission of a

crime and intentionally provides help to the principal actor to
avoid apprehension and conviction.

A collaborator would be someone who aids, counsels or otherwise encourages the main criminal actor in the commission of a
crime in the capacities described in categories 2-4. Typically accessories after the fact are prosecuted separately and more leniently
because the law sees the first three categories as similar in that they
all refer to the commission of a crime, whereas the fourth category
makes the perpetrator less blameworthy as it seeks to stymie the
police instead of committing the actual crime.

In order for someone to incur accomplice liability the actor
would have to have solicited, aided, agreed to aid, or attempted to
aid the principal in planning or committing the crime. This implies
that the crime makes necessary some active participation by the
accomplice, and that the behavior in question had some effect.
Moreover, there has to exist a nexus between the actor charged
with aiding and abetting and the principal in the commission of
the crime. An accomplice differs from an accessory in that an accomplice is present at the actual crime. Furnishing moral support
and encouragement in the performance of the crime would be considered "aiding" the principal in the commission of the crime.[434] As
Judge McClellan, a late nineteenth century judge put it, a defendant is not required to provide much help to a perpetrator to incur
liability:

> "The assistance given . . . need not contribute to the criminal re-
> sult in the sense that but for it the result would not have ensued.
> It is quite sufficient if it facilitated a result that would have tran-
> spired without it. It is quite enough if the aid merely renders it
> easier for the principal actor to accomplish the end intended by
> him and the aider and abettor, though in all human possibility
> the end would have been attained without it."[435]

As general legal principles, a person willingly involving himself in a crime is responsible for offenses that result in that initial criminal act, and would be an accessory or accomplice in said criminal act. As the English legal authority William Blackstone defined in his famous *Commentaries*, "An accessory is he who is not the chief actor in the offense, nor present at its performance, but is someway concerned therein, either before or after the fact committed."

Also, helping criminals escape justice is a criminal offense. Again, as Blackstone defined in his *Commentaries*:

> "An accessory after the fact may be, where a person, knowing a felony to have been committed, receives, relieves, comforts, or assists the felon. Therefore, to make an accessory *ex post facto*, it is in the first place requisite that he knows of the felony committed. In the next place, he must receive, relieve, comfort, or assist him. And, generally, any assistance whatever given to a felon, to hinder his being apprehended, tried, or suffering punishment, makes the assistor an accessory. As furnishing him with a horse to escape his pursuers, money or victuals to support him, a house or other shelter to conceal him, or open force and violence to rescue or protect him."[436]

For accessory after the fact liability to exist, three requirements must be met. First, the crime must have been committed by the time aid was provided. Second, the accessory must actually know, not just suspect, that a crime was committed. Third, the aid must be given mainly, but not exclusively, to avoid apprehension, conviction or punishment of the wanted criminal. Acts such as harboring a known felon or aiding him in his escape qualify as a basis for accessory liability. More generally, this applies to the sort of behavior that concerns that which obstructs justice.[437]

The Catholic Church agrees: according to the Catechism of the Catholic Church, if we "protect evildoers," then "we have a responsibility for the sins committed by others."[438]

The United Nations' Universal Declaration of Human Rights, promulgated on December 10, 1948, stipulates several international norms that are relevant to assessing the offenses of Christian clergy during the Nazi period, especially articles 2, 3, 5, 7, 8, 9, 10, 12, 15, 16, 17, 21, 22, 23 and 27. Article 7 of the Statute of the International Criminal Tribunal for Yugoslavia defines individual criminal responsibility. It states specifically that "a person who planned, instigated, ordered, committed or otherwise aided and abetted in the planning, preparation or execution" of such crimes "shall be individually responsible for the crime" and also that "The fact that any of the acts . . . was committed by a subordinate does not relieve his superior of criminal responsibility if he knew or had reason to know that the subordinate was about to commit such acts or had done so and the superior failed to take the necessary and reasonable measures to prevent such acts or to punish the perpetrators thereof."[439] Under these provisions, the defendant would be liable if he "acted in the awareness of the substantial likelihood that a criminal act or omission would occur as a consequence of his conduct."[440] Article 86 of Additional Protocol I to the 1949 Geneva Conventions, entitled "failure to act," in paragraph 1 imposes responsibility for grave breaches which result from a "failure to act when under a duty to do so."

# 14

## Indictable Material

The roster of transgressions of clergy and other members of the Catholic and Protestant churches, as well as the churches as religious organizations and the Vatican as a political entity, include:

- Defamation
- Incitement
- Being accessories to human rights violations
- Being collaborators serving in criminal organizations
- Obstructing justice
- Seeking clemency for convicted war criminals
- Resisting the extradition of potential German war criminals
- Hiding fugitives in Vatican properties
- Aiding and abetting the escape of mass murderers
- Receiving and profiting from stolen property
- Abusing diplomatic privileges.[441]

### Genealogical Records

Both Protestant and Catholic churches collaborated with the Nazis by giving them full access to Church baptismal (genealogical) records. The Church only refused to release said records in the name of "pastoral secrecy" for Catholics who had converted from Judaism. These records were essential to determine who was a Jew according to Germany's Nuremberg race laws, and the church collaborated wholeheartedly with the Nazi authorities in the process of identification of the Jewish population. A priest wrote in the *Klerusblatt* (the official organ of the Bavarian priests' association) in September 1934: "We have always unselfishly worked for the people without regard for gratitude or ingratitude. We shall also do our best to help in this service to the people." The consequence of the Church's cooperation by providing this service to the Nazis was dismissal from jobs and loss of livelihood during the 1930s, and deportation and physical destruction once the war had began.[442]

Germany's race laws were intended to allow to pseudo-scientifically identify who was ethnically a Jew. Catholic and Protestant bishops and priests gladly provided the Nazis the baptismal information that made the general implementation of the race laws possible by identifying who was a Christian, and therefore by omission who was a Jew. This allowed the Nazis to gradually turn Jews into a socially dead people and to eliminate them from German society.[443]

If Pius XII had wanted to really protect the Jews while retaining the Vatican's neutrality, he could have discreetly enjoined all parish priests throughout Europe to destroy their genealogical records. This action would have prevented or at least hindered the Germans from being able to identify the Jews that lived among the Christian population in the thousands of cities and villages that came under their occupation. However, he did nothing of the sort, even though he and Church officials knew that their participation in the identification of Jews as non-Christians would lead to the extermination of those Jews.[444] The Nazis could have eventually gathered the religious/ethnic information from the censuses they were conducting, however, nothing really prevented Jews to lie about their ethnic background in the census once they realized what that information led to. *Only the baptismal records unequivocally identified who was a Christian, and therefore, who was a Jew.*[445]

Making church genealogical records available to the German authorities constitutes a case of criminal facilitation as it provided the authorities with the means and opportunity to commit a crime. Therefore, all bishops and priests who willingly collaborated with the Nazis by furnishing them with baptismal records bear legal guilt as they were rendering aid to persons who intended to commit human rights violations and thus were accomplices in the commitment of those crimes.

## Clergy Serving in the Military

Catholic and Protestant clergy served in the German armed forces providing succor to the soldiers, many of whom were mass murderers. About a thousand Catholic priests and Protestant ministers looked after the spiritual needs of the Germans who served in the *Einsatzgruppen* killing squads, Order Police battalions, in the death camps, and the army. As far as we know, virtually none of them ever raised a voice against the slaughter of the Jews. Since the end of the war, the Church has made many attempts to counter allegations of inaction to save or protect Jews. However, it has never put forth evidence that shows either directives to the clergy to instruct the soldiers that murdering Jews was a crime and a sin, or evidence of those instructions from the chaplains themselves regardless of whether they acted on *motu proprio*—that is, their own volition—or following superior orders. Thus, it is reasonable to assume that documentation of such directives does not exist (although, in all fairness, we will not know with certainty until the Vatican Secret Archives covering the WWII period are open). There is testimony of less than ten cases of people who tried to obstruct the massacres then taking place, out of one thousand serving in the armed forces. However, a close examination of the records shows all clear-cut cases of resistance were of people who were not actually military chaplains, but were rather of men close to them. This fact heightens the inactions of the chaplains even further.[446]

Both Catholic and Protestant German military chaplains supported the perpetrators by blessing and condoning their crimes
through the things they did, things they said, and things they did
not say. An obvious example of their actions is the group absolution of soldiers.[447] Ultimately, the presence of priests in the killing
fields, the vast majority of which were at best silent in the face of
the monstrous deeds of the faithful under their care, served to legitimize the annihilation to the executioners and led them to think
that despite the blood on their hands they were still decent people
who continued to be loved by their church and God.[448] After the
war, Franz Stangl, commandant of the Sobibór and Treblinka
death camps, found solace for his role in mass murder from the
involvement of Christian clergy during the assault on the Jews.[449]

*Field clergy giving the blessing in a religious service for German soldiers.*
*Bundesarchiv, Bild 146-2005-0193, Henisch*

All clergy who aided and abetted the murderers in the mobile
killing squads, police battalion units, the SS and/or any army units
involved in the mass murder of Jews had the right and moral obligation to at least try to stop the perpetrators from committing their

crimes, yet the vast majority chose not to admonish them to refrain from killing Jews. Having done this aiding and abetting on site, side by side with the actual perpetrators, made these clergy collaborators serving in criminal organizations and therefore accomplices implicated in criminal deeds. The very fact they were with the perpetrators during their criminal enterprise providing spiritual support and words of encouragement is *at least* morally reprehensible. Those chaplains that stayed behind in the garrison or headquarters and therefore were not physically present when the crimes were perpetrated, but that provided moral support to the perpetrators before and/or after the crimes were committed, were accessories to the crime of mass murder. That they were not ordered by their superiors in the episcopate and the Holy See to either stay away or if not to at least instruct the faithful that what they were doing was a crime and a mortal sin is inexcusable. Those directly involved in mass murder were guilty of Crimes Against Humanity.

## Acts of Omission

There is no doubt that the failure to prevent unjust harm is a grave offense, particularly when the harm in question is mass murder. In cases such as this, failure to warn and failure to act would be morally indefensible and sufficiently blameworthy to justify criminalization. This offense of omission becomes worse when the entity that could have prevented, or at least mitigated the effects of that harm, chose not to act despite low risk to itself and had a moral and legal duty to do so.

Just like a psychologist that knows his patient intends to kill someone the therapist does not know, or a teacher that learns one of his students intends to murder someone the teacher does not know, the "special relationship" between the therapist and patient and between teacher and student, and the knowledge of the intent to murder, imposes a moral and legal duty on both the therapist and teacher to alert the police, the potential victim, or both.

The Church, ecclesiastical leaders, and priests with the knowledge that the Nazis intended to round the Jews up, deport and murder them, chose to remain silent and failed to warn the victims. Apart from the immorality of a potential defensive claim that the clergy had no "special relationship" with the Jews and therefore were not obligated to warn them, it is indisputable that the clergy had a "special relationship" with the Christian murderers whose souls were in their care, and that they could "foresee" that the Germans intended to kill the Jews. Therefore, that they chose not to alert the victims would have made them legally guilty because the special relationship to the murderers establishes legal duty. In some countries this would be considered a civil case of negligence or failure to warn and would be handled as a civil case. In the Church's own terms it is a sin. According to Church Father Saint Ambrose, "He who knows evil is being done, and does nothing to stop it, is guilty with the evildoer" and in the Church's own language, by being silent or passive observers people incur "a responsibility for the sins committed by others" by "not hindering them when we have an obligation to do so."[450] If this were not so, then the moral basis of the Church would be demonstrably absent.

In the case of the Catholic and Evangelical churches, they were both in their own eyes and in those of the faithful formally charged with preventing grave moral harm. Such an act of omission is equivalent to a choice to let the harm occur and therefore shows approval of the harmful act. That popes Pius XI and XII, other Vatican officials, and clergy around Europe failed to speak out loudly, openly, frequently and unequivocally against the discrimination and murder of the Jews shows at the very least a monumental moral failing. Their lack of dissent and support for the antisemitic laws enacted in Europe directly facilitated the commitment of human rights violations. Silence rendered the silent morally co-guilty in the crimes taking place in front of their very eyes.

It could be even argued that the Church had a greater moral duty to help the Jews given that *Kristallnacht*, Babi Yar and Auschwitz were perpetrated by Christians brought up in the Church's centuries-old antisemitic teachings.[451]

## Support for Slovakia

The country of Slovakia is of particular interest to this study because its president and many of the officials in the government during the war were Catholic priests. In practical terms this means they subscribed to the tenets of Christianity, and that they owed allegiance and obedience to the Pope when it came to religious matters. The priests of the Catholic Church of Slovakia were more than just influential: they were the political founders and leaders of the newly independent state. Their government instituted comprehensive antisemitic laws modeled on Germany's and instigated the deportation of the country's Jews. The German government had even commented with "undisguised gratification" that the antisemitic laws in Slovakia "had been enacted in a state headed by a member of the Catholic clergy."[452]

President-priest Tiso, who boasted of Slovakia's Catholic principles, preached in a holiday mass in August 1942 as the first wave of Jews were being expelled and sent to the death camps, that the deportation of the Jews was a Christian act because Slovakia had to free itself of "its pests."[453] When a Rabbi asked the papal ambassador to intervene in the deportation of innocent Jewish children and infants from Slovakia to Auschwitz, the ambassador is reported to have said: "There is no innocent blood of Jewish children in the world. All Jewish blood is guilty. You have to die. This is the punishment that has been awaiting you, because of that sin [deicide]."[454] Belief that the Jews deserved their fate as punishment for killing Christ was pervasive among the clergy. As Archbishop Kametko of Nietra said in response to a similar plea:

"They will slaughter all of you there [the death camps], old and young alike, women and children, at once—it is the punishment that you deserve for the death of our Lord and Redeemer, Jesus Christ—you have only one solution. Come over to our religion and I will work to annul this decree."[455]

The Vatican's main concern when they complained several times to the Slovak government about the deportations—complaints that were mostly about Catholics that had converted from Judaism or those in mixed marriages and none of which had been expressed publicly—was that the avowedly Catholic regime would implicate the Church and the Pope in mass murder (see section "Church's Plausible Deniability Strategy"). There was no public condemnation or excommunication. By allowing Father Tiso and the other priests who contributed and gave blessings to the deportations and mass murder to remain Catholics and administer the sacraments, the Vatican showed that they believed that people could represent the Catholic Church in its most sacred duties even if they were complicit in the mass murder of Jews.[456]

The Slovak Catholic Church and all its members, including those priests that made up the Slovak government, owed allegiance to the Pope and the Vatican as well as to their own country. Legally they might be considered as agents of the Vatican. The Holy See had the moral duty to instruct their subordinates in Slovakia to halt the discrimination and deportation of Jews. Their few diplomatic entreaties were not enough.

All those people in Slovakia who participated in the mass murder of Jews by promulgating illegal anti-Jewish legislation designed to deprive the Jewish population of their human rights, who were complicit in their deportation, or in other ways, would be guilty of Crimes Against Humanity.

## Support for Croatia

The puppet state of Croatia offers another valuable example of the role of the Vatican during the execution of the "Final Solution." In Croatia a satellite Nazi state was established with the pious Catholic *Poglavnik*, Ante Pavelić, at the helm of the terrorist organization that brutally ruled the country, the Ustasha. Moreover, many other members of the ruling elite were priests.

Like France, Croatia is <u>one of the Church's most beloved na-</u><u>tions and a bulwark against Orthodox schismatics</u>. The Holy See looked on Croatia as "<u>the frontier of Christianity</u>."[457] The fact that Croatia proudly proclaimed its Catholic tradition and allegiance to the Vatican and the Pope make their preference to diplomacy in the face of genocide more shameful. <u>Secretary Maglione instructed</u> <u>the apostolic visitor in Croatia that when making any complaint</u> <u>against the misery of the Jews "...</u> <u>he should recommend in a dis-</u><u>creet manner,</u> that would <u>not be interpreted as an official appeal</u>." By not complaining officially to Pavelić in 1941, the Pope forfeited a premium opportunity before the official beginning of the German genocidal campaign against the Jews. This was because the <u>main victims of the Ustasha were Serbian Orthodox Christians</u>, which meant the Pope would not have interfered in any way with Hitler's plans for the Jews.[458]

*On the left, Alojzije Stepinac, Roman-Catholic Archbishop of Zagreb 1937-1960 with Ante Pavelić, leader of the Ustasha. On the right, Ante Pavelić walks with Giuseppe Ramiro Marcone, who was appointed papal legate to Croatia on June 13, 1941.*

Many priests themselves committed mass murder of Orthodox Serbs and Jews, including as commanders of approximately half of the twenty death camps set up by the Ustasha.[459] During the rule of the barbaric Ustasha regime, half a million innocent civilians were slaughtered, many of them using medieval methods: eyes were gouged out, limbs severed, intestines and other internal organs ripped from the bodies of the living. Some were slaughtered like beasts, their throats cut from ear to ear with special knives or saws. Others died from blows to their heads with sledgehammers. Many more were simply burned alive.[460] These were Crimes Against Humanity as defined in Article 6(c) of the Charter of the International Military Tribunal.[461] Also, a huge amount of treasure was plundered from murdered Orthodox Christians and Jews and later sent to the Vatican and possibly deposited in the Vatican Bank (see below, "Profiting from Stolen Property").

During the Croatian genocide the Vatican had compiled a list of Croatian priests who had participated in massacres of Orthodox Serbs and Jews with the intention of disciplining them after the war. At least one of them, a Franciscan friar called Miroslav Filipović, continued to act as a member of his order as commandant of the notorious Croat concentration camp, Jasenovac, while committing the most heinous atrocities. Sometimes he wore his Franciscan robes while perpetrating his crimes. There is no evidence that he was excommunicated from the Catholic Church, although he was removed from his order. After the war he was tried in Belgrade and found guilty. He was hanged wearing his friar's robes. Most of the fugitive clerics, however, were not only not arrested, they were housed in Vatican properties, sheltered, clothed and fed, and eventually helped evade justice so they could regroup to fight Communism.[462]

## Obstruction of Justice

As we saw earlier, toward the end of the war the Vatican set up the Ratlines, which were purposely established for the Vatican's economic benefit and to aid and abet the escape of wanted war criminals. The motivation for this criminal act was ostensibly to create an "army" of "freedom fighters" for the upcoming fight against Communism. Other factors that played in the decision to do this was the conviction that the Nazi and fascist murderers they were helping escape had not really done anything wrong, that they were being unjustly persecuted by vindictive Allied victors, and that it was simply a matter of Christian charity to help them. In achieving the goal of providing the means and logistics for the escape, a cabal of prelates and priests in the Vatican, going all the way up to the top and with the help and consent of some elements in British and American intelligence, committed a number of crimes.

Instead of smuggling Jewish survivors into Palestine or Argentina, the Vatican smuggled Eichmann, Pavelić and Stangl and many more war criminals responsible for crimes against humanity to safe havens around the world, particularly Argentina, Canada, the United States, Great Britain and Australia.

A scandal almost erupted in the press over Bishop Hudal's Nazi sympathies and smuggling efforts. Instead of publicly denouncing him, the Vatican replaced him with the much less conspicuous and much more efficient Father Draganović. Father Draganović's network, assisted by several religious orders in printing false identity cards, procured Red Cross passports under false pretenses and provided transport under false names. Ultimately the Vatican provided many more Nazis with false passports than they provided Jews with false baptismal certificates.

Pius XII was fully aware of Pavelić's background and of the atrocities his regime committed. There is evidence to show that the Vatican knew it was sheltering wanted war criminals. The Pope's diplomatic messages reveal an active role of intercession on their behalf. Also, it would be impossible to argue that the Ratlines were the work of rogue elements in the Vatican, as the evidence shows Draganović operated with the highest official authorization to direct the smuggling of wanted war criminals.

264 | SIX MILLION CRUCIFIXIONS

The Ratlines were expressly set up to rescue the guilty, as the innocent had no need for false identity papers. Preventing international justice apprehend and try wanted war criminals makes the Vatican an accessory after the fact and constitutes a crime of obstruction of justice. There is overwhelming evidence to convict the Vatican for perversion of the course of justice.[463]

## Profiting from Stolen Property

Another potential count in an indictment against the Vatican would have been receiving and profiting from stolen property. Agents of the Vatican knowingly received and used stolen or fraudulently obtained identity papers from the Red Cross. Also, the Vatican received property stolen from the victims of the Nazis into the Vatican Bank and profited from it. The Ratlines were established as much for the Vatican's battle against Communism as for economic benefit. Stolen Nazi gold was smuggled out of Switzerland (who during the war had acted as Germany's secret accomplice in the Third Reich's monetary crimes[464]) to safety in the only financial institution with total diplomatic immunity and that can never be audited: the Vatican Bank. From there, the plundered loot eventually made it on to the Nazi diaspora in Argentina where it was invested in a number of Argentinean businesses. Much of this stolen treasure, in gold bullion from the treasuries of the plundered countries the Germans conquered, as well as gold coins and ingots made from gold stolen from murdered Jews (both from jewelry as well as gold teeth extracted from their corpses), conceivably made it back to Germany years later. It is quite likely that this treasure was used to partly fuel the rapid German economic revival of the postwar period, the *Wirtschaftswunder* ("economic miracle").

Ultimately, to understand why the Vatican was motivated to help smuggle the Nazis' plundered loot through the Vatican Bank we need to understand that the Vatican's concern was with protecting their considerable investments in the Third Reich. As more information emerges from declassified files in Argentina, Yugoslavia,

Washington, London and other capitals that may know about Pius XII's secrets, the clearer it becomes that the trail of laundered Nazi money leads inexorably back to the Vatican. Only the opening of the Vatican Secret Archives can shed more light on this sad chapter in the Vatican's history.

There is evidence that shows that the Vatican received and more likely than not profited from stolen property, and there is a considerable amount of circumstantial evidence to point that the Vatican was peripherally involved in money laundering, mostly of the Ustasha looted treasure. In conclusion, there is sufficient evidence to accuse the Vatican of receiving and profiting from stolen property. There is overwhelming evidence that they engaged in the traffic of illicitly obtained or stolen identity documents.[465]

## Abuse of Diplomatic Privileges

When the war ended many of the wanted war criminals ended up in custody of the Allies in POW camps. Sometimes the authorities did not know the identities of the wanted war criminals they already held. Vatican diplomats intervened with Allied authorities to obtain official travel documents that allowed Father Draganović, Bishop Hudal, Bishop Bučko and others to travel and enter prisoner camps and thus organize their clandestine war criminal smuggling network under the cover of official religious duties. Furthermore, Vatican diplomatic channels were used to convey false representations to obtain the release of Nazi murderers and collaborators.

Vatican facilities—monasteries and other Church facilities in the Vatican—were used to house transient war criminals as part of the process of spiriting them out of Europe. Getting to and from those Vatican properties meant the criminals had to travel protected from the authorities that were trying to apprehend them. Thus, to protect these fugitive war criminals from arrest they were escorted in vehicles with Vatican diplomatic plates.

It would have been impossible to set up and operate the Rat-lines without the Vatican's diplomatic protection. Both Pius XII and Montini were experienced diplomats who knew what they were doing. Their actions were meant to subvert hostile states (i.e. those where Communism was taking hold) through armed revolution. As had been the case during the war, Communism was the mortal foe the Vatican was determined to vanquish at all costs. These actions show a clear pattern of violation of diplomatic norms and constitute a crime of abuse of diplomatic privileges in which the Vatican became an accessory to the escape of the fugitive criminals it was sheltering.[466]

## Crimes Against Humanity

When discussing Crimes Against Humanity we must make a distinction between "historic" crimes, that is, crimes committed decades or even centuries ago, and those committed in recent times. The perpetrators of these "historic" crimes range from the popes all the way down to ordinary Christian peasants, and included bishops, priests and Church organizations such as the Inquisition. During the Middle Ages there were many secular rulers responsible for crimes against the Jewish population as well, although during the age of faith everyone was influenced in one way or another by the teachings of the Church. Since the perpetrators of these "historic" crimes are dead, crimes perpetrated a long time ago cannot be prosecuted.

If they could, however, these crimes would have included:

- Imprisonment and deprivation of physical liberty, manifested in acts of the Inquisition in which they incarcerated Jews and *conversos* (converted Jews), and forcing Jews into squalid ghettos;

- Persecutions on racial, ethnic, cultural, or religious grounds, including the intentional and severe deprivation of fundamental rights such as forcing Jews to wear distinctive clothing, preventing them from working in most professions, owning land or real estate, attacking their religion and burning their sacred books, etc.;

- Torture, by intentionally inflicting severe physical and mental pain or suffering on Jews with the intent of extracting confessions of a spurious nature;

- Murder, by burning Jews at the stake who refused to convert to Christianity, as a result of fantastic accusations such as well poisoning or the Blood Libel, and through the hate toward Jews clergy fomented that incited the Christian mob to massacre Jews during the Crusades;

- Deportation or forced transfer of the Jewish population through expulsion, perpetrated both by the secular rulers of those countries Jews lived in (usually backed and/or promoted by the Inquisition) and by the popes;

- The crime of apartheid, including forced preaching, forced conversion, ghettoization and economic plunder of Inquisition victims and other inhumane acts such as the abduction of Jewish children to be brought up as Christians.

All the acts listed above were perpetrated with the purpose of systematically oppressing Jews and were committed with the intent of establishing and maintaining Christian domination over Jews. That the Catholic and Protestant churches acted as callously as they did during the Holocaust having this type of record should bring them eternal shame.

During WWII many people perpetrated crimes against humanity. This section only focuses on members of the clergy. There were many Croatian Catholic priests who committed mass murder, including as commanders of approximately half of the twenty death camps set up by the Ustasha. In Slovakia, all clergy who were members of the government and instituted comprehensive antisemitic laws, as well as everyone who participated in the mass murder of Jews by collaborating in their deportation or in other ways would be guilty of Crimes Against Humanity. Lastly, all clergy who were serving in the German or Croatian armed forces and were directly involved in mass murder would be guilty of Crimes Against Humanity.


## Defamation and Incitement

The antisemitism the Church had spread around Europe for centuries was a powerful motivator for Christians to perform anti-Jewish actions. It is not surprising that someone would act this way to defend themselves from the "Jewish Problem," if they believed the Jews were Christ-killers, or minions of the Devil, or Bolshevik revolutionaries bent on destroying civilization and religion, or evil capitalist financiers committed to cause global depression and taking over the world, or spiritual defilers of Christian minds. At the time of the Second World War all these were common accusations comprising the standard and traditional Catholic Church's antisemitic litany. Thus, through the centuries, the Church conditioned people to see Jews as demonic and a threat to society. The vast majority of supporters of the Nazi regime were committed to resolve the "Jewish Problem." Given this objective the "new" Nazi antisemitism was at the very least acceptable to millions of Germans and their helpers throughout occupied Europe brought up in an environment created by the "old" antisemitism created by the Church.[467]

As we have seen earlier in this book, there were many instances throughout history in which clerics and Christian writers have incited Christians to hate Jews and Judaism and even instigated them to commit acts of violence or take arbitrary measures against the Jews. The murder of thousands of Jews during the Crusades prompted the popes to promulgate the bull *Sicut Judaeis* to protect them from the expressly Christian rabble, while at the same time the popes and prelates continued to disseminate those pernicious negative teachings that engendered the hatred and violence on the first place. Even during the war there were instances of incitement against the Jews, for instance, in the pronouncements of the Slovak and Hungarian Catholic churches.

*An anti-Jewish sign posted on a street in Dresden reads, "The Jews are the children of the devil. Tar and sulfur, where should I put my hatchlings when the whole world knows where they are coming from." Below the large sign are two smaller ones that read, "The Jews are our misfortune."*

One notorious form of incitement and defamation was the medieval Passion Play, a dramatic performance of Jesus' Passion during his last agonizing hours as recorded in the Gospels. These Passion Plays were very popular throughout Christian Europe in the late Middle Ages. They gradually moved out of the church and monastery into the streets and the stage, where the dramatization of Jesus' suffering became a very effective way of representing the tortures and pain inflicted on him. It was held every year in Lent and typically the devout audience, incensed by the literature and sermons intended to help them meditate on the Passion and the strong iconography and anti-Jewish message that helped them visualize it, went out after the performance on a violent rampage against Jews.[468]

Also, the play makes its anti-Jewish message worse as it falsely portrays Pilate as dedicated to justice, enlightened and merciful instead of viciously brutal and rash as his record truly shows. The play (as do the Gospels) also portrays Jews as bloodthirsty and malevolent and diminish Pilate's role in the crucifixion. Even though Jesus and his disciples lived and died as Jews, the play obscures this by calling him "Christ" and never by his Hebrew name. The net result is that the play portrays the general Jewish population as a polar opposite of Jesus and his disciples.[469]

The seventeenth century Passion Play at Oberammergau in Germany emerged in this context. This was and still is the most important staging of the play. In 1949 and 1959, Catholic cardinals offered the residents of Oberammergau the official blessing of the Church as they looked forward to the productions of the succeeding years.[470] Hitler supported passion plays:

> "It is vital that the Passion Play be continued at Oberammergau; for never has the menace of Jewry been so convincingly portrayed as in this presentation of what happened in the times of the Romans. There one sees in Pontius Pilate a Roman racially and intellectually so superior, that he stands out like a firm, clean rock in the middle of the whole muck and mire of Jewry."[471]

The case of Julius Streicher, publisher of the notoriously antisemitic publication *Der Stürmer* during the Nazi years, is particularly interesting. Streicher showed to what extremes Christian antisemitism could lead to. Streicher, who called himself "Judeophobe Number 1," was blinded by his hatred of Jews. *Der Stürmer*, whose slogan "The Jews are our misfortune", echoed Martin Luther's writings on Jews, was well known for its repeated portrayal of the blood libel, its claim that the Jews were responsible for the worldwide economic depression, and were responsible for the crippling unemployment and inflation which afflicted Germany during the 1920s. Moreover, the paper also claimed that the Jews were white slavers responsible for most of Germany's prostitutes. A frequently repeated theme was the sexual violation of ethnically German women by Jews in which Streicher made gruesome stereotypical portrayals of Jews in sexually charged encounters. His repeated portrayal of Jews as evil and subhuman, combined with the religious undertones of identification with the devil, quotations from Luther, the Talmud and the Hebrew Bible extracted out of context to portray the Jews in the worst possible light, played a critical role in the gradual dehumanization and marginalization of the Jews in the eyes of the German population. All of these actions helped to create the environment in which the extermination of the Jewish people was possible.

In the 1930s Streicher expressed admiration in *Der Stürmer* for the antisemitism of the Vatican publication *La Cività Cattolica*. Much of his ideology and hatred for Jews stemmed from the teachings of Martin Luther, who as Hitler said, "saw the Jew as we are only beginning to see him today."[472] Just like Hitler and many Christian clerics in Germany at the time, Streicher addressed his audience in language that was familiar to them, and that they could relate to. His use of language with a religious tenor in the paper, billbords and books was critical to clearly impress the tender reader's mind: "Without a solution of the Jewish question there will be no salvation for mankind." In billboards he often used the phrase, "He who fights the Jews battles the Devil." In the children's book *The Poisonous Mushroom*, published by *Der Stürmer* in 1938, the Jews are not only responsible for Jesus' death, they are "children of the Devil and human murderers." In this way Nazi propaganda fully incorporated the legacy of biblical imagery (e.g. from John 8) and the common Christian medieval slander of ritual murder. A story in *The Poisonous Mushroom* tells of a German girl who is waiting to be examined by a Jewish doctor: "Her eyes stare into the face of the Jewish doctor, and this face is the face of the devil. In the middle of this devil's face is a huge crooked nose. Behind the spectacles two criminal eyes. And the thick lips are grinning, a grinning that expresses: 'Now I've got you at last, you little German girl!'"[473]

Hinter den Brillengläsern funkeln zwei Verbrecheraugen und um die wulstigen Lippen spielt ein Grinsen.

*The Poisonous Mushroom.*

At a Nuremberg gathering during Christmas in 1936, Streicher addressed two thousand children: "Do you know who the Devil is?" he asked his breathlessly listening audience. "The Jew, the Jew!" replied two thousand children's voices.

During his trial before the International Military Tribunal at Nuremberg almost a decade later, Streicher argued in his defense that he had never said anything about the Jews that Martin Luther had not said four hundred years earlier. Streicher said, "Luther would very probably sit in my place in the defendants' dock today, if this book [Concerning the Jews and their Lies] had been taken into consideration by the Prosecution."

One of the prosecutors at Nuremberg, Lieutenant-Colonel Baldwin, delivered the following closing statements in the case against Streicher:

". . . No Government in the world, before the Nazis came to power, could have embarked upon and put into effect a policy of mass extermination in the way in which they did, without having a people who would back them and support them, and without having a large number of people, men and women, who were prepared to put their hands to their bloody murder. . . .

It was to the task of educating the people, of producing murderers, educating and poisoning them with hate, that Streicher set himself; and for twenty-five years he has continued unrelentingly the education—if you can call it so—the perversion of the people and of the youth of Germany. And he has gone on and on as he saw the results of his work bearing fruit. . . .

That is the crime that he has committed. It is the submission of the prosecution that he made these things possible, made these crimes possible, which could never have happened, had it not been for him and for those like him. He led the propaganda and the education of the German people in those ways. Without him the Kaltenbrunners, the Himmlers, the General Stroops, would have had nobody to carry out their orders. And, as we have seen, he has concentrated upon the youth and the childhood of Germany. In its extent his crime is probably greater and more far-reaching than that of any of the other defendants. The misery that they caused finished with their incarceration. The effects of this man's crimes, of the poison that he has injected into the minds of millions and millions of young boys and girls and young men and women, lives on. He leaves behind him a legacy of almost a whole people poisoned with hate, sadism, and murder, and perverted by him. That German people remain a problem and perhaps a menace to the rest of civilization for generations to come."[474]

At Nuremberg the underlying legal principle of Julius Streicher's prosecution and conviction was incitement to murder and extermination.[475] The Nuremberg Trial set the precedent of accusing someone of incitement and of using hateful speech. Just like Streicher and *Der Stürmer*, there were dozens of popes and other Christian prelates, priests and general Christian writers, from Augustine to Luther to the leaders of the German churches still living and everyone in between, who throughout the centuries made attacks on the human dignity of the Jewish people. They accomplished this by making insulting false claims about Jews, by slandering Jews by making malicious, disparaging and defamatory statements about them, by inciting the Christian faithful to a paroxysm of violence every year by perpetuating the deicide charge, by fostering hatred through sermons, liturgy, sacred writings and passion plays and by continuously libeling Jews. Just like Streicher, they were also "judeophobes." If Streicher was accused of leading the education of the German people in perverse ways, of concentrating on the youth and childhood of Germany, of injecting the poison of hate in the minds of millions of Germans—a poison that "lives on"—so could the Church. Had it not been for *Der Stürmer* and its publisher, German fascism would not have been able to educate in such a short period of time those mass murderers who put into effect the criminal plans of Hitler and his thugs by murdering almost six million European Jews.[476] And had it not been for Christianity's teachings about Jews, there would not have been a *Der Stürmer* or a Streicher.

## Counts for Indictment

Had the Allies set up a trial to bring members of the clergy to justice at the end of the war, the indictment could have included the following charges:

| | CHARGE | REASON(S) |
|---|---|---|
| 1 | Defamation | Attacking the human dignity of Jews by insulting, maliciously disparaging or slandering them through negative and false portrayal of Jews and Judaism in Christian traditions, doctrine, liturgy and lectionaries (Hate Speech) |
| 2 | Incitement | • Incitement to hate Jews and Judaism through sermons and Passion Plays<br>• Incitement to violence by perpetuating the deicide charge<br>• Incitement to violence through the use of libel |
| 3 | Complicity in human rights violations | • Help provided to facilitate the identification of future victims<br>• Encouragement to follow illegal orders<br>• Approval of antisemitic racial laws |
| 4 | Accessory or complicity in crimes against humanity | Role clergy played while serving in criminal organizations (mobile killing squads, death camps, army, police battalions, etc.) |
| 5 | Failure to warn/act | • Neglecting to warn Jews of impending roundups and what they meant<br>• Failure to warn and to act forcefully to prevent discrimination and deportation of Slovakian Jews<br>• Failure to warn and to act forcefully to prevent the genocide of Croatian Orthodox Serbs and Jews |

| CHARGE | | REASON(S) |
| --- | --- | --- |
| 6 | Obstruction of Justice | Aiding and abetting the escape of wanted war criminals |
| 7 | Profiting from stolen property | • Receiving and using stolen or fraudulently obtained identity papers<br>• Receiving and profiting from stolen property<br>• Money laundering |
| 8 | Abuse of diplomatic privileges | • Conveying false representations to obtain the release of Nazi murderers and collaborators<br>• Obtaining official travel documents under the cover of official religious duties with the intent of organizing a clandestine war criminal smuggling network<br>• Housing fugitive war criminals in Vatican properties<br>• Escorting fugitive war criminals in vehicles with Vatican diplomatic plates |
| 9 | Crimes against humanity (historic) | • Murder<br>• Deportation or forced transfer of the population<br>• Imprisonment or other severe deprivation of physical liberty<br>• Torture<br>• Persecution against Jews on racial, ethnic, cultural, or religious grounds<br>• The crime of apartheid<br>• Other inhumane acts of a similar character intentionally causing great suffering, or serious injury to body or to mental or physical health. |

| CHARGE | | REASON(S) |
|---|---|---|
| 10 | Crimes against human-ity (WWII) | • Institution of comprehensive antisemitic laws in Slovakia<br>• Deportation from Slovakia<br>• Mass murder by Ustasha Catholic priests in Croatia |

Table 2: Counts for indictment

# 15

## Conclusions

Between four and five in the morning on August 19, 1942 the men of Police Battalion 101 entered the Polish town of Łomazy. They rapidly scoured the small town to round up the Jews. They shot all those that could not move wherever they found them, on the streets, in their homes, in their beds: old, infirm, and the young. Together with the Germans came about forty or fifty auxiliaries—mainly Ukrainians—who were willing collaborators that had been recruited to do the actual killing under German supervision. They gathered all the Jews in a holding area while a group of Jews outfitted with spades was forced to excavate a large pit for the execution in a wooded area about a thousand yards away. The Germans and the auxiliaries meanwhile had breakfast, including vodka.

The Germans made the Jews go on a death march to the execution area, shooting all stragglers along the way, and made them undress once they got there. At the same time they took any and all valuables in the possession of their victims. Some of them had to wait naked under the strong sun for hours and got severely sun burnt. Still, this was nothing compared to the fate that awaited them. Once the killing operation was ready to begin, groups of fifteen to twenty Jews at a time were forced to run into the execution pit through a gauntlet of Germans who jeered and beat them with the butts of their rifles. The company commander made twenty to twenty-five bearded elderly Jews undress and crawl into the grave and instructed the non-commissioned officers of the company to rain blows on the Jews with clubs as they did that. The Germans subsequently shot dead the severely beaten Jews, which in their minds were archetypical Jews.

*The German Gendarmerie and Ukrainian Schutzmannschaft collected these Jews during the liquidation of the Mizocz ghetto, which held roughly 1,700 Jews. On the eve of the ghetto's liquidation (October 13, 1942), some of the inhabitants rose up against the Germans and were defeated after a short battle. The remaining members of the community were transported from the ghetto to this ravine in the Sdolbunov Gebietskommissariat, south of Rovno, where they were executed.*

The execution pit presented a ghastly scene. The Jews were forced to go in and lay themselves face down. The auxiliaries standing in the pit shot each Jew in the back of their head with their rifle, spreading blood, brains and pieces of bone from the blown skulls everywhere. The following group of Jews had to lay down on top of their bloodied predecessors whose skulls had been bursted. In this manner, the pit gradually filled up. The auxiliaries, who had been drinking steadily, were drunk and thus tended to miss their shots, even at close range. This produced a gruesome scene as many of the Jews were injured but not killed by the bullets, which meant the successive groups of Jews had to lay down on bloodied bodies in their death throes, squirming in agony and uttering hair-raising screams. As if this were not ghastly enough, the pit had been dug below the water table. The rising water mixed with blood, bone splinters and pieces of brain matter reached as high as the knees of the auxiliaries doing the shooting, and made the corpses float about the whole area. Most men participated in the executions, which went on for a few hours. Eventually the pit was filled with bodies and blood. Approximately 1,700 Jewish men, women and children were murdered in this gruesome way. Except for the first group of victims, all the rest had to hear the screams of agony of their fellow Jews as they were bludgeoned into the pit, and then shot to death. They then had to go on the same journey themselves. Late in the afternoon, when the slaughter was complete, a few remaining Jews were forced to cover the mass grave with dirt. Some of the Jews still writhing in the pit were therefore buried alive. The Germans then liquidated the grave-sealing Jews.[477]

The horrific method in which this town was made *Judenfrei*—like so many others in the Eastern Front—raises many questions. What motivated the perpetrators to so willingly round up, deport and slaughter thousands of people in the most hellish way? Why was it that they did not excuse themselves from this task when their commanders gave them the choice and when there was no consequence to do so? Why was it they willingly took pictures of themselves and their victims to share with their friends and families back home? Why did they feel it necessary to degrade, humiliate and torture their victims instead of just mechanically shooting them? Clearly if someone had been opposed to the killing they would not have sadistically tormented these men, particularly suffering old men. These are not the actions of reluctant functionaries blindly obeying orders. Their willingness and in most cases eagerness to exterminate Jews, and to do so in the ways they did, was predicated on the basis of a profound, visceral hatred toward Jews instilled in them almost from the moment they could understand language, a hatred that went much deeper than the racial propaganda of the day.

*1937 poster titled "Judaism against Christianity: the Jewish war of destruction against the Christian Church." Part of the text reads: "Two thousand years ago the Jews nailed Christ to the Cross. He died while they smirked mockingly. This crucifixion was the greatest ritual murder of all time. Why did it happen? Why do Jews persecute Christ with their hatred? Why do they insult him even today? Why do Soviet Jews burn down the churches? Why do they torture the clergy to death? Why do they eradicate Christianity wherever they can?" Bundesarchiv, Plak 003-020-028-T1, Fips*

In the American South black slaves suffered immeasurably, yet they were not slated for systematic extermination as an ethnic group, even though their white masters thought of them as subhuman and not much more than beasts of burden. The Germans and their helpers went far beyond because they felt the Jews were guilty of monstrous crimes and were dangerous. They exterminated Jews because they felt they were defending themselves from what they perceived to be a demonic influence in their Christian way of life.

The perpetrators inflicted unspeakable pain and suffering on their victims, and then killed them, because they were taking revenge for Capitalism, for Communism, for revolution, for the defeat in WWI, for unemployment, for economic depression, for taking the best jobs, and any number of baseless accusations, all successors in modern guise and language to the accusations of ritual murder, causing the Black Plague, associating with the Devil, poisoning wells, desecrating the host, defiling Christian minds and of killing Christ.

It is hard to accept that the Vicars of Christ, including some who were named saints by the Catholic Church and who were supposedly endowed with spiritual infallibility, could be responsible for the brutal repression, degradation, forced impoverishment and imprisonment of an entire people over the course of so many generations. Even in those cases when the popes and high prelates of the Catholic Church attempted to defend Jews, they did so while at the same time holding on to and spreading the hateful teachings that made that defense necessary. On the Protestant side of Christianity, things were not that much better. As we have seen in this book, anti-Jewish teachings are pervasive at all levels of Christianity irrespective of denomination: in the Christian Bible and other sacred texts, in liturgy, in art, in sermons and as a consequence also in social talk and behaviors.[478]

Even though the type of antisemitism prevalent in the years leading to and during the Second World War was no longer theologically based, it is indisputable that the often politically motivated, secular and racial hatred that blamed the Jews for all the ills of the world and drove so many people to murder them during the war was built on a solid foundation of anti-Jewish enmity and contempt learned from Christian teachings. The reason the peoples of Europe developed the ideas of modern antisemitism, succeeded in disseminating them so quickly, and felt no compunction in collaborating in the execution of the "Final Solution of the Jewish Question" is because as the inheritors of a legacy of sixteen centuries of Christian conditioning of hostility toward Jews they believed there was indeed a "Jewish Question" that had to be resolved. Ultimately, they were predisposed to absorb any new idea that conformed to a worldview in which Jews were malevolent, hateful and perceived to be dangerous, and which provided them with a way to eliminate the perceived problem.

It may be tempting to dismiss this connection, particularly when the racial aspect of the hatred was so prevalent in Nazi propaganda and ideology. However, that racial propaganda was either nonexistent or very minimal in the small towns and villages in those countries in the East where most Jews lived and where they were murdered in the most gruesome ways. In those areas the hatred toward Jews cannot be explained by blaming it on years of relentless anti-Jewish racial propaganda alone. In Poland, Latvia, Lithuania, Belarus, Russia, Ukraine, Hungary and other countries overran by Germany, the Nazis found no shortage of local people willing to denounce Jews, to hunt them down, and to act as auxiliaries in their massacre. In those areas there was no shortage of people satisfied with the fate reserved for the Jews. Germany's Minister of Propaganda Joseph Goebbels believed that the power of Nazi antisemitism stemmed from repetition, rather than from accuracy: *"If you repeat a lie often enough, it becomes the truth."* In those areas in the East the lies people had heard repeated *ad nauseam* all their lives were not that Jews were *Untermenschen*—subhumans that were interchangeably called bloodsuckers, rats, germs, vampires and parasites that had to be eradicated—but rather that they were Christ-killers, that their perfidy had led to their divine rejection, that they were cursed and doomed to eternal and deserved suffering, that they were minions of the Devil, and that they were a malevolent force bent on the destruction of Christian civilization. In all the areas where Jews were demonized, humiliated, dehumanized and murdered the common denominator was Christianity and its ancestral enmity toward Jews.

Also, it is undeniable that thousands of clergy of all levels in both churches wholeheartedly supported the Nazi persecution of the Jews by providing the German government with material assistance to identify the Jews, by providing succor to the mass murderers in the killing fields and death camps, and by encouraging the faithful to be loyal to the *Führer* in his infinite hatred of Jews despite their full knowledge of the consequences of that hatred. Even though they did not call for the slaughter of the Jews, many church leaders, from Pope Pius XII all the way down to parish priests everywhere, actively or passively supported their persecution by continuing to promote a feeling of animosity toward Jews in their publications and sermons and by approving and supporting the criminal anti-Jewish racial laws promulgated by Germany and its allies. In Croatia many Catholic priests committed the most heinous atrocities and the Slovakian Catholic Church was complicit in the deportation of Slovakia's Jews to their deaths, all while the Vatican essentially stood by silently.

Moreover, the Vatican has shown no remorse or acknowledgment of any of this and has provided the planning, means and logistics necessary to make possible the escape of wanted war criminals from international justice. Furthermore, the Vatican has used its financial apparatus to enable the laundering of Nazi treasure plundered from invaded countries and murdered Jews to safe havens around the world.

After the war the occupational authorities in Germany set up a number of trials to bring to justice the most egregious perpetrators of war crimes. The first and most famous of these trials was the international trial of the major war criminals set up in Nuremberg. There were twelve subsequent trials held by the Americans there and others in the jurisdictions of the other occupational powers. Additionally, there were many more held by local courts. The German Catholic bishops did not think these were fair trials and claimed that the Germans had suffered enough already, and sought clemency for the convicted war criminals. The bishops were mostly successful in this quest, and in so doing they committed an immoral act, as they knew exactly what kind of men they were protecting.

There were some positive actions. During the war the Vatican pursued a policy of rescue through quiet diplomacy. There is some evidence to show that at times the Vatican did indeed save some Jews this way. In addition, there were many cases of individual clergy—some of them with explicit and all of them with implicit approval of the Pope—who, acting on their own volition were successful in saving the lives of Jews. Hundreds, if not thousands of righteous Catholics, operating through convent and monastery networks, through individual parish communities, within diocesan structures, or as individual believers, saved thousands of Jews. There were many Catholics who sacrificed themselves, sometimes even with their own lives, for Jews.[479] However, in absolute terms, only a small fraction of European Christians objected to the elimination of the Jews and just a minuscule number took active steps to protect them. That was nowhere near enough when those being slaughtered counted in the millions.

No one, neither the Catholic or Protestant churches nor the Pope had the power to make Hitler desist from his genocidal campaign. However, if the pontiff and his clergy, in association with leaders of the Protestant churches, had opposed antisemitism and the ongoing annihilation of the Jews consistently, vigorously and as a united front of the two churches, they may have succeeded in creating a moral revolt against genocide. The churches should have used any and all outlets available: Vatican Radio, the BBC and other Allied radio broadcasts with reach in the German-occupied territories, on diplomatic communiqués and démarches, on encyclicals and pastoral letters read from the pulpits everywhere, on the myriad religious publications still in circulation during the war and that reached all theaters, in direct contact between clergy and the faithful (especially those in the armed services), and through printed flyers such as those the Allies were already regularly dropping from the air on occupied countries.[480] The likelihood of Nazi retaliation would have been very close to nil. The Pope, who during the war still ruled autocratically over an independent state with a functioning diplomatic corps, as well as over a fully operational, giant transnational organization of influential prelates and priests not subject to the ban on freedom of speech and who had global presence and reach, should have done this everywhere, loudly and plainly, and he should have done it relentlessly and through every means of communication available to the Vatican. The Pope's prevarications vis-à-vis the genocide meant he was perceived—willingly or not—to favor the Germans and tacitly approve of the extermination of the Jews.

Direct appeals to the faithful would not have stopped Hitler or those who followed him blindly, but it would have hindered him greatly. The number of ordinary individuals who were willing to kill in Hitler's name and to fight in his wars would have been greatly reduced. This included ordinary people such as train engineers, people manufacturing and delivering poison gas or men in uniform committing atrocities. One of the reasons the Germans were so successful in murdering so many Jews is because they were capable of recruiting thousands of willing collaborators everywhere they went, collaborators steeped in anti-Jewish teachings who were happy to contribute to the elimination of the Jews in their midst, and because entire populations were passive onlookers at best. Making Christians everywhere in Europe know in no uncertain terms that the genocidal campaign against the Jews was illegal, immoral and a sin to participate in would have forced Hitler to redouble his efforts to continue with the exterminatory operations in secret and only use brainwashed, fanatical henchmen. This would have by necessity slowed Hitler down considerably given that that constituted only a very small number of people in absolute terms. Direct appeals to the faithful would have likely inspired more people to hide Jews. These appeals would have led more people to become rescuers with a concomitant reduction of the number of victims.

The church leaders must have known that promoting hatred by maligning the Jews, particularly when that hatred led to their annihilation, was more than immoral: it was illegal. They must have known that sheltering and helping wanted criminals escape justice was illegal. They must have known that receiving and profiting from plundered war loot was a violation of the law. It is not possible to excuse oneself from these crimes simply because perhaps there was no specific statute stating these things were illegal. The *ex post facto* legal principle requires that the perpetrator believe that he is acting within the law and that he is acting in good faith. No one can argue that the clergy that provided the means to identify Jews, who were subsequently deprived of their livelihood and then of their lives, were acting within the law and in good faith. No one can argue that the priests and prelates who helped known criminals responsible for the murder of millions of people escape to safe havens were acting within the law and were acting in good faith. And no one can argue that persevering in the millenarian disparagement campaign against the Jews the Church and its minions had been involved in since the times of Emperor Constantine was acting in good faith.

Therefore, the proper authorities at the end of the war should have initiated both criminal and civil legal proceedings against the Catholic and Protestant churches and the Vatican as organizations. Also, those authorities should have indicted all clergy who may have collaborated in assisting wanted war criminals escape Justice, as well as all those who may have had a role in the denigration, discrimination, persecution and/or extermination of the Jews, with the objective of redressing these crimes and disgraceful and sinful offenses. Originally, a second international trial at Nuremberg was to have focused primarily on the activities of German finance and industry during the Third Reich. The so-called "Industrialists Trial" was widely regarded as of equal importance to the prosecution of the Nazi and SS high command. After the laborious and sometimes confrontational process of working with the other Allied powers to establish the first Nuremberg trial, the United States vetoed this plan. The U.S. then declared in the autumn of 1945 that it would refuse to participate in any further international trials and would hold separate prosecutions on its own. The U.S. did indeed hold twelve trials subsequently before the Nuremberg Military Tribunals. In the other occupation zones similar trials took place. *None of them was against any member of the clergy.* It is the argument of the author that a third international trial should have been set up against the Churches and clergy. To this date, no member of the Catholic or Protestant Churches was made to account for their crimes before, during and after the Second World War.

If the verdict on a trial had shown culpability then the Vatican should have been compelled to surrender any ill-gotten gains it may have acquired from its conduct during the war and subsequent years. Furthermore, the proper ecclesiastical authorities should have been enjoined to make all the necessary changes to Christian theology, traditions, doctrine, liturgy and sacred texts to expunge the supersessionistic, vicious and defamatory anti-Jewish polemic included in them, as well as remove and/or correct all the oral and written Christian teachings that created, promoted and/or encouraged the negative perception of the Jewish people over the last two millennia.

# Epilogue

*"We feel we owe no greater debt to Our office and to Our time than to testify to the truth with Apostolic Firmness: 'to give testimony to the truth.'. . . In fulfillment of this, Our duty, we shall not let Ourselves be influenced by earthly considerations. . ."*

*Pope Pius XII*

# 16

## Cleaning Up the Ashes

Antisemitism did not disappear with the demise of the Third Reich. Centuries of anti-Jewish teachings were so pervasive that even before the stench of death dissipated from Poland in the postwar period new pogroms were conducted there against the surviving Jews.

In the Polish town of Kielce an outbreak of anti-Jewish violence, sparked by blood libel, resulted in a pogrom in which thirty-seven Polish Jews were murdered out of about two hundred survivors who had returned home after World War II.[481] Two more Jews in the trains passing through Kielce also lost their lives. Two or three Gentile Poles were killed by the Jews defending themselves, while nine were sentenced to death later. The brutality of the Kielce pogrom put an end to the hopes of many Jews that they would be able to resettle in Poland after the end of Germany's occupation.

Many ambassadors complained about the Polish Catholic Church's reaction to violence against Jews. The Polish primate, Cardinal Hlond, condemned the murders, but attributed them not to racial causes but to rumor concerning killing of Polish children by Jews. Hlond also put a blame for deterioration in Polish-Jewish relations on the Jews "occupying leading positions in Poland in state life." Cardinal Adam Stefan Sapieha, who was reported to have said the Jews brought it on themselves, echoed this position. Pope Pius XII did not condemn the pogroms because he claimed

294 | SIX MILLION CRUCIFIXIONS

that it was difficult to communicate with the Church in Poland because of the Iron Curtain. Other assaults on Jews occurred in Poland: between November 1944 and October 1945 attacks occurred frequently, resulting in the death of three hundred and fifty-one Polish Jews. In other Catholic countries in Eastern Europe postwar pogroms killed hundreds more. Retaining the same mindset the Church had had during the Holocaust, the 1947 pastoral letter of the Polish bishops made neither a general nor a particular condemnation of the Kielce pogrom or of antisemitism. Independent groups were formed to analyze what caused the Kielce pogrom. As was to be expected, their findings differed from those of Pope Pius and Cardinal Hlond. In essence, the Research Committee of Deported Jews concluded that traditional Christian antisemitism conditioned Poles to hate Jews, and the International Emergency Conference to Combat Antisemitism discovered that even though the people responsible for the Kielce pogrom associated Jews with Communists, that type of incident had "something of a religious character about them."[482]

Following the aftermath of the genocidal campaign against the Jews, once the war in Europe concluded, the Allies set up a series of trials to bring to Justice the Nazi perpetrators. The first of these trials was held in Nuremberg, and on the dock were some of the top men in the Nazi hierarchy.

Leaders of the German Protestant and Catholic Churches did not believe that trying these Nazi leaders was the *just* thing to do. Bishop Galen, who dared to challenge the Nazis during the euthanasia program during the 1930s, published an address after the war in 1945 in which he attacked the Nuremberg "show trials." According to Galen, the trials were not about justice but rather about the defamation of the German people. He went as far as to make the disgraceful claim that the prisons of the occupying authorities were worse than the Nazi concentration camps of Eastern Europe. This was published in Rome, as the occupying authorities would not have allowed it in Germany. The German bishops perceived this as the Vatican's disapproval of punishment of German war criminals, which led them to begin a campaign to have imprisoned criminals freed and have the sentences of those condemned to death commuted to incarceration.[483] This trend got to be so bad that the American bishop Aloisius Muench, Pius XII's own envoy to occupied western Germany after the war, feared a public relations disaster and "wrote to the Vatican warning the Pope to desist from his efforts to have convicted war criminals excused." This advice was not heeded: it was Pope Pius who wanted to intercede on behalf of the convicted war criminals. To him, Germany had been at the center of his diplomatic plans before, during and after the war. Just like before and during the conflict, a strong Germany was instrumental to stop the Soviet menace.[484]

The German bishops asserted that both the Nuremberg and subsequent zonal army trials were a product of power politics and represented victor's justice, and that they were unfair because there was no law that stated the criminality of the acts when they were perpetrated. It seems that to these bishops there really was no law against murdering Jews as, according to them, these laws were "hitherto unknown in Germany."[485]

The relentless lobbying of the Catholic bishops on General Clay (the military governor of the U.S. Zone in Germany) and John J. McCloy (the first high commissioner of occupied Germany) for clemency for convicted war criminals paid off. Eventually the efforts of the episcopate, combined with the new Cold War realities, convinced the American occupational authorities to commute the number of death sentences to a fourth of what the courts had originally ruled. The bishops were eager to appear as the defenders of the German people. In so doing they sought clemency for those convicted of wartime atrocities and made the despicable and untruthful claim that the occupational authorities were mistreating Germans in prisons as cruelly and unwarrantedly as the Germans had done to Jews. In the end, almost all the sentences to convicted war criminals were reduced to lesser penalties.[486]

To protect the Church's reputation and whitewash the actions of the Church, his own and those of the Church hierarchy, Pope

Pius XII falsely stated immediately after the war that German Catholics were heroes and martyrs, and that most Catholics had vehemently opposed Nazism. He did this even after the Americans and the British had shown him photographs of the death camps and the British ambassador had suggested that the Holy See send representatives to the concentration camps so they could judge by themselves the extent of German—including Catholic—barbarity. These things did not go unnoticed by German and Austrian bishops. They empowered the Austrian episcopacy to make the outrageous claim that "no group had to make greater sacrifice in terms of property and wealth, of freedom and health, of life and blood as Christ's church." This could not be farther from the truth.[487] Even though the Nazis increasingly opposed the Church and killed some clergy, they did it more because they were Slavic and/or opposers of Nazism on political grounds than because they were Catholic. As Hitler had declared in the Reichstag in 1939, "the German priest as servant of God we shall protect, the priest as political enemy of the German State we shall destroy."[488] Even though Nazism despised the Church, most Catholics wholeheartedly embraced Nazism after the Concordat between Nazi Germany and the Vatican was signed.

In May 1945, after having learned of Hitler's death, Cardinal Bertram of Breslau ordered that "a solemn requiem mass be held in commemoration of the *Führer*. . ." so that the Almighty's son, Hitler, be admitted to paradise. A solemn requiem mass is celebrated only for a believing member of the Church and if it is in the public interest of the Church. Hitler was not a believing member of the Church and only a Church deeply steeped in their own anti-Jewish teachings and the grotesque twist to them that Hitler gave them could think that a solemn requiem for Hitler was a good, moral thing to do and that it was in the Church's public interest.[489]

Even after the war, after the extent of the genocide was made widely known, Italian Catholic textbooks still contained things like: "This people will be torn from their land . . . scattered through the world . . . under the burden of a divine curse which will accompany them through the course of their history."[490] This was pervasive in other Catholic countries as well. In a postwar French Catholic textbook: "The Jews remain those that reject Christ, and those whose ancestors solemnly asked that his blood fall upon them," and in a Spanish Catholic textbook: "The wretched Jews could not imagine the accumulation of calamities that would befall them and their descendants for having taken upon themselves the responsibility for the blood of the Just One, the Son of God."

The German Protestant minister Niemöller, who at first supported Hitler's rise to power, then became disillusioned and fought the Nazis and was eventually confined in a concentration camp. Still, he could not detach himself from the antisemitic maelstrom he and his fellow Germans were engulfed in. In 1946, when he finally comprehended the consequences of Christian antisemitism, he declared:

"Christianity in Germany bears a greater responsibility before God than the National Socialists, the SS and the Gestapo. We ought to have recognized the Lord Jesus in the brother who suffered and was persecuted despite him being a communist or a Jew. . . . Are not we Christians much more to blame, am I not much more guilty, than many who bathed their hands in blood?"[491]

During the same year he wrote a short poem based on the sentiments expressed on his speeches:

First they came for the Communists, but I was not a Communist so I did not speak out.

Then they came for the Socialists and the Trade Unionists but I was not one of them so I did not speak out.

Then they came for the Jews but I was not Jewish so I did not speak out.

And when they came for me, there was no one left to speak out for me.

## Post-War German Righteous Catholics

In Freiburg in Germany a few righteous Catholics, in true Christian sprit, appalled by the Holocaust and concerned about the fate of the Jewish survivors, worked tirelessly to secure restitution for them. This group was known as the Freiburg Circle. As a result of their lobbying, the Catholic Church had made it clear to the faithful that compensation and restitution constituted a moral obligation for both individuals and country. This was affirmed in annual church meetings until 1950. By then, however, almost nothing had been done either at the state or federal level, and compensation for Holocaust victims ceased to be a high priority for church leaders, who no longer maintained their call for indemnification. This also reflected the guidance they were receiving from the Holy See, which was not even minimally pressing on this matter. As Commissioner McCloy observed, German solicitude extended more toward the perpetrators than toward its victims and survivors. In his view, this applied to church leaders as well.

However, not everyone felt this way. The Freiburg Circle and others continued to fight for restitution. Konrad Adenauer, Germany's first postwar Chancellor and himself a Catholic, said that "unspeakable crimes were committed in the name of the German people, crimes which oblige us to moral and material restitution." This and her frustration with the Church led Gertrude Luckner from the Freiburg Circle to shift her focus from the Church to the government.[492]

In 1950 Karl Thieme, also from the Freiburg Circle, visited Rome to promote the Seelisberg theses. The French Jewish historian Jules Isaac, together with other Catholics, had formulated this document. Isaac had futilely met with Pope Pius six months before with the same purpose. These theses were meant to be a framework for the elimination of Christian falsehoods about Jews and Judaism. Even though Thieme received no official curial statement, he got tentative approval. Thieme also met with the Pope's German Jesuit confidant, Robert Leiber, who expressed hope that one day the Pope would make a statement on Christian-Jewish reconciliation. The Pope never did. Confronting Christian antisemitism was a low priority for him. Moreover, the group that produced the theses called for the recognition of the State of Israel, which the Vatican still refused to do at that time. The Vatican would shamefully continue in this refusal until 1993, forty-five years after its founding and fourteen years after its greatest foe, Egypt, had recognized its right to exist in 1979. The Vatican was one of the last states in the world to do so.[493]

*Gertrude Luckner, who worked tirelessly for Christian-Jewish reconciliation.*

The efforts for compensation and restitution were mostly futile until 1959 when Germany finally awoke to feelings of guilt about the Holocaust. By then the German economy had been growing at a record pace, in part likely fueled by the loot plundered by the Nazis and laundered by the Swiss banks and the Vatican. One of the reasons the bishops changed their minds about restitution then was because Pope Pius had died the previous year. Since Pius XII had had a very special bond with Germany the bishops had been reluctant to speak out while he was still alive and thus risk severing that link.

## The Second Vatican Council

The Dead Sea Scrolls discovered at the end of the 1940s and beginning of the 1950s showed great vitality in Judaism shortly before the time of Christ, despite contrary traditional Christian teachings. That, and the election of Angelo Roncalli to the papacy, had a profound influence in Catholicism in its relations to Jews. Roncalli took the name John XXIII.

During the war he had fought tirelessly to save Jews, and as the Pope he intended to finally eliminate the antisemitism that had fueled the hatred toward them. His removal of the word "perfidi-ous" from the Good Friday prayer, which referred to Jews as "per-fidious Jews," together with his subsequent renouncing of all nega-tive references of Jews such as allusions to their "veiled hearts" and "blindness," probably prompted French historian Jules Isaac to want to make a second attempt at Jewish-Christian relations re-form after his first ineffectual efforts with Pope Pius XII. Not sur-prisingly, the meeting with John XXIII was much more produc-tive. Shortly after the meeting, the Pope instructed Cardinal Bea to include Judaism in the agenda for the Second Vatican Council he had convened. In the agenda the bishops had originally included the topic of the relationship between the Church and non-Christian religions, but Judaism was conspicuously absent. John XXIII rectified the situation by including Jews in the Council's deliberations.

From the beginning of the Council the word "deicide" was at the center of the debate over the declaration on Jews. As we have seen, this accusation was at the heart of Christian animosity toward them. Most Council fathers, if not all, had been brought up with the teachings that all Jews of Christ's day were responsible for his crucifixion and that there was a curse on the Jewish People. The Council fathers were concerned and reluctant to contradict Scripture, which conveyed the notion that Jews had crucified Jesus. Still, in light of what had happened to the Jews twenty years earlier, most of the fathers wanted the term expunged from Christian teachings. In the second draft of the resolution they wrote that "the Chosen People cannot without injustice be termed a deicidal one."

*On the left, a commonly found roadside cross during Nazi-era Germany. The accusation of deicide was fully incorporated in the Christian psyche by the time the Nazis came to power, as the illustration on the right from the antisemitic German children's book,* Der Giftpilz *(The Poisonous Mushroom) shows. As this German mother explains to her children, "When you see a cross, then think of the horrible murder by the Jews on Golgotha."*

When John XXIII died in 1963, before the conclusion of the *Nostra Aetate* (Latin for "In Our Times") declaration on Jews, progress slowed down. Most of the Council fathers still wanted to honor the late Pope's wish for a strong statement freeing Jews from the accusation of deicide. This elicited worldwide praise. However, the politics of the time got in the way. The Arab countries lobbied intensely against a favorable statement about Jews, and the fathers feared that Catholics living in Arab states may suffer retaliation. Cardinal Montini, whose role during the war as one of Pius' closest advisors we discussed earlier, was elected as Pope Paul VI. He sought a watered-down version of the declaration that would not free Jews from the accusation of deicide. The term was inserted three times in the drafts, and removed another three times as a result of the conflicting goals. Pope Paul sided with the conservative fathers with a sermon he gave on Passion Sunday in 1965 when he directly accused the Jews of deicide. As *L'Osservatore Romano* reported, in his sermon the Pope said that when Jesus revealed himself to his Jewish brethren they "derided, scorned and ridiculed him, and, finally, killed him."[494] Nothing could be farther from the spirit of the Council as had been set by his predecessor, Pope John XXIII.

*The Second Vatican Council.*

The final pronouncement was a compromise, yet it was still a remarkable document. The *Nostra Aetate* declaration stated that the crucifixion "cannot be blamed upon all the Jews then living, without distinction, nor upon the Jews of today." In addition to this, the fathers declared that the Jews are not "repudiated or cursed by God." These statements marked the beginning of the end of over sixteen centuries of Christian antisemitism.[495]

During the protracted debates, non-German fathers repeatedly brought up the issues of Christian antisemitism and the Holocaust: "The injustices of the centuries cry out for amends" (Ritter); "How many [Jews] died because Christians did not care and kept silent?" (Cushing); "A truly Christian declaration cannot omit the fact the Jewish people have been subjected to centuries of injustices and atrocities by Christians" (O'Boyle) and many others. These statements provided a general understanding that *Nostra Aetate* was an implicit acknowledgement of Christian guilt for the Holocaust and for Christian antisemitism since the beginning of the Christian movement. The declaration however fell short of including an explicit apology for centuries of Christian antisemitism. Yet, even though it did declare that the Church "deplores the hatred, persecutions, and displays of antisemitism directed against the Jews of any time and from any source," it is unquestionable that the declaration would have been more emphatic and bolder had Pope John XXIII lived until 1965.[496]

## Toward a Better Understanding: Building on *Nostra Aetate*

The Vatican embraced the revolutionary new ideas in *Nostra Aetate*. In 1974 the Holy See gave further instructions on how to interpret the declaration with the "Guidelines for Implementation of *Nostra Aetate*." After that, in 1985, the Vatican issued the "Notes on the Correct Way to Present the Jews and Judaism in the Preaching and Catechesis of the Catholic Church." In 1998, after eleven years in the making and more than half a century after the Holocaust, the Vatican, under Pope John Paul II, issued the statement *We Remember: A Reflection on the Shoah*. This was a well-intentioned document but it fell short of being absolutely truthful. Moreover, the document was simply too little, too late. It was mostly a defensive apologetic attempt to exonerate the Church. We Remember missed an opportunity to make an appraisal and reckoning with centuries of Christian antisemitism and what role it may have had as it transformed into something lethal in the Second World War.

An analysis of what was actually published shows how little the Church acknowledges and how much it denies: "The Shoah was the work of a thoroughly modern neo-pagan regime. Its anti-Semitism had its roots outside of Christianity." As we had seen, the Nazi regime may have been neo-pagan but the vast majority of its members were very much Christian, and despite the regime's efforts, they staunchly remained that way. Claiming that Nazi antisemitism had its roots outside Christianity is a misleading half-truth because even though Christian doctrine states that anyone can be baptized, as we saw earlier racial antisemitism had been pursued and enforced by the Inquisition since the Middle Ages, and was supported by the German church during the Nazi years and the Jesuits even beyond. As we have seen in this book, Christian anti-Judaism is the foundation on which Nazi antisemitism was built. The roots of Nazi antisemitism are indisputably *inside* Christianity. Moreover, We Remember does not mention the prevarications of the wartime pope, Pius XII, when confronted with the plight of the Jews. The document states that the Pope, who never mentioned the Jews in his public pronouncements during the war, was responsible for saving hundreds of thousands of Jewish lives, however that claim is not substantiated by the available documents.

Making statements like "Sentiments of anti-Judaism in some Christian quarters and the gap which existed between the Church and the Jewish people led to a generalized discrimination. . ." or "[Jews] were looked upon with a certain suspicion and mistrust. In times of crisis such as famine, war, pestilence or social tensions, the Jewish minority was sometimes taken as a scapegoat and became the victim of violence, looting, even massacres" fails to make clear that it was not just "a certain suspicion and mistrust" that led Christians to act the way they did toward Jews, but rather a systematic, continuous persecution by theologians, Church leaders, priests and laymen who instituted a policy of hatred, discrimination and humiliation and spread it through the catechism, canon law, liturgy, pulpits and schools with the intention of reducing the Jews to a position of subservience and inferiority, a position in which, to use St. Augustine's expression, they could survive but never thrive.

Reading this document with no knowledge of history would give the reader the impression that "the Church as such" played no role in paving the road to the Holocaust, as if the Church's teachings long before and during the war had nothing to do with what happened. One would get the impression the responsibility was on the shoulders of just some rotten apples, some misguided "sons and daughters of the Church" who built an entire edifice of hatred out of thin air.

In contrast, the American Catholic bishops were clear and forthcoming. As they explained in their 2001 booklet *Catholic Teaching on the Shoah: Implementing the Holy See's We Remember*, "Christian anti-Judaism did lay the groundwork for racial, genocidal antisemitism by stigmatizing not only Judaism but Jews themselves for opprobrium and contempt. So the Nazi theories tragically found fertile soil in which to plant the horror of an unprecedented attempt at genocide. . . . *We Remember*'s call for the Church's ongoing repentance for these sins [against Jews], will involve for most Christians an assumption of responsibility for our collective Christian past, not personal guilt. . . . the Church, have every reason to assume responsibility to ensure that nothing like it can ever happen again."[497]

The French bishops also rejected the Vatican's half-truths and made a more honest "Declaration of Repentance" in 1997, certainly a more forthright *mea culpa* than *We Remember*:

> "It is important to admit the primary role, if not direct, then indirect, played by the constantly repeated anti-Jewish stereotypes wrongly perpetuated among Christians in the historical process that led to the Holocaust. . . .

According to theologians it is a well-attested fact that a tradition of anti-Judaism affected Christian doctrine and teachings, theology and apologetics, preaching and liturgy in various degrees and prevailed among Christians throughout the centuries until Vatican Council II. This soil nurtured the poisonous plant of contempt for Jews with its legacy of serious consequences, which until our century, have been difficult to remove. Wounds resulting from this contempt are still open and unhealed.

To the extent that the priests and leaders of the Church for so long allowed the teaching of contempt to develop and fostered in Christian communities a collective religious culture which permanently affected and deformed mentalities, they bear a serious responsibility. One can conclude that even though they condemned the pagan roots of antisemitic theories, they failed to challenge these secular thoughts and attitudes by not clarifying understandings as they should have.

As a result consciences were often lethargic, their capacity considerably weakened in face of the sudden appearance of national socialist antisemitism's criminal violence, a diabolic and extreme form of contempt for Jews based in categories of race and blood, openly directed at the physical elimination of the Jewish people."

There were many more statements like these from other Christian countries.

The Vatican, however, seems to be above this level of contrition. The French bishops, especially in light of the example set by the Holy See, must be commended for having mustered the strength to issue this declaration and offer their honest and heartfelt apology:

"Today we confess that silence was a mistake. We also acknowledge that the Church of France at that time failed in its mission of educating consciences and that she thus bears with the Christian people the responsibility of not having helped rescue in the early stages when protest and protection were possible and necessary, even though there were numerous acts of courage later on.

We acknowledge this reality today because this failure of the Church of France and its responsibility toward the Jewish people are part of its history. We confess this sin. We beg God's forgiveness and ask the Jewish people to hear our words of repentance."[498]

## Last Thoughts

*Six Million Crucifixions* examines the root causes of antisemitism in Christianity and how that prepared the soil for the modern antisemitism that led to the extermination of six million Jews during the Second World War. Its focus is on those things that engendered antisemitism and made it evolve and flourish over the last two thousand years, eventually colliding with modern ideas of racial superiority. As we have seen, this led to the extermination of millions of innocent human beings whose only fault was to have been born a Jew. This book also provides background information about the role the Church played during the years of the Third Reich and its immediate postwar aftermath.

Some of the information and allegations contained in this book will be corroborated or repudiated when and if the information contained in the Vatican's Secret Archives and Vatican Bank are opened to researchers. Given that under normal circumstances the Vatican has a policy of keeping the documents in the Archives secret for seventy-five years after the events they cover, and that these documents are likely to be self-incriminating and might be destroyed, the international justice entity that would have handled this case should have subpoenaed these records at the end of the war. Without these documents the evidence available may have not been sufficient for a conviction on some of the counts in a potential indictment.

There is no question that forcing the Jews into ghettos, coercing them to wear distinctive clothing, preventing them from working in most professions, owing land or real estate, pressing them to convert to Christianity and burning them at the stake if they refused, etcetera, were particularly odious offenses that constituted serious attacks on human dignity, grave humiliation, or a degradation of an entire group of human beings. They were not isolated or sporadic events, but were part either of Church policy or of a wide practice of atrocities or abuse tolerated or condoned by the Church over a period of centuries.

It is important to realize that the Christian background of persecution, discrimination, demonization, segregation, vilification and victimization of Jews and Judaism as presented in this book constitutes a crime against humanity and would have been prosecutable were it not for the fact that the perpetrators were dead. However, the Churches and the Vatican may be liable in a civil court. The Vatican has actively concealed many of the documents pertaining to its actions during the war and its aftermath. Concealment by the defendant should toll (that is, extend) the statute of limitations, which could make a trial against the people responsible possible even years after the events. In any case, even though the modern Church may not be responsible for any orally or written antisemitism created, taught and disseminated by their predecessors all the way back to the foundational texts of Christianity, it is responsible for continuing to teach and disseminate them today. If someone wrote and published something in today's Germany falsely accusing someone else of murder, of being evil and demonic, and systematically taught this to millions of people, they would be prosecuted and incarcerated. In today's legal parlance, the antisemitism still embedded in many Christian texts is simply Hate Speech. Persevering in the usage of those texts—given what they led to—is at best an immorality of colossal proportions.

A combination of unique factors made possible the Holocaust, the greatest crime in human history: total control of the machinery of state by the Nazi totalitarian regime; the active or passive collaboration of most of the German population; the collaboration of like-minded peoples in the territories occupied by the invading German armies and the deeply ingrained antisemitism common to all Christian countries. Even though one cannot trace a straight line of causal connection linking the Christian Bible to the barbarous actions of the Nazis, it is indisputable that New Testament and later Christian writings shaped the hostile perception and attitudes Christians held of Jews and justified aggressive and many times destructive actions toward them throughout Christian history. Christian teachings about Jews were the common factor in the underlying motivation of all forms of collaboration in the persecution of Jews that took place in those areas conquered by the Germans. Even though other elements contributed to the fantastic notions the Germans and others held about Jews, the Church's antisemitism was a necessary but not sufficient cause of the extermination of the Jews during the Second World War. Christian teachings about Jews were the "nitroglycerin" that formed the basis of the "dynamite" the modern antisemites manufactured by adding other ingredients. The Nazis simply had to light the match.

Our conclusions and recommendations are harsh, and are sure to be unpopular. However, we believe them to be based on careful analysis and evaluation of the historical record, and to be just and fair. It is our belief that the outcome of the proposed legal proceedings would have cleared the path to the expunction of those aspects of Christian teachings that led to immeasurable suffering, and when taken to their natural logical conclusions, to mass death. Also, it is our expectation that one of the outcomes of these proceedings would have been the establishment of measures of reparation and the restoration of the Jewish people's good name as regarded as just. Lastly, it is our conviction and hope that the elimination of the supersessionism and antisemitism in Christianity would have ushered in a new age of forgiveness, reconciliation and brotherhood between Jews and Christians.

# Appendices

"*A monstrous people, having neither hearth nor home, without a country and of all countries; once the most fortunate people in the world, now the evil spirit and the detestation of the world; wretched, scorned by all, having become in their wretchedness by a curse the mockery of even the most moderate.*"

*Bishop Jacques-Benigne Bossuet*

# I

## In Their Own Words

*"In the Christian world—I do not say on the part of the
Church as such—erroneous and unjust interpretations of the
New Testament regarding the Jewish people and their alleged
culpability have circulated for too long."*

*Pope John Paul II*

Readers of this book may find it hard to believe that the Christian churches may have promoted so much evil for so long. They would be right to be amazed by it, and by the fact that the Church succeeded to promote evil with impunity. It is indeed astonishing how much hatred was instilled in the minds of so many generations of Christians, and it is appalling to realize what those teachings eventually led to. But hard as it may be to accept, this is what the historical record shows. For those who believe that attitudes and actions against Jews throughout history were simply the errors and failures of a few "sons and daughters of the Church" "in the Christian world" who acted independently and perhaps even despite what "the Church as such" taught, we will simply let the source texts and the pronouncements of some of the infallible Vicars of Christ speak for themselves:

**The Jews are cursed for murdering Jesus.**

"When Pilate saw that he was getting nowhere, but that instead an uproar was starting, he took water and washed his hands in front of the crowd. 'I am innocent of this man's blood,' he said. 'It is your responsibility!' All the people answered, 'Let his blood be on us and on our children!'" (Matthew 27: 24-25)

*Pope Saint Peter I:* "Having brought the apostles, they made them appear before the Sanhedrin to be questioned by the high priest. 'We gave you strict orders not to teach in this name,' he said. 'Yet you have filled Jerusalem with your teaching and are determined to make us guilty of this man's blood." Peter and the other apostles replied: "We must obey God rather than men! The God of our fathers raised Jesus from the dead—whom you had killed by hanging him on a tree." (Acts 5:27-30)

*Pope Clement VIII:* "The Bible itself says that the Jews are an accursed people."

**The Jews are cursed to be traitors like Judas.**

"Judas Iscariot, who became a traitor." (Luke 6:16)

". . . the Jews, who killed the Lord Jesus and the prophets and also drove us out. They displease God and are hostile to all men . . . In this way they always heap up their sins to the limit. The wrath of God has come upon them at last." (1 Thessalonians 2:15-16)

*Pope Innocent III:* "When Jews are admitted out of pity into familiar intercourse with Christians, they repay their hosts, according to the popular proverb, after the fashion of the rat hidden in the sack, or the snake in the bosom, or of the burning brand in one's lap."

*Pope Gregory IX:* "Ungrateful for favors and forgetful of benefits, the Jews return insult for kindness and impious contempt for goodness." (Epistle to the Hierarchy of Germany)

*Pope Stephen III:* "With great sorrow and mortal anxiety, We have heard that the Jews have in a Christian land the same rights as Christians, that Christian men and women live under the same roof with these traitors and defile their souls day and night with blasphemies." (Epistle to the Bishop of Norbonne)

*Pope Innocent IV:* "The wicked perfidy of the Jews—from whose hearts Our Savior did not remove the veil because of their enormous crimes but caused them justly to continue in their blindness, commit acts of shame which engender astonishment in those who hear, and terror in those who discover it." (The Wicked Perfidy of the Jews)

*Pope Saint Gregory the Great:* "Furthermore, I must tell you that I have been led to praise God the more for your work by what I have learnt from the report of my most beloved son Probinus the presbyter; namely that, your Excellency having issued a certain ordinance against the perfidy of the Jews, those to whom it related attempted to bend the rectitude of your mind by offering a sum of money; which your Excellency scorned, and, seeking to satisfy the judgment of Almighty God, preferred innocence to gold." (Epistle to Rechared, King of the Visigoths)

*Pope Saint Gregory VII:* "We exhort your Royal Majesty [King Alfonse VI of Castile], not to further tolerate that the Jews rule Christians and have power over them. For to allow that Christians are subordinated to Jews and are delivered to their whims, means to oppress the Church of God, means to revile Christ himself." (Regesta IX. 2)

*Pope Innocent III:* "They shall not appear in public at all on the days of lamentation and on passion Sunday; because some of them on such days, as we have heard, do not blush to parade in very ornate dress and are not afraid to mock Christians who are presenting a memorial of the most sacred passion and are displaying signs of grief. What we most strictly forbid however, is that they dare in any way to break out in derision of the Redeemer." (Fourth Ecumenical Lateran Council)

*Pope Gregory IX:* "We order all our brother bishops absolutely to suppress the blasphemy of Jews in your dioceses, churches, and communities, so that they do not dare raise their necks, bent under eternal slavery, to revile the Redeemer."

*Pope Innocent III:* "We therefore renew in this canon, on account of the boldness of the offenders, what the Council of Toledo providently decreed in this matter: we forbid Jews to be appointed to public offices, since under cover of them they are very hostile to Christians." (Fourth Ecumenical Lateran Council)

*Pope Saint Gregory I:* "It has come to my ears that certain men of perverse spirit have sown among you some things that are wrong and opposed to the holy faith, so as to forbid any work being done on the Sabbath day. What else can I call these but preachers of Antichrist, who, when he comes, will cause the Sabbath day as well as the Lord's day to be kept free from all work. For, because he pretends to die and rise again, he wishes the Lord's day to be had in reverence; and, because he compels the people to judaize that he may bring back the outward rite of the law, and subject the perfidy of the Jews to himself, he wishes the Sabbath to be observed." (Epistles, Book XIII:1)

## The Jews are cursed to be unscrupulous money-grubbers, like Judas.

"Judas Iscariot went to the chief priests and asked, 'What are you willing to give me if I hand him over to you?' So they counted out for him thirty silver coins. From then on Judas watched for an opportunity to hand him over." (Matthew 26:14-16)

*Pope Saint Pius V:* "Besides usury, through which Jews everywhere have sucked dry the property of impoverished Christians, they are accomplices of thieves and robbers." (Hebraeorum Gens)

*Pope Benedict XIV:* "Because the Jews control businesses selling liquor and even wine, they are therefore allowed to supervise the collection of public revenues. They have also gained control of inns, bankrupt estates, villages and public land by means of which they have subjugated poor Christian farmers. . . The most serious is that some households of the great have employed a Jew as 'Superintendent-of-the-Household'; in this capacity, they not only administer domestic and economic matters, but they also ceaselessly exhibit and flaunt authority over the Christians they are living with. It is now even commonplace for Christians and Jews to intermingle anywhere. But what is even less comprehensible is that Jews fearlessly keep Christians of both sexes in their houses as their domestics, bound to their service. Furthermore, by means of their particular practice of commerce, they amass a great store of money and then by an exorbitant rate of interest utterly destroy the wealth and inheritance of Christians." (A Quo Primum)

*Pope Clement VIII:* "All the world suffers from the usury of the Jews, their monopolies and deceit. They have brought many unfortunate people into a state of poverty, especially the farmers, working class people and the very poor. . . . Their ethical and moral doctrines as well as their deeds rightly deserve to be exposed to criticism in whatever country they happen to live." (Caeca et obdurata)

*Pope Innocent III:* "The more the Christian religion is restrained from usurious practices, so much the more does the perfidy of the Jews grow in these matters, so that within a short time they are exhausting the resources of the Christians. Wishing therefore to see that Christians are not savagely oppressed by Jews in this matter, we ordain by this synodal decree that if Jews in the future, on any pretext, extort oppressive and excessive interest from Christians, then they are to be removed from contact with Christians until they have made adequate satisfaction for the immoderate burden. Christians too, if need be, shall be compelled by ecclesiastical censure, without the possibility of an appeal, to abstain from commerce with them. We enjoin upon princes, not to be hostile to Christians on this account, but rather to be zealous in restraining Jews from so great oppression." (Fourth Ecumenical Lateran Council)

**The Jews are cursed to be outcasts like Cain, segregated from the rest of the society within which they live.**

"And while they were in the field, Cain attacked his brother Abel and killed him. . . . The Lord said, 'What have you done? Listen! Your brother's blood cries out to me from the ground. Now you are under a curse and driven from the ground, which opened its mouth to receive your brother's blood from your hand. When you work the ground, it will no longer yield its crops for you. You will be a restless wanderer on the earth.'" (Genesis 4:8-12)

*Pope Innocent III:* "The Lord made Cain a wanderer and a fugitive over the earth, but set a mark upon him, making his head to shake, lest anyone finding him should slay him. Thus the Jews, against whom the blood of Christ calls out, although they ought not to be wiped out, nevertheless, as wanderers they must remain upon the Earth until their faces are filled with shame and they seek the name of the Lord Jesus Christ." (Epistle to the Count of Nevers)

*Pope Saint Sylvester I:* "Concerning the prohibition of usury and base gain by the clergy; and concerning the prohibition against conversing or eating with the Jews. No priest shall set money out at interest or take unfair profit or be friendly or sociable with Jews; nor should anyone take food or drink with the Jews; for if this was decreed by the holy apostles, it is incumbent upon the faithful to obey their command; and the synod shall excommunicate any one who does not comply with this order." (First Ecumenical Council of Nicea)

*Pope Eugene IV:* "We decree and order that from now on, and for all time, Christians shall not eat or drink with the Jews, nor admit them to feasts, nor cohabit with them, nor bathe with them. . . . They cannot live among Christians, but in a certain street, separated and segregated from Christians, and outside which they cannot under any pretext have houses." (Decree, 1442)

*Pope Alexander III:* "Our ways of life and those of the Jews are utterly different, and Jews will easily pervert the souls of simple folk to their superstition and unbelief if such folk are living in continual and intimate intercourse with them." (Ad Haec)

**The Jews are cursed to be distinguished from everyone else by an identifying mark, like Cain.**

"Then the Lord put a mark on Cain." (Genesis 4:15)

*Pope Martin V:* "However, we received a short time ago through credible reports knowledge to our great alarm, that various Jews of both sexes in Cafas and other cities, lands and places overseas, which fall under the jurisdiction of Christians, are of obstinate mind and, in order to conceal swindling and wickedness, wear no special sign on their clothing, so that they are not recognizable as Jews. They are not ashamed to give themselves out as Christians before many Christians of both sexes of these cities, districts and places mentioned, who could not in fact identify them, and consequently commit shameful things and crimes." (Sedes Apostolica)

*Pope Eugene IV:* "We decree and order that from now on, and for all time . . . All and every single Jew, of whatever sex and age, must everywhere wear the distinctive dress and known marks by which they can be evidently distinguished from Christians." (Bull. Rom. Pont., V, 67)

*Pope Saint Pius V:* "In order to make an end of all doubt concerning the color of the cap and the sign of the women, we declare that the color must be yellow." (Romanus Pontifex)


**The Jews are cursed to be outcasts, periodically ejected from the nations amongst whom they live, like Cain.**

"You will be a restless wanderer on the earth." (Genesis 4:12)

*Pope Leo VII:* "Let the Gospel be preached unto them and, if they remain obstinate, let them be expelled."

*Pope Saint Pius V:* "With full understanding and in exercising of the apostolic powers, we withdraw from the Jews and their rule (and recognize no right or claim) all properties, which the Jews have in their possession in this city of Rome or other places of our domain of rule." (Cum Nos Super)

*Pope Paul IV:* "It is too absurd and pointless that the Jews, whom their own guilt condemns to slavery, under the pretense that Christian piety suffers and tolerates their coexistence, pay back [with wickedness] the mercy received from Christians." (Cum Nimis Absurdum)

*Pope Adrian I:* "Since certain, erring in the superstitions of the Hebrews, have thought to mock at Christ our God, and feigning to be converted to the religion of Christ do deny him, and in private and secretly keep the Sabbath and observe other Jewish customs, we decree that such persons be not received to communion, nor to prayers, nor into the Church; but let them be openly Hebrew according to their religion, and let them not bring their children to baptism, nor purchase or possess a slave." (Second Ecumenical Council of Nicea)

*Pope Innocent IV:* "We who long with all our hearts for the salvation of souls, grant you full authority by these present letters to banish the Jews, either in your own person or through the agency of others, especially since, as we have been informed, they do not abide by the regulations drawn up for them by this Holy See." (To the King of France)

*Pope Saint Pius V:* "The Jewish people fell from the heights because of their faithlessness and condemned their Redeemer to a shameful death. Their godlessness has assumed such forms that, for the salvation of our own people, it becomes necessary to prevent their disease. Besides usury, through which Jews everywhere have sucked dry the property of impoverished Christians, they are accomplices of thieves and robbers; and the most damaging aspect of the matter is that they allure the unsuspecting through magical incantations, superstition, and witchcraft to the Synagogue of Satan and boast of being able to predict the future. We have carefully investigated how this revolting sect abuses the name of Christ and how harmful they are to those whose life is threatened by their deceit. On account of these and other serious matters, and because of the gravity of their crimes which increase day to day more and more, We order that, within ninety days, all Jews in our entire earthly realm of justice—in all towns, districts, and places—must depart these regions. After this time limit shall all at the present or in the future, who dwell or wander into that city or other already mentioned, be affected, their property confiscated and handed over to the Siscus, and they shall becomes slaves of the Roman Church, live in perpetual servitude and the Roman Church shall have the same rights over them as the remaining [worldly] lords over slaves and property." (Hebraeorum Gens)

## The Jews are cursed to be slaves, like Ishmael and Esau.

"And the Lord said unto her, Two nations are in your womb, and two peoples from within you will be separated; one people will be stronger than the other, and the older [Esau] will serve the younger [Jacob]." (Genesis 25:23)

"His son [Ishmael] by the slave woman was born in the ordinary way; but his son by the free woman [Isaac] was born as the result of a promise. These things may be taken figuratively, for the women represent two covenants. One covenant is from Mount Sinai and bears children who are to be slaves: This is Hagar. Now Hagar stands for Mount Sinai in Arabia and corresponds to the present city of Jerusalem, because she is in slavery with her children." (Galatians 4:23-25)

*Pope Innocent III:* "The Jews, by their own guilt, are consigned to perpetual servitude because they crucified the Lord." (To the Archbishops of Sens and Paris)

*Pope Innocent IV:* "And that you [King Saint Louis IX] order both the aforesaid abusive books [The Talmud] condemned by the same doctors and generally all the books with their glosses which were examined and condemned by them to be burned by fire wherever they can be found throughout your entire kingdom, strictly forbidding that Jews henceforth have Christian nurses or servants, that the sons of a free woman may not serve the sons of a bondwoman, but as slaves condemned by the Lord, whose death they wickedly plotted, they at least outwardly recognize themselves as slaves of those whom the death of Christ made free and themselves slaves. So we may commend the zeal of your sincerity in the Lord with due praises." (The Wicked Perfidy of the Jews)

*Pope Benedict XIV:* "It is fitting for Jews to serve Christians, but not for Christians to serve Jews. On the contrary, the Jews, as slaves rejected by that Savior whose death they wickedly contrived, should recognize themselves in fact and in creed the slaves of those whom the death of Christ has set free, even as it has rendered them bondmen." (Quoting Pope Innocent III, "Etsi Judaeos")

*Pope Gregory IX:* "They ought to know the yoke of perpetual enslavement because of their guilt. See to it that the perfidious Jews never in the future become insolent, but that they always suffer publicly the shame of their sin in servile fear." (Epistle to the Hierarchy of Germany)

*Pope Alexander III:* "We declare that the evidence of Christians is to be accepted against Jews in every case, since Jews employ their own witnesses against Christians—and that those who prefer Jews to Christians in this matter are to lie under anathema, since Jews ought to be slaves to Christians." (Third Lateran Ecumenical Council, Canon 26)

*Pope Innocent III:* "Crucifiers of Christ ought to be held in continual subjection." (Epistle to the Hierarchy of France)

**Modern Popes.**

*Pope Pius IX:* "It is from them [the Jews] that the synagogue of Satan, which gathers its troops against the Church of Christ, takes its strength." (Syllabus of Errors)

*Pope Pius IX:* By rejecting Christianity, Jews had become "*dogs*" and "we have today in Rome unfortunately too many of these dogs, and we hear them barking in all the streets, and going around molesting people everywhere." (In a speech after Italian forces liberated Rome.)

*Pope Pius XI:* "One of the most evil and strongest influences that is felt here [Poland], perhaps the strongest and most evil, is that of the Jews." (Letter of Ratti to Gasparri.)

*Pope Pius XI:* ". . . the Christ who took His human nature from a people that was to crucify Him." (Mit brennender Sorge)

Not all popes spoke this way, and even the ones who did also protected Jews at other times. However, as we saw earlier, this pattern of ambivalence led to perennial suffering for the Jewish population who lived amongst Christians. It could not have been any different given that the Church was teaching contempt toward Jews one day and attempting to protect them the next when the flock, having assimilated the teachings of hatred, reacted violently against them.

In conclusion, it is our hope that as Pope John Paul II said, the Church will not be "afraid of the truth that emerges from history and is ready to acknowledge mistakes wherever they have been identified."[499]

And it is also our hope that the Church will find the strength and wherewithal to follow its own doctrine and fulfill its moral duty of repair:

"Many sins wrong our neighbor. One must do what is possible in order to repair the harm (e.g., return stolen goods, restore the reputation of someone slandered, pay compensation for injuries). Simple justice requires as much."[500]

# II

## Pontifical Bulls

*"The Catholic Church considered the Jews pestilent for
fifteen hundred years, put them into ghettos, etc., because it
recognized the Jews for what they were. . . . I am moving
back toward the time in which a fifteen-hundred-year-long
tradition was implemented. . . . I recognize the representatives of this race as pestilent for the state and for the church
and perhaps I am thereby doing Christianity a great service
for pushing them out of schools and public functions."*

*Adolf Hitler*

W hat follows is a list of the principal pontifical bulls dealing
with the Jews issued by various popes throughout history:

| POPE | BULL | DATE | OBJECT |
|------|------|------|--------|
| Honorius III | Sicut judaeis non debet esse licentia | Nov. 7, 1217 | It is forbidden to force the Jews to baptism or molest them. |

| POPE | BULL | DATE | OBJECT |
|------|------|------|--------|
| Honorius III | Ad nostram noveritis audientiam | Apr 29, 1221 | Jews are obliged to carry a distinctive badge. Forbidden to fill public office. |
| Gregory IX | Sufficere debuerat perfidioe judoerum perfidia | Mar 5, 1233 | Jews forbidden to employ Christian servants. |
| Innocent IV | Impia judoerum perfidia | May 9, 1244 | French King ordered to burn the Talmud. Jews forbidden to employ Christian nurses. |
| Clement IV | Turbato corde | Jul 26, 1267 | Christians forbidden to embrace Judaism. |
| Gregory X | Turbato corde | Mar 1, 1274 | Same as previous. |
| Nicolas III | Vineam Sorec | Aug. 4, 1278 | Preaching to the Jews. |
| Nicolas IV | Turbato corde | Sept. 5, 1288 | Christians forbidden to embrace Judaism. |
| John XXII | Ex Parte Vestra | Aug. 12, 1317 | Relapse of converts. |
| John XXII | Cum sit absurdum | Jun 19, 1320 | Converted Jews need not be despoiled. |
| Urban V | Sicuti judaeis non debet | Jun 7, 1365 | Forbidden to molest Jews or to force them to baptism. |

| POPE | BULL | DATE | OBJECT |
|------|------|------|--------|
| Martin V | Sedes apostolica | Jun 3, 1425 | Jews obliged to wear distinctive badge. |
| Eugene IV | Dudum ad nostram audientiam | Aug. 4, 1442 | Jews forbidden to live with Christians or fill public functions, etc. |
| Calixtus III | Si ad reprimendos | May 28, 1456 | Confirmed the preceding bull. |
| Paul III | Cupientes judaeos | Mar 21, 1542 | Privileges in favor of neophytes. |
| Paul III | Illius, qui pro dominici | Feb. 19, 1543 | Establishment of a monastery for catechumens and neophytes. |
| Jules III | Pastoris aeterni vices | Aug. 31, 1554 | Tax in favor of neophytes. |
| Paul IV | Cum nimis absurdum | Jul 14, 1555 | Jews forbidden to live in common with Christians, to practice any industry, etc. |
| Paul IV | Dudum postquam | Mar 23, 1556 | Tax in favor of neophytes. |
| Paul IV | Cum inter ceteras | Jan. 26, 1562 | Bull relative to monastery of catechumens. |
| Paul IV | Dudum e felicis recordationis | Feb. 27, 1562 | Bull confirming that of Paul III. |
| Pius V | Romanus Pontifex | Apr 19, 1566 | Bull confirming that of Paul IV. |

| POPE | BULL | DATE | OBJECT |
|------|------|------|--------|
| Pius V | Sacrosanctae catholicae ecclesiae | Nov. 29, 1566 | Bull relating to convent of neophytes. |
| Pius V | Cum nos nuper | Jan. 19, 1567 | Jews are forbidden to own real estate. |
| Pius V | Hebraeorum gens | Feb. 26, 1569 | Expulsion of Jews from Church States except Rome and Ancona. |
| Gregory XIII | Vices Ejus nos | Sept. 1, 1577 | Obligatory preaching. Creation of college of neophytes. |
| Gregory XIII | Antiqua judaeorum impro-bitas | Jul 1, 1581 | Against blasphemers. |
| Gregory XIII | Sancta Mater Ec-clesiae | Sept. 1, 1584 | Obligatory preaching. |
| Sixtus V | Christiana pietas | Oct. 22, 1586 | Privileges granted to Jews. |
| Clement VIII | Cum saepe ac-cidere | Feb. 28, 1592 | Jews of Avignon forbidden to sell new goods. |
| Clement VIII | Caeca et obdurata | Feb. 25, 1593 | Confirmation of the Bull of Paul III. Jews forbidden to dwell outside of Rome, Ancona, and Avignon. |

| POPE | BULL | DATE | OBJECT |
|------|------|------|--------|
| Clement VIII | Cum Hae- braeorum malitia | Feb. 28, 1593 | It is forbidden to read the Talmud. |
| Paul V | Apostolicae servi- tutis | Jul 31, 1610 | Regulars (of monks) obliged to learn He- brew. |
| Paul V | Exponi nobis nu- per fecistis | Aug. 7, 1610 | Bull relating to the dowries of Jewish women. |
| Urban VIII | Sedes apostolica | Apr 22, 1625 | Jews declared heretical in Portugal. |
| Urban VIII | Injuncti nobis | Aug. 20, 1626 | Privileges granted to the monastery of catechu- mens. |
| Urban VIII | Cum sicut accep- timus | Oct. 18, 1635 | Obligation to feed poor Jews imprisoned for debt. |
| Urban VIII | Cum allias piae | Mar 17, 1636 | Synagogues of the Duchies of Ferarri and Urban, to pay a tax of 10 ecus. |
| Alexander VII | Verbi aeterni | Dec. 1, 1657 | Bull relating to rights of neophytes regarding Jus Gasaga. |
| Alexander VII | Ad ea per quae | Nov. 15, 1658 | Jus Gasaga. |

| POPE | BULL | DATE | OBJECT |
|------|------|------|--------|
| Alexander VII | Ad apostolicae dignitatis | May 23, 1662 | Concordat between the college of neophytes and German college. |
| Alexander VII | Illius, qui illuminat | Mar 6, 1663 | Privileges favoring the fraternities of neophytes. |
| Alexander VIII | Animarum saluti | Mar 30, 1690 | Bull relating to the neophytes in the Indies. |
| Innocent XII | Ad radicitus submovendum | Aug. 31, 1692 | Abolition of special jurisdiction. |
| Clement XI | Propagandae per unicersum | Mar 11, 1704 | Confirmation and extension of Paul III regarding neophytes. |
| Clement XI | Essendoci stato rappresentato | Jan. 21, 1705 | Powers of Vicar of Rome in jurisdiction of catechumens and neophytes. |
| Clement XI | Salvatoris nostri vices | Jan. 2, 1712 | Transfer to "Pii Operai" the work of the catechumens. |
| Innocent XIII | Ex injuncto nobis | Jan. 18, 1724 | Prohibits sale of new objects. |
| Benoit XIII | Nuper, pro parte dilectorum | Jan. 8, 1726 | Establishment of dowries for young girl neophytes. |

| POPE | BULL | DATE | OBJECT |
|------|------|------|--------|
| Benoit XIII | Emanavit nuper | Feb. 14, 1727 | Necessary conditions for imposing baptism on a Jew. |
| Benoit XIII | Alias emanarunt | Mar 21, 1729 | Forbidding the sale of new goods. |
| Benoit XIV | Postremomens | Feb. 28, 1747 | The baptism of Jews. |
| Benoit XIV | Apostolici Ministerii munus | Sept. 16, 1747 | Right of repudiation of neophytes. |
| Benoit XIV | Singulari Nobis consoldtioni | Feb. 9, 1749 | Marriages between Jews and Christians. |
| Benoit XIV | Elapso proxime Anno | Feb. 20, 1751 | Concerning Jewish heretics. |
| Benoit XIV | Probe te meminisse | Dec. 15, 1751 | Baptism of Jewish children. |
| Benoit XIV | Beatus Andreas | Feb. 22, 1755 | Martyrdom of a child by Jews. |

<u>Table 3</u>: Papal bulls dealing with Jews

Almost none of the pontifical bulls promulgated after those by Benoit XIV dealt directly with Jews but rather were generally related to doctrinal issues.[501]

# Glossary

**Ancien Régime:** French for "Old Regime." Refers to the aristocratic social and political system that existed in France prior to the French Revolution.

**Apocryphal Gospels:** Refers to those New Testament books that give account of Jesus and his teachings, but are not regarded as canonical, that is, part of the officially recognized New Testament.

**Bolshevism:** Political movement in the Soviet Union founded by Vladimir Lenin that came to power in the October Revolution of 1917. The movement was later to become Communism under Joseph Stalin.

**Canonical Gospels:** The four gospels accepted as part of the New Testament officially sanctioned by the Church.

**Caritas:** Latin for "charity." Refers to the Christian theological concept of unlimited love and kindness toward all others.

**Catechism:** Doctrinal manuals traditionally used in the Christian religion for religious teaching.

**Catechumens, House of:** A special house established by the Church for the Catholic education of converts to Catholicism.

**Church hierarchy:** Refers to the various ranks of ministers in the Christian churches, such as Pope, Archbishop, Bishop, Priest, Pastor, etc. Generally speaking, the term is used to refer to the authorities of the church.

**Confessing Church:** A schismatic Protestant church, which arose in Nazi Germany as an attempt to oppose state-sponsored efforts to nazify the German Protestant Church.

**Conversos:** Spanish for "converted." Refers to Jews who converted to Catholicism in Spain, particularly during the 14$^{th}$ and 15$^{th}$ centuries.

**Convivencia:** Spanish for "coexistence." Refers to the years between 711 to 1492 CE in Spain in which Christians, Jews and Muslims coexisted in relative peace. The period was immensely fruitful in the arts and sciences.

**Curia:** The Roman Curia is the administrative apparatus of the Catholic Church, with the Pope at the head and the Church hierarchy below.

**Deicide:** The term means the killing of a god, but is used specifically to refer to the crucifixion of Jesus. Christianity associated the guilt for the death of Jesus with the Jews, causing a long history of vindictive persecution. The Catholic Church officially repudiated the accusation of deicide after the Second Vatican Council in 1965.

**Einsatzgruppen:** SS paramilitary units created with the specific purpose of following the German armed forces on the Eastern Front during WWII to systematically kill communist commissars, intellectuals, Gypsies, and particularly Jews, of which they murdered about 1.3 million.

**Episcopate:** The collective body of all bishops of a church.

**Euthanasia Program:** A program in Nazi Germany designed to kill the incurably sick. The program was in effect between 1939 and 1941 during which physicians killed over 70,000 people.

**Evangelical Church:** A federation of various regional Protestant German churches.

**Final Solution of the Jewish Question:** A euphemistic term used in Nazi Germany to refer to the planning and execution of the systematic genocide of European Jews during WWII.

**Freedom Fighters:** Term used to refer to individuals British and American Allies recruited to fight Communist ascendance and influence after WWII. Many of these "freedom fighters" were ex-Nazis or ex-Ustasha, whom the Allies deemed experienced and useful in the fight against Communism, often ignoring these people's genocidal background.

**Freiburg Circle:** A discussion group of anti-Nazi professors that after WWII became involved in work of restitution for the Jewish victims of Nazi Germany.

**Gentile:** Non-Jewish peoples.

**Gestapo:** Nazi Germany's brutal secret police.

**Godfearer:** Term used in the Christian Bible to refer to non-Jews who practiced Judaism in varying degrees, without becoming Jews.

**Great War:** The First World War.

**Greater German Reich:** The name given to the German Reich (empire) after 1943. It refers to the German territory proper as well as all the other lands added to the Reich through military conquest.

**Holy See:** The Episcopal jurisdiction of the Bishop of Rome (the Pope), forming the central government of the Catholic Church.

**Homily:** A commentary that follows a reading of scripture, considered by many people as synonymous with a sermon.

**Index of Forbidden Books:** The list of publications the Roman Catholic Church prohibited the faithful from reading. The Index remained in effect until 1966.

**Inquisition:** An institution of the Catholic Church charged with trying and convicting heretics.

**Judenrein:** German for "cleansed of Jews."

**Judenfrei**: German for "free of Jews." The Germans used the term during WWII to refer to an area that no longer had any Jews (who had been deported and/or murdered).

**Kristallnacht:** The "Night of Broken Glass." Refers to an anti-Jewish pogrom in Nazi Germany and Austria on November 9, 1938.

**Kulturkampf:** German for "culture struggle." Refers to policies enacted between 1871 and 1878 by the Chancellor of the German Empire, Otto von Bismark, to curtail the influence of the Roman Catholic Church.

**Lebensraum:** German for "living space." Refers to the space Germans during the Nazi years felt they needed to expand. In practical terms it meant lands to the East of Germany, where the local Slavic and Jewish population was to be exterminated.

**Manichean:** Refers to the dualistic contrast or conflict between opposites.

**Mein Kampf:** German for "my struggle." A book Adolf Hitler wrote early on in his political career outlining his political and racial ideologies.

**Mishnah:** Hebrew for "repetition." The Mishnah is the first written redaction of the Jewish oral tradition and the first major work of Rabbinic Judaism. Subsequent Rabbinic commentaries, combined with the Mishnah, comprise the Talmud.

**Mosaic Law:** The law of Moses, the Five Books of Moses, or the Pentateuch. This includes the Commandments, or Biblical law.

**Motu Proprio:** Latin for "on his own impulse." Refers to a document issued by the Pope on his own initiative, but as a general expression means acts performed by someone of his own volition.

**Nuncio:** Officially known as Apostolic Nuncio, it's an ecclesiastical diplomatic title given to a permanent diplomatic representative of the Holy See to a state, i.e and ambassador.

**Ordnungspolizei:** The name of the regular German police force during the Nazi years. The police battalions of the Ordnungspolizei were separate military formations ostensibly responsible for anti-partisan duties, but ultimately responsible for rounding up and murdering hundreds of thousands of Jews and other minorities persecuted by the Germans during WWII.

**Orthodox schismatics:** Refers to the Eastern Orthodox Church, as a splinter group of mainline Catholicism.

**Pale of Settlement:** The term given to a region of Imperial Russia along its western border where Jews were allowed to reside and beyond which they were not.

**Papal Bull:** Papal communication of public nature.

**Passion:** The term used to describe the events and suffering of Jesus in the hours leading to and including his trial and execution.

**Poglavnik:** A term coined by the Ustasha, the Croatian fascist group that ruled over the Nazi puppet state of Croatia during WWII, meaning "leader."

**Pogrom:** A form of riot directed against Jews and characterized by physical assault and murder, as well as the destruction of their homes, businesses, and religious centers.

**Prelate:** A high-ranking member of a church clergy.

**Primate:** Typically an archbishop with authority over all the regional sees.

**Realpolitik:** German for "real" or "practical" and "politics." Refers to politics based on practical considerations, as opposed to ideological notions.

338 | SIX MILLION CRUCIFIXIONS

**Res, non verba:** Latin for "actions, not words."

**Seelisberg Thesis:** A document drafted by the Jewish French historian Jules Isaac together with other Catholics, meant to be a framework for the elimination of Christian falsehoods about Jews and Judaism.

**Shoah:** A Hebrew word connoting catastrophe, calamity, disaster, or destruction. Many Jews prefer the term to the word "Holocaust."

**Sonderkommandos:** Sub-units of the SS Einsatzgruppen, the German mobile killing squads mainly responsible for murdering Jews in the wake of the German army's expansion on the Eastern Front. The unrelated Jewish Sonderkommandos were squads of Jewish prisoners selected to dispose of the corpses of fellow Jews in the death camps.

**SS:** Schutzstaffel, German for "Protective Echelon." The SS was a major organization of the Nazi Party that wielded immense power in Nazi Germany. They were in charge of executing the "Final Solution of the Jewish Question."

**Talmud:** Hebrew for "instruction, learning." The Talmud is a central text in Judaism composed of the Mishnah, which is the first written collection of Judaism's Oral Law, and the Gemara, which is a compendium of rabbinic discussions and interpretation of the Mishnah.

**Third Reich:** The commonly used term to describe Germany under the government of Adolf Hitler and the Nazi Party from 1933 to 1945.

**Torah:** Hebrew for "teaching" or "instruction." Refers to the Pentateuch or Five Books of Moses and contains Judaism's legal and ethical religious texts.

**Untermensch:** German term for "sub-human" used in Nazi racial ideology to describe "inferior races" such as Jews, Gypsies, Poles and other Slavic peoples like Russians, Serbs, Ukrainians and, generally, anyone who was not an "Aryan."

**Ustasha:** The Ustasha was a Croatian fascist anti-Yugoslav separatist movement that acted as a terrorist organization prior to WWII, but was installed as a Nazi puppet state as the Independent State of Croatia after the German invasion of Yugoslavia. The Ustasha were responsible for the gruesome murder of hundreds of thousands of Orthodox Serbs, Jews and Roma. The Ustasha were determined to ethnically cleanse Yugoslavia and make it a purely Catholic state. After WWII many priests who had been members of the movement worked on the Vatican Ratlines that spirited thousands of wanted war criminals out of Europe.

**Vatican Bank:** The Istituto per le Opere di Religione (Italian for "Institute for Works of Religion") was founded on June 27, 1942 by Pope Pius XII, and is commonly known as the Vatican Bank. Ostensibly created to fund works of charity, it has been embroiled in much controversy and scandal due to its alleged connections to money laundering from stolen treasure from the victims of the Ustasha and the Nazis during WWII and its aftermath, as well as mafia drug money in more recent years.

**Vatican Secret Archives:** The Vatican Secret Archives are located in Vatican City and contain all the acts promulgated by the Holy See, as well as state papers, correspondence and papal account books. Traditionally the documents in the archives remain closed to researchers for 75 years after the period they cover.

**Volk:** German term meaning, "people" or "nation." During the Nazi years the term was used extensively, and generally in the sense of "German people."

**Waffen SS:** The military branch of the SS.

**Wehrmacht:** The German Armed Forces.

**Yiddish:** Literally, "Jewish." Yiddish is a High German language of Ashkenazi origin conventionally written in the Hebrew alphabet and commonly used by the Jews of central and eastern Europe before the Holocaust.

# Notes

1 Bauer's interview with Littell is available online at: http://www1.yadvashem.org/odot_pdf/Microsoft%20Word%20-%203725.pdf.

2 Address at the conclusion of the symposium organized by the "Pave the Way Foundation," September 19, 2008. http://www.vatican.va/holy_father/benedict_xvi/speeches/2008/september/documents/hf_ben-xvi_spe_20080918_pave-the-way_en.html.

3 Jeremy Cohen, *Christ Killers*, pp. 23-24.

4 James Carroll, *Constantine's Sword*, pp. 232-233.

5 Élie Berger, *Les Registres d'Innocent IV*, Paris, 1884, p.403, quoted in Léon Poliakov, *The History of Anti-Semitism*, p. 61.

6 Joshua Trachtenberg, *The Devil and the Jews*, p. 166.

7 Jeremy Cohen, *Christ Killers*, p. 27.

8 Ibid., p. 31.

9 Léon Poliakov, *The History of Anti-Semitism*, pp. 19-20, 184 & Jules Isaac, *Jesus and Israel*, p. 20 & Jeremy Cohen, *Christ Killers*, p. 29.

10 Daniel J. Goldhagen, *Hitler's Willing Executioners*, p. 49.

11 Jeremy Cohen, *Christ Killers*, p. 28.

12 Melito of Sardis, Sermon *"On the Passover,"* trans., intro, and commentary in Richard C. White (Lexington, KY: Lexington Theological Seminary, 1976) p. 47.

13 Walter Zwi Bacharach, Anti Jewish Prejudices in German Catholic Sermons, p. 8.

14 James Carroll, *Constantine's Sword*, p. 185.

15 Chrysostom cited in Ruether, *Faith and Fratricide*, p. 177. See also James Carroll, *Constantine's Sword*, pp. 190-191.

16 Jeremy Cohen, *Christ Killers*, p. 120.

17 Friedrich Heer, *God's First Love*, p. 66.

18 "The Chronicle of Solomon bar Simson," in Eidelberg, *The Jews and the Crusaders*, p. 25. See also James Carroll, *Constantine's Sword*, p. 261.

19 Joshua Trachtenberg, *The Devil and the Jews*, p. 167-168.

20 See Leviticus 17:11, etc.

21 James Carroll, *Constantine's Sword*, pp. 272-273.

22 Saul Friedländer, *Nazi Germany and the Jews*, p. 84.

23 James Carroll, *Constantine's Sword*, p. 277.

24 Ibid., p. 338.

25 Joshua Trachtenberg, *The Devil and the Jews*, p. 106.

26 Quoted in James Carroll, *Constantine's Sword*, p. 339.

27 Ibid., p. 277.

28 Ibid., p. 306.

29 Ibid., p. 340.

30 Fourth Lateran Council, Constitutions 1: "On the Catholic Faith," in Tanner, *Decrees of the Ecumenical Councils*, p. 230.

31 Fourth Lateran Council, Constitutions 68: "That Jews Should Be Distinguished from Christians in their Dress," in Tanner, *Decrees of the Ecumenical Councils*, p. 266. See also James Carroll, *Constantine's Sword*, p. 282.

32 Raul Hilberg, *The Destruction of the European Jews*, p. 17 n21. The *Einsatzgruppen* (mobile killing squads attached to the German Army) and Police Battalions responsible for killing Jews in the Eastern Front killed by shooting, gassing, burning, bludgeoning and other creative and sadistic methods of execution. Just like the Ustashi butchers in Croatia, it seems that sometimes the German murderers drew inspiration from lessons learned from the Inquisition in their "purification" zest. As *SS-Hauptscharführer* Adolf Ruche testified in the *Einsatzgruppen* trial at Nuremberg, "They brought eight Jews, men and women, with them. The Latvians guarded the Jews, while Harter and Hauser erected a funeral pyre with their own hands. The Jews were bound, put on the pile alive, drenched with gasoline and burned." Nuremberg Military Tribunal, 1946; Vol. 4:448. There were many instances in which hundreds of Jews were locked in synagogues or barns and burned alive. (See photograph on page 211.)

33 Cantate Domino, in Tanner, *Decrees of the Ecumenical Councils*, p. 578.

34 James Carroll, *Constantine's Sword*, p. 365.

35 Ibid., p. 306.

36 Quoted in Ibid., p. 333.

37 Quoted in Ibid., p. 336.

38 Quoted in Ibid., p. 337.

39 Daniel J. Goldhagen, *A Moral Reckoning*, pp. 199, 186 and *Catechism of the Catholic Church*, parag. 674.

40 Richard L. Rubenstein, John K. Roth, *Approaches to Auschwitz*, p. 261, 271.

41 On the rabbinic tradition and the origins of the Talmud, and on the attempt to establish theological authority over Jewish belief see James Carroll, *Constantine's Sword*, p. 307.

42 Quoted in Ibid., p. 310.

43 Jeremy Cohen, *Christ Killers*, pp. 88-89.

44 Quoted in James Carroll, *Constantine's Sword*, p. 308.

45 On the Talmud trial in Paris see Ibid., p. 309.

46 Ibid., p. 308.

47 On the placing of the Talmud on the Index of Forbidden Books in 1559, see Ibid., pp. 373-375.

48 Quoted in David Kertzer, *The Kidnapping of Edgardo Mortara*, p. 14.

49 James Carroll, *Constantine's Sword*, pp. 340-341.

50 Ibid., p. 346.

51 Quoted in Ibid., pp. 360-361.

52 Quoted in Ibid., p. 369.

53 Quoted in Ibid., p. 371.

54 Friedrich Heer, *God's First Love*, p. 130.

55 James Carroll, *Constantine's Sword*, p. 368.

56 Luther, Martin. *On the Jews and Their Lies*, cited in Michael, Robert. "Luther, Luther Scholars, and the Jews," Encounter 46 (1985) No. 4:343-344.

57 Martin Luther, *On the Jews and Their Lies* (1543 C.E.).

58 Quoted in Raul Hilberg, *The Destruction of the European Jews*, p. 16. The Nazis used the slogan "The Jews are our misfortune" extensively.

59 Ibid., pp. 15, 21, 31

60 Quoted in James Carroll, *Constantine's Sword*, p. 364.

61 Cum Nimis Absurdum, quoted in Ibid., 375.

62 Ibid., pp. 375-376.

63 Romans 11:15, in The Jerusalem Bible. See also James Carroll, *Constantine's Sword*, p. 379.

64 Raul Hilberg, *The Destruction of the European Jews*, pp. 10, 13.

344 | SIX MILLION CRUCIFIXIONS

65 James Carroll, *Constantine's Sword*, pp. 531-532.

66 Ibid., p. 479.

67 Friedrich Heer, *God's First Love*, pp. 172-3, 221. On Jewish contribution to German literature see *Ibid.*, p. 225.

68 Ibid., p. 174.

69 Daniel J. Goldhagen, *A Moral Reckoning*, pp. 152-153.

70 Joshua Trachtenberg, *The Devil and the Jews*, p. 215.

71 James Carroll, *Constantine's Sword*, pp.422-423.

72 On modern antisemitism see Ibid., p. 425.

73 Friedrich Heer, *God's First Love*, p. 257.

74 Ibid., p. 174.

75 Ibid., p. 258.

76 Saul Friedländer, *Nazi Germany and the Jews*, pp. 85-86.

77 James Carroll, *Constantine's Sword*, pp. 446-447.

78 Joshua Trachtenberg, *The Devil and the Jews*, pp. 219-220.

79 Friedrich Heer, *God's First Love*, p. 253.

80 Joshua Trachtenberg, *The Devil and the Jews*, pp. 188-189.

81 Ibid., pp. 190-193.

82 James Carroll, *Constantine's Sword*, p. 432.

83 Ibid., p. 434.

84 Ibid., p. 445.

85 Saul Friedländer, *Nazi Germany and the Jews*, p. 84.

86 See Burns, *Dreyfus*, p. 96 and James Carroll, *Constantine's Sword*, p. 454.

87 Émile Zola, quoted in "Quand Zola S'Engageait pour le Capitaine Dreyfus," *La Croix*, January 12, 1998, p. 12.

88 James Carroll, *Constantine's Sword*, pp. 453-454.

89 Quoted in The New York Times, February 9, 1994. See also James Carroll, *Constantine's Sword*, p. 456.

90 Quoted in Burns, *Dreyfus*, p. 243.

91 *Syllabus of Errors*, quoted in James Carroll, *Constantine's Sword*, p. 442. See also Charles Coulombe, *Vicars of Christ: A History of the Popes*, pp. 462-463.

92 James Carroll, *Constantine's Sword*, pp. 442-443.

93 Daniel J. Goldhagen, *A Moral Reckoning*, p. 197. See also David Kertzer, *The Popes Against the Jews*, pp. 106-130.

94 See David Kertzer, *The Popes Against the Jews* & James Carroll, *Constantine's Sword*, pp. 670, 676.

95 ASV, ANV, b. 192, prot. 238, Ratti to Gaspari (November 2, 1918), ff. 565-575. Quoted in David Kertzer, *The Popes Against the Jews*, p. 249.

96 Ratti to Gasparri (January 9, 1919), reproduced in Wilk, vol. 3 (1997), pp. 250-261. Quoted in David Kertzer, *The Popes Against the Jews*, p. 251. See also Daniel J. Goldhagen, *A Moral Reckoning*, p. 81.

97 Quoted in John Loftus & Mark Aarons, *Unholy Trinity*, pp. 5, 9, 10.

98 Quoted in Friedrich Heer, *God's First Love*, pp. 354-355. See also Garry Wills, *Papal Sin*, pp. 19, 32.

99 Michael Phayer, *The Catholic Church and the Holocaust*, p. 224.

100 Pius XI had actually said late in his life that "spiritually we are all semites." Quoted in Ibid., pp. 4-5.

101 Ibid., p. 19 & Saul Friedländer, *Nazi Germany and the Jews*, p. 223.

102 Pius XII quoted in Saul Friedländer, *Pius XII and the Third Reich: A Documentation*. See also Garry Wills, *Papal Sin*, p. 35.

103 Quoted in Michael Phayer, *The Catholic Church and the Holocaust*, p. 44.

104 Alberto Melloni, Fra Istanbul, Atene e la guerra. La missione di A.G. Roncalli (1935-1944), p. 240. See also Daniel J. Goldhagen, *A Moral Reckoning*, p. 159.

105 Quoted in Friedrich Heer, *God's First Love*, p. 333.

106 Michael Phayer, *The Catholic Church and the Holocaust*, pp. 64-65. Osborne quoted in Garry Wills, *Papal Sin*, p. 66.

107 For more on Pope Benedict VIII's beliefs about Jews see Hans Kühner, Der Antisemitismus der Kirche, *Verlag Die Waage*, Zurich, 1976, p.108.

108 J.S., ZStL, 208 AR-Z 24/63, p. 1371. Quoted in Daniel J. Goldhagen, *Hitler's Willing Executioners*, p. 452.

109 Quoted in Friedrich Heer, *God's First Love*, p. 292. Also see *Ibid.*, pp. 294-295.

110 Adolf Hitler, *Mein Kampf*, pp. 46, 125, 152.

111 Quoted in Guenter Lewy, *The Catholic Church and Nazi Germany*, p. 26.

112 *Akten deutscher Bischöfe*, vol. 1, pp. 100-102. Quoted in Saul Friedländer, *Nazi Germany and the Jews*, p. 47. See also Walter Zwi Bacharach, *Anti Jewish Prejudices in German Catholic Sermons*, p. 111.

113 Quoted in Walter Zwi Bacharach, *Anti Jewish Prejudices in German Catholic Sermons*, pp. 111-112.

114 Quoted in Friedrich Heer, *God's First Love*, p. 293.

115 Kurt Meier, *Die Deutschen Christen*, Göttingen: Vandenhoeck & Ruprecht, 1964, p. 8.

116 George Orwell, *The Prevention of Literature*, 1946.

117 See Walter Zwi Bacharach, *Anti Jewish Prejudices in German Catholic Sermons*, p. 67.

118 Raphael Patai, ed., *The Complete Diaries of Theodr Herzl*, vol. 4, (New York: Herzl Press, 1960), pp. 1,593-1,594 and 1,602-1,604. Quoted in Daniel J. Goldhagen, *A Moral Reckoning*, p. 239.

119 Quoted in John Roth, Carol Rittner, eds., *Pope Pius XII and the Holocaust*, p. 190.

120 Quoted in Michael Phayer, *The Catholic Church and the Holocaust*, p. 50.

121 Ibid., p. 176

122 See Kurt Hruby, "Antizionismus, Antijudaismus und chrsitlicher Antizionismus," *Freiburger Rundbrief* 22, no. 81/84 (1970): 11-18. Quoted in Michael Phayer, *The Catholic Church and the Holocaust*, p. 264 n. 82.

123 The Vatican refused to recognize the State of Israel until 1993. Quoted in Daniel J. Goldhagen, *A Moral Reckoning*, pp. 239-240.

124 Ibid., pp. 264-265.

125 Quoted in Jeremy Cohen, *Christ Killers*, pp. 31-32.

126 See Jules Isaac, *The Teaching of Contempt*, pp. 34-35 & Daniel J. Goldhagen, *Hitler's Willing Executioners*, p. 42.

127 Jules Isaac, The Teaching of Contempt, p. 33

128 Quoted in Dagobert David Runes, *The Jew and the Cross*, p. 61.

129 Quoted in Daniel J. Goldhagen, *Hitler's Willing Executioners*, p. 50.

130 Quoted in James Carroll, *Constantine's Sword*, p. 213. Also see Ruether, *Faith and Fratricide*, p. 173.

131 See Jeremy Cohen, *Christ Killers*, p. 83. Quoted in James Carroll, *Constantine's Sword*, pp. 217-218.

132 James Carroll, *Constantine's Sword*, p. 219.

133 Ibid., p. 365.

134 *Sicut Judaeis* and St. Bernard quoted in Ibid., pp. 269-271. See also Jeremy Cohen, *Christ Killers*, p. 83 & Joshua Trachtenberg, *The Devil and the Jews*, p. 181.

135 Daniel J. Goldhagen, *Hitler's Willing Executioners*, p. 50.

136 Quoted in Léon Poliakov, *The History of Anti-Semitism*, p. 123.

R. Hoch ruth. The Deputy

347

137 Joshua Trachtenberg, *The Devil and the Jews*, p. 187.

138 Quoted in Jeremy Cohen, *Christ Killers*, pp. 89, 202.

139 Joshua Trachtenberg, *The Devil and the Jews*, pp. 18-19, 31 & William Shakespeare, *The Merchant of Venice*, III, i, 22 and II, ii, 27.

140 Joshua Trachtenberg, *The Devil and the Jews*, p. 43.

141 See Walter Zwi Bacharach, *Anti Jewish Prejudices in German Catholic Sermons*, p. 151.

142 Joshua Trachtenberg, *The Devil and the Jews*, pp. 174, 175, 176.

143 Ibid., pp. 180-181.

144 Ibid., p. 196.

145 Ibid., p. 210.

146 Jules Isaac, *Jesus and Israel*, pp. 11-14, 74, 22.

147 Ibid., p. 33. Incontrovertible proof of this was found in the Dead Sea Scrolls after WWII.

148 Ibid., p. 49.

149 Saint Augustine, *The City of God*, XVIII, p. 46. Quoted in Jules Isaac, *The Teaching of Contempt*, p. 45.

150 And in fact, the Jewish community in Babylon—today's Iraq—was a large and prosperous one until their expulsion following the founding of the State of Israel in 1948.

151 See Jules Isaac, *The Teaching of Contempt*, pp. 45, 54, 66-67, 69-70 and for more on the main dispersion of Jews in the Assyrian and Babylonian invasions see Jules Isaac, *Jesus and Israel*, pp. 89-93. Jacques-Bénigne Bossuet, the most outstanding pulpit preacher of seventeenth century French Catholicism, who believed that "The Jews are the scum of humanity" (Heer, Friedrich, *God's First Love*, p. 343) wrote about the putatively dispersed Jews: "A monstrous people, having neither hearth nor home, without a country and of all countries; once the most fortunate people in the world, now the evil spirit and the detestation of the world; wretched, scorned by all, having become in their wretchedness by a curse the mockery of even the most moderate." Poliakov, Léon, *The History of Anti-Semitism*, p. 184.

152 Jules Isaac, *Jesus and Israel*, pp. 94-101.

153 Ibid., p. 177.

154 1 Thessalonians 2:14-15.

155 And of course, one must point to the obvious fact in Christian theology that if Jesus *had* to die to redeem mankind, then it was immaterial who was responsi-

ble for his death. It could even be argued Christian believers should be grateful that someone killed him and therefore made possible their own salvation. See Jules Isaac, *Jesus and Israel*, pp. 233, 264.

156 Ibid., pp. 285, 296-297, 310.

157 Jules Isaac, *The Teaching of Contempt*, pp. 128, 135-136.

158 Ibid., pp. 142-144.

159 Jules Isaac, *Jesus and Israel*, p. 385.

160 Quoted in James Carroll, *Constantine's Sword*, p. 347.

161 Ibid., pp. 374-375.

162 Ibid., pp. 347-348.

163 Padberg et al, *First Thirty Jesuit Congregations*, pp. 204, 232, 534, 625. Quoted in James Carroll, *Constantine's Sword*, pp. 382-383. See also Daniel J. Goldhagen, *A Moral Reckoning*, p.154.

164 Sermon of December 31, 1933, in Faulhaber, *Judaism, Christianity and Germany*, p. 107. Quoted in Guenter Lewy, *The Catholic Church and Nazi Germany*, p. 275.

165 Adam, *Theologische Quartalschrift*, CXIV (1933), pp. 60-62. Quoted in Guenter Lewy, *The Catholic Church and Nazi Germany*, p. 279. See also Daniel J. Goldhagen, *A Moral Reckoning*, p. 157.

166 "Katholische Grundsätze für den Religionsunterricht in unserer Zeit," *AB Freiburg*, no 9, March 4, 1936, p. 61. Quoted in Guenter Lewy, *The Catholic Church and Nazi Germany*, p. 163. See pp. 162-166 for further examples of the church's use of racial language.

167 Daniel J. Goldhagen, *A Moral Reckoning*, p. 154.

168 Quoted in Georges Passelecq and Bernard Suchecky, *The Hidden Encyclical of Pius XI*, p. 246. See also Daniel J. Goldhagen, *A Moral Reckoning*, p. 39.

169 *Humani Generis Unitas*, paragraph 1142, quoted in Georges Passelecq and Bernard Suchecky, *The Hidden Encyclical of Pius XI*, p. 252. Gundlach quotation about "assimilated Jews" in *Ibid.*, p. 48 (Lexicon für Theologie und Kirche, Vol 1, second edition (Herder, 1930), pp. 504-505. See also Garry Wills, *Papal Sin*, pp. 35-36.

170 Garry Wills, *Papal Sin*, pp. 39-40.

171 Oreglia, *La Civiltà Cattolica*, 1880, IV, pp. 109-110, 112. Quoted in Daniel J. Goldhagen, *A Moral Reckoning*, p. 79.

172 F. Saverio Rondina, "La morale giudaica," *La Civiltà Cattolica* 1893, I, pp. 145-153. Quoted in David Kertzer, *The Popes Against the Jews*, pp. 145-146.

173 Quoted in James Carroll, *Constantine's Sword*, p. 457.

174 "L'antisemitismo in Francia," *L'Osservatore Romano*, 1 Iuglio 1892, p. 1. Quoted in David Kertzer, *The Popes Against the Jews*, p. 147.

175 "L'antisemitismo in Francia," *L'Osservatore Romano*, 2 Iuglio 1892, p. 1. Quoted in David Kertzer, *The Popes Against the Jews*, p. 148.

176 E. Rosa, "Cattolicismo e Nazismo: Idee chiare e pericolosi equivoci," *L'Osservatore Romano*, June 10, 1938, 2. Quoted in Susan Zuccotti, *Under His Very Windows*, p. 30.

177 "Un'omelia del Vescovo di Cremona: La chiesa e gli ebrei," *L'Osservatore Romano*, January 15, 1939, 2. Quoted in Susan Zuccotti, *Under His Very Windows*, pp. 54-55.

178 *La Croix*, January 18, 19, 1898. Quoted in James Carroll, *Constantine's Sword*, p. 459.

179 *La Croix*, January 19, 1898. Quoted in James Carroll, *Constantine's Sword*, pp. 459-460.

180 See James Carroll, *Constantine's Sword*, p. 460.

181 Quoted in Burns, *Dreyfus*, p. 152. See also James Carroll, *Constantine's Sword*, p. 462.

182 Charles Coughlin, quoted in Brinkley, *Voices of Protest*, pp. 266, 270-271. See also James Carroll, *Constantine's Sword*, p. 438.

183 William Manchester, *The Glory And The Dream*, 1974, Bantam Books, p. 176.

184 Pastoral letter of January 30, 1939, *AB Freiburg*, no. 3, February 8, 1939, p. 15. See also Daniel J. Goldhagen, *A Moral Reckoning*, p. 165.

185 Pastoral letter of March 25, 1941, *AB Freiburg*, no. 9, March 27, 1941, p. 388. See also Daniel J. Goldhagen, *Hitler's Willing Executioners*, p. 109.

186 Pastoral letter for Lent 1939, *AB Limburg*, no. 1, February 6, 1939, pp. 1-8.

187 Quoted in John Loftus & Mark Aarons, *Unholy Trinity*, p. 129.

188 Lillian Freudmann, *Antisemitism in the New Testament*, p. 284.

189 For an inventory of antisemitism in lectionaries and recommendations on expunging them of antisemitic polemic see Norman A. Beck, *Removing Anti-Jewish Polemic from our Christian Lectionaries: A Proposal* (http://jcrelations.net/en/?id=737), Norman A. Beck, *Mature Christianity: The Recognition and Repudiation of the Anti-Jewish Polemic of the New Testament*, Norman A. Beck, *Mature Christianity in the 21st Century* and Lillian Freudmann, *Antisemitism in the New Testament*.

190 Jeremy Cohen, *Christ Killers*, pp. 33-35.

191 John 8:42-45, 47, New International Version.

192 James Carroll, *Constantine's Sword*, p. 93.

193 Walter Zwi Bacharach, *Anti Jewish Prejudices in German Catholic Sermons*, p. 11.

194 Ibid., pp. 11-12, 21.

195 *Beyond Good and Evil*, Friedrich Nietzsche.

196 As an example of what's in the liturgical cycle we can mention the "Reproaches" from the American Catholic Church prayer book. These are antisemitic chants blaming the Jews for the death of Jesus. They take the form of Jesus retelling how good he was to the Jews, and how bad they were to him: Some examples: "My people, what have I done to you? How have I offended you? Answer me! I led you out of Egypt, from slavery to freedom, but you led your Savior to the cross" and "For your sake I scourged your captors and their first-born sons, but you brought your scourges down on me . . . I led you on your way in a pillar of cloud, but you led me to Pilate's court. . . . For you I struck down the kings of Canaan, but you struck my head with a reed. . . . I raised you to the height of majesty, but you raised me high on a cross." Even though these statements are put on the lips of Jesus, they do not appear anywhere in Scripture. They are traditional works that incite antipathy toward Jews that date from the ninth century, and are considered to be optional. Despite the libelous message, forty percent of the parishes in the U.S. chant them at the peak of the liturgical cycle. See Daniel J. Goldhagen, *A Moral Reckoning*, p. 206.

197 Walter Zwi Bacharach, *Anti Jewish Prejudices in German Catholic Sermons*, pp. 20-21, 24 n.13 & Joshua Trachtenberg, *The Devil and the Jews*, p. 216.

198 Quoted in Walter Zwi Bacharach, *Anti Jewish Prejudices in German Catholic Sermons*, pp. 77, 79.

199 Joseph Deharbe, 1869. Quoted in Ibid., p. 116.

200 Georg Patiss, 1882. Quoted in Ibid., p. 117.

201 Jeremy Cohen, *Christ Killers*, pp. 207-208. The *Judensau* was removed from most of the churches and cathedrals where it had been originally placed centuries ago, but can still be found in many places around Europe: Aarschot (Notre Dame Church), Bamberg Cathedral, Basel Cathedral, Brandenburg Cathedral, Cadolzburg, Colmar (St Martin Cathedral), Eberswalde, Erfurt Cathedral, Gniezno Cathedral, Heilsbronn Cathedral, Cologne (underside of a choir-stall seat in the Cathedral, probably the earliest example, and in Church of St. Severin), Lemgo (St Marien), Magdeburg Cathedral, Metz Cathedral, Nuremberg (St Sebaldus Church), Regensburg Cathedral, Remagen (Gate post), Upp-

sala Cathedral, Wiener Neustadt in Austria, Wimpfen (Church of St. Peter), Wittenberg (Town church), Xanten Cathedral, Zerbst (St Nicolas Church).

202 Walter Zwi Bacharach, *Anti Jewish Prejudices in German Catholic Sermons*, p. 113.

203 Quoted in Ibid., p. 117. See also p.113.

204 See Ibid., p. 114.

205 Quoted in Ibid., p. 115. We probably need to thank Hitler for this misguided conception of Jewish scientists, as otherwise the Germans might have developed nuclear weapons ahead of the Allies.

206 Quoted in Ibid., pp. 117, 118.

207 Quoted in Ibid., pp. 118, 123 n.36.

208 Ibid., p. 132.

209 For the equivalent laws promulgated by the Nazis see Raul Hilberg, *The Destruction of the European Jews*, pp. 11-12.

210 Karl Bachem, Vorgeschichte, Geschichte und Politik der Deutschen Zentrumspartei, vol. VIII (Cologne, 1931), p. 262. See also Guenter Lewy, *The Catholic Church and Nazi Germany*, pp. 4-5.

211 James Carroll, *Constantine's Sword*, p. 29.

212 Guenter Lewy, *The Catholic Church and Nazi Germany*, p. 292 & Doris Bergen, The Ecclesiastical Final Solution, in Michael Berenbaum, Abraham J. Peck, *The Holocaust and History*, p. 566.

213 Garry Wills, *Papal Sin*, p. 18.

214 Walter Zwi Bacharach, *Anti Jewish Prejudices in German Catholic Sermons*, p. 110.

215 Quoted in Eugene J. Fisher in *National Catholic Register*, October 27, 1998.

216 On the various points being made here of how Christian teachings prepared the German population for Nazi indoctrination, see Walter Zwi Bacharach, *Anti Jewish Prejudices in German Catholic Sermons*, p. 138.

217 Werner May, *Deutscher National-Katechismus*, 2nd edition (Breslau: Verlag von Heinrich Handel, 1934).

218 Ibid., p. 139.

219 Farinaccci speech on "The Church and the Jews" at Milan's Institute for Fascist Culture, 1939. Quoted in David Kertzer, *The Popes Against the Jews*, p. 283.

220 John Cornwell, *Hitler's Pope*, pp. 108-109.

221 Quoted in Ibid., p. 109.

222 Ibid., p. 81.

223 Adolf Hitler, speaking in the Reichstag on January 30, 1934.

224 Quoted in Matheson, *Third Reich and the Christian Churches*, pp. 6-7.

225 Quoted in Ibid., p. 10.

226 Quoted in James Carroll, *Constantine's Sword*, p. 498.

227 John Cornwell, *Hitler's Pope*, p. 84.

228 "Wir Stehen zum Kreuz," *Der Deutsche Weg*, IV (January 18, 1937), p. 1, quoted in Guenter Lewy, *The Catholic Church and Nazi Germany*, p. 211.

229 Quoted in John Cornwell, *Hitler's Pope*, p. 156. See also James Carroll, *Constantine's Sword*, pp. 498-499.

230 *Völkischer Beobachter*, quoted in Schrader, *Church and State in Germany*, p. 8.

231 Quoted in John Cornwell, *Hitler's Pope*, p. 130.

232 James Carroll, *Constantine's Sword*, p. 505.

233 Quoted in Helmreich, *German Churches under Hitler*, pp. 275-276. See also James Carroll, *Constantine's Sword*, p. 505.

234 Quoted in Guenter Lewy, *The Catholic Church and Nazi Germany*, p. 90.

235 Quoted in James Carroll, *Constantine's Sword*, pp. 507. See also p. 506.

236 F. Schühlein, "Geschichte der Juden," *Lexicon für Theologie und Kirche*, 2nd rev. ed. (Freiburg, Br., 1933), V, 687. Quoted in Guenter Lewy, *The Catholic Church and Nazi Germany*, p. 279.

237 Gustav Lehmacher, S.J., "Rassenwerte," Stimmen der Zeit, CXXVI (1933), 81. Quoted in Guenter Lewy, *The Catholic Church and Nazi Germany*, p. 279.

238 "Verdient die katholische Kirche den Namen 'Judenkirche'?," *Klerusblatt*, XVIII (1937), 542. Quoted in Guenter Lewy, *The Catholic Church and Nazi Germany*, p. 279.

239 Theodor Bolger, O.S.B., *Der Glaube von gestern und heute* (Cologne, 1939), p. 150. Quoted in Guenter Lewy, *The Catholic Church and Nazi Germany*, p. 279.

240 *AKD Mitteilugsblatt*, no. 6, May 15, 1934, p. 8. See also Guenter Lewy, *The Catholic Church and Nazi Germany*, pp. 278, 279.

241 Quoted in James Carroll, *Constantine's Sword*, p. 683 n.23.

242 Vatican SRS, Baviera, letter from Pacelli to Gasparri, April 18, 1919, folio 37. Quoted in John Cornwell, *Hitler's Pope*, pp. 74-79.

243 Original is at ASV, ANV, b. 193, "Relazione finale della Missione di Mons. Ratti in Polonia redatta da Mons. Pellegrinetti, Luglio 1921," f. 431; the pub-

lished version is in Cavalleri 1990, pp. 148-149. Quoted in David Kertzer, *The Popes Against the Jews*, p. 260. See also Daniel J. Goldhagen, *A Moral Reckoning*, p. 81.

244 John Loftus & Mark Aarons, *Unholy Trinity*, p. 294.

245 The account of the talk is in Faulhaber's summary report in the *DA Limburg*, 561/2 C. Quoted in Guenter Lewy, *The Catholic Church and Nazi Germany*, pp. 207-208.

246 Gröber, *Handbuch der religiösen Gegenwartsfragen*, articles "Bolschewismus," p. 86, "Marxismus," p. 404, 87, "Kunst," p. 372. Quoted in Guenter Lewy, *The Catholic Church and Nazi Germany*, p. 277.

247 Quoted in Michael Phayer, *The Catholic Church and the Holocaust*, p. 35.

248 Guenter Lewy, *The Catholic Church and Nazi Germany*, p. 224.

249 Gröber, *Kirche, Vaterland und Vaterlandsliebe*, pp. 103-104. See also Guenter Lewy, *The Catholic Church and Nazi Germany*, p. 225.

250 "Gemeinsames Wort der deutschen Bischöfe," *Martinus-Blatt*, no. 38, September 17, 1939.

251 W. K., "Das Recht des deutschen Volkes auf Lebensraum," *Bistumsblatt Erzdiözese Breslau*, no. 7 February 18, 1940, p. 44. See also Guenter Lewy, *The Catholic Church and Nazi Germany*, pp. 227-228.

252 Guenter Lewy, *The Catholic Church and Nazi Germany*, pp. 232-233.

253 *AB Breslau*, no. 21, November 14, 1940, p. 164. See also Guenter Lewy, *The Catholic Church and Nazi Germany*, p. 229.

254 Pastoral letter of January 25, 1941, *AB Ermland*, no. 2, February 1, 1941, pp. 13-14.

255 Pastoral letter of September 24, 1941, *AB Eichstätt*, September 25, 1941, p. 71.

256 Quoted in Guenter Lewy, *The Catholic Church and Nazi Germany*, p. 231.

257 Ibid., p. 233.

258 Ibid., p. 234.

259 *Badischer Beobachter*, no. 272, October 10, 1933, cited in Müller, *Katolische Episkopat*, pp. 72-73.

260 Bergen to Papen, June 1, 1933. *Documents on German Foreign Policy*, C, I, doc. 278, p. 507.

261 *Germania*, no. 255, September 16, 1933, and *Badischer Beobachter*, no. 254, September 22, 1933, cited in Müller, *Katolische Episkopat*, pp. 76-77. See also Guenter Lewy, *The Catholic Church and Nazi Germany*, p. 106.

262 Quoted in Michael Phayer, *The Catholic Church and the Holocaust*, p. 69.

263 See Paul's Epistle to the Romans 13:1-7.

264 Michael Phayer, *The Catholic Church and the Holocaust*, p. 75.

265 Reported in *Kölnische Volkszeitung*, no. 171, June 27, 1933, quoted in Müller, *Katolische Episkopat*, p. 78. See also Guenter Lewy, *The Catholic Church and Nazi Germany*, p. 100.

266 Quoted in Daniel J. Goldhagen, *Hitler's Willing Executioners*, pp. 108-109, 111.

267 Martin Niemöller, *Here Stand I!*, Chicago: Willett, Clarke & Co., 1937, p. 19. See also Daniel J. Goldhagen, *Hitler's Willing Executioners*, p. 112.

268 Quoted in Saul Friedländer, *Nazi Germany and the Jews*, p. 45.

269 Stewart W. Herman, *It's Your Souls We Want* (New York: Harper & Brothers, 1943), p. 234. Quoted in Daniel J. Goldhagen, *Hitler's Willing Executioners*, pp. 111-112.

270 Susan Zuccotti, *Under His Very Windows*, p. 108.

271 Ibid., p. 112.

272 Quoted in Israel Gutman, *Encyclopedia of the Holocaust*, p. 1137.

273 Michael Phayer, *The Catholic Church and the Holocaust*, p. 43.

274 ADSS, IX, doc. 174, notes of the Secretariat of State, May 5, 1943, 274. Quoted in Susan Zuccotti, *Under His Very Windows*, pp. 109-110.

275 The Russians blamed the Germans and the Germans blamed the Russians. The Soviet government finally acknowledged in 1990 that the Katyn massacre had been carried out by the Soviet secret police.

276 ADSS, VII, doc. 282, Roncalli to Montini, July 8, 1943, 473-76, 474. Quoted in Susan Zuccotti, *Under His Very Windows*, p. 110. See also Daniel J. Goldhagen, *A Moral Reckoning*, p. 151.

277 Quoted in Guenter Lewy, *The Catholic Church and Nazi Germany*, p. 301.

278 Weizsäcker to the Foreign Ministry, October 17, 1943, PA Bonn, Inland IIg, 192. Quoted in Guenter Lewy, *The Catholic Church and Nazi Germany*, p. 301. See also Garry Wills, *Papal Sin*, p. 16. The expression "under his very windows" comes from the German Ambassador's report to his superiors: "I can confirm the reaction of the Vatican to the removal of Jews from Rome...The Curia is dumbfounded, particularly as the action took place under the very windows of the pope, as it were." This also provides the title for Zuccotti's book. Susan Zuccotti, *Under His Very Windows*, Epigraph & p.162.

279 Weizsäcker to the Foreign Ministry, October 28, 1943, *PA Bonn*, Inland IIg, 192. Quoted in Guenter Lewy, *The Catholic Church and Nazi Germany*, 301. See also Garry Wills, *Papal Sin*, p. 16.

280 The numbers do not match exactly with the actual numbers sent, indicating a sloppy log entry. Quoted in James Carroll, *Constantine's Sword*, p. 524.

281 Quoted in John Morley, *Vatican Diplomacy and the Jews*, pp. 92-93. See also Daniel J. Goldhagen, *A Moral Reckoning*, pp. 169, 309 n77.

282 Quoted in Saul Friedländer, *Pius XII and the Third Reich: A Documentation*, p. 138. See also Daniel J. Goldhagen, *A Moral Reckoning*, p. 170 and Michael Phayer, *The Catholic Church and the Holocaust*, p. 76.

283 *Actes et Documents du Saint Siège relatifs à la Seconde Guerre Mondiale* (French for Acts and Documents of the Holy See related to the Second World War), ADSS henceforth, IX, doc. 390, notes of the Secretariat of State, October 1943, Tacchi Venturi to Maglione, October 25, 1943, 525-26. See also Daniel J. Goldhagen, *A Moral Reckoning*, p. 170 and Susan Zuccotti, *Under His Very Windows*, p. 167.

284 Daniel J. Goldhagen, *A Moral Reckoning*, p. 170 & Susan Zuccotti, *Under His Very Windows*, pp. 217-218.

285 Tiso quoted in Rittner, Smith and Stenfeld, Editors., *The Holocaust and the Christian World: Reflections of the Past, Challenges for the Future*, p. 106. See also Daniel J. Goldhagen, *A Moral Reckoning*, pp. 64, 170-171. Tardini quoted in John Morley, *Vatican Diplomacy and the Jews*, pp. 92-93.

286 Daniel J. Goldhagen, *A Moral Reckoning*, p. 158.

287 Quoted in James Carroll, *Constantine's Sword*, pp. 486-187. Ghandi successfully used the same strategy of "passive resistance" in India against the British Empire decades later.

288 Ibid., p. 490.

289 Ibid., p. 492.

290 Pastoral letter of the Bavarian bishops read on June 21, 1936, *AB Regensburg*, no. 10, August 4, 1936, p. 86. Quoted in Guenter Lewy, *The Catholic Church and Nazi Germany*, p. 168.

291 Sermon on February 6, 1936, Faulhaber, *Münchener Kardinalspredigten*, 1st series, p. 17. Quoted in Guenter Lewy, *The Catholic Church and Nazi Germany*, p. 306.

292 Sermon on July 13, 1941, Heinrich Portmann, ed., *Bischof Galen spricht* (Freiburg, Br. 1946), p. 49. Quoted in Guenter Lewy, *The Catholic Church and Nazi Germany*, p. 306.

293 Catechism of the Catholic Church, parag. 1736.

294 Daniel J. Goldhagen, *A Moral Reckoning*, p. 178.

295 James Carroll, *Constantine's Sword*, pp. 271-272.

296 Quoted in Daniel J. Goldhagen, *A Moral Reckoning*, p. 49. Interestingly enough, Vatican Radio found time and the will to broadcast news, analysis, homilies and religious addresses in forty languages.

297 Daniel J. Goldhagen, *Hitler's Willing Executioners*, p. 112. The proclamation is in *Kirchliches Jahrbuch für die Evangelische Kirche in Deutschland, 1933-1944* (Gütersloh: C. Bertelsmann Verlag, 1948), p. 481.

298 Quoted in Daniel J. Goldhagen, *A Moral Reckoning*, p. 67.

299 Quoted in Ibid., p. 65.

300 Quoted in Yitzhak Arad, "The Christian Churches and the Persecution of Jews in the Occupied Territories of the USSR," in *The Holocaust and the Christian World: Reflections on the Past, Challenges for the Future*, Carol Rittner, Stephen D. Smith and Irena Steinfeldt, eds., London: Kuperard for the Beth Shalom Holocaust Memorial Centre and the Yad Vashem International School for Holocaust Studies, 2000, p. 110.

301 John Morley, *Vatican Diplomacy and the Jews*, p. 203.

302 Walter Zwi Bacharach, *Anti Jewish Prejudices in German Catholic Sermons*, p. 109.

303 Michael Phayer, *The Catholic Church and the Holocaust*, p. 67. Pius XII claimed to have done this repeatedly, though: "in the past we condemned repeatedly the persecutions that a fanatical antisemitism unleashed against the Hebrew people." *Acta Apostolicae Sedis: Commentarium Officiale*, Vol. 38 (1946) p. 322; Address to the delegates of the Supreme Council of the Arab people of Palestine.

304 Quoted in Hanna Arendt, *Eichmann in Jerusalem: A Report on the Banality of Evil*, pp. 200-201.

305 Doris L. Bergen, Between God and Hitler: German Military Chaplains and the Crimes of the Third Reich, in *In God's Name*, edited by Omer Bartov, Phyllis Mack, p. 128-130 & Daniel J. Goldhagen, *A Moral Reckoning*, pp. 62-63.

306 Doris L. Bergen, Between God and Hitler: German Military Chaplains and the Crimes of the Third Reich, in *In God's Name*, edited by Omer Bartov, Phyllis Mack, pp. 124-126.

307 Quoted in Daniel J. Goldhagen, *A Moral Reckoning*, p. 63.

308 Pastoral letter of August 1942, copy in *DA Mainz*, K/3. Quoted in Guenter Lewy, *The Catholic Church and Nazi Germany*, p. 241.

309 From "See, a virgin will conceive in her womb and will bear a son, and they will call his name Emmanuel." Isaiah 7:14. "Emmanuel" is translated as "God with us."

310 Guenter Lewy, *The Catholic Church and Nazi Germany*, pp. 239-240.

311 Heinrich Böll, "Brief an einen jungen Katholiken," *Erzählungen, Hörspiele, Aufsätze* (Cologne, 1961), pp. 381-382. Quoted in Guenter Lewy, *The Catholic Church and Nazi Germany*, p. 241.

312 Doris L. Bergen, German Military Chaplains in World War II and the Dilemmas of Legitimacy. *Church History* 70(2), (2001). See Hans Richard Nevermann, "Warum zog ich nicht die Notbremse? Erinnerungen 40 Jahre nach dem Überfall auf die Sowjetunion," Junge Kirche 6 (1981): 282-84 & Heinz Keller, "Ob das der Herrgott von uns will?," in Brandt, *Priester in Uniform*, pp. 130-31. Keller was with the 2d Medical Corps, 46th Infantry Division in the Crimea and the Caucasus.

313 Guenter Lewy, *The Catholic Church and Nazi Germany*, p. 107.

314 Quoted in James Carroll, *Constantine's Sword*, p. 29.

315 Daniel J. Goldhagen, *A Moral Reckoning*, p. 60. Quoted in Guenter Lewy, *The Catholic Church and Nazi Germany*, p. 265.

316 James Carroll, *Constantine's Sword*, pp. 29-30 & Deborah Lipstadt, *Aryan Nation*.

317 Guenter Lewy, *The Catholic Church and Nazi Germany*, p. 289.

318 Quoted in Carol Rittner, Stephen D. Smith, and Irena Steinfeldt, eds., *The Holocaust and the Christian World: Reflections of the Past, Challenges for the Future* (New York, Continuum, 2000), p. 242. See also Daniel J. Goldhagen, *A Moral Reckoning*, p. 52.

319 Carol Rittner, Stephen D. Smith, and Irena Steinfeldt, eds., *The Holocaust and the Christian World: Reflections of the Past, Challenges for the Future*, p. 242.

320 Quoted in Ibid., pp. 244-245.

321 Ready for Martyrdom, *Time Magazine*, Monday, Sep. 27, 1943.

322 Daniel J. Goldhagen, *A Moral Reckoning*, pp. 50-52.

323 The Roads to Rome, *Time Magazine*, January 7, 1946.

324 Quoted in Michael Phayer, *The Catholic Church and the Holocaust*, p. 76.

325 Ibid., pp. 57, 222.

326 Quoted in Ibid., p. 144.

327 Quoted in Guenter Lewy, *The Catholic Church and Nazi Germany*, pp. 284.

328 John Morley, *Vatican Diplomacy and the Jews*, p. 112.

329 Quoted in Lawrence Elliott, *I Will be Called John*, p. 164. Roncalli would later become Pope John XXIII and call the Second Vatican Council to address Catholicism's anti-Judaism.

330 Barry Rubin, *Istanbul Intrigues*, p. 214.

331 Ira Hirschmann, *Caution to the Winds*, pp. 181-182.

332 As reported in Haaretz from documentation discovered by Prof. Dina Porat, who headed the Project for the Study of Anti-Semitism at Tel Aviv University, http://www.haaretz.com/hasen/spages/795016.html. In public, however, Roncalli always said his work on behalf of the Jews was at the behest of Pope Pius XII.

333 Quoted in William R. Perl, *The Holocaust Conspiracy*, pp. 198-199.

334 Quoted in Saul Friedländer, *Pius XII and the Third Reich: A Documentation*, p. 115.

335 Tisserant to Suhard, June 11, 1940, in a private letter captured by the Germans. Published from the files of the German Chancellery (*BA Koblenz*, R 43 II/1440a) by Eberhard Jäckel, "Zur Politik des Heiligen Stuhls im Zweiten Weltkrieg: Ein ergänzendes Dokument," *Geschichte in Wissenschaft und Unterricht*, XV (1964), 45. Quoted in Guenter Lewy, *The Catholic Church and Nazi Germany*, p. 307. Cardinal Tisserant, however, was involved in the Ratlines.

336 Daniel J. Goldhagen, *A Moral Reckoning*, p. 50. It must also be questioned how much worse the Pope thought the situation of the Jews could possibly get.

337 Quoted in William R. Perl, *The Holocaust Conspiracy*, pp. 204-205.

338 Charles R. Gallagher, *Vatican Secret Diplomacy: Joseph P. Hurley and Pope Pius XII*, p. 132.

339 Ibid., pp. 86, 98.

340 Ibid., p. 102.

341 Ibid., pp. 103, 104.

342 Ibid., pp. 99-100.

343 Quoted in Ibid., pp. 148-149. See also p. 152.

344 Susan Zuccotti, *Under His Very Windows*, pp. 38-41.

345 Ibid., pp. 53-54.

346 The ambassador's report is reproduced in "Pope Pius XII and the Jews," *Jewish Spectator* (Feb. 1964), pp. 13-17. Quoted in Daniel J. Goldhagen, *A Moral Reckoning*, p. 149.

347 Daniel J. Goldhagen, *A Moral Reckoning*, p. 149.

348 Letter of Father Tacchi Venturi to Cardinal Maglione, 29 August 1943. Quoted in Daniel J. Goldhagen, *A Moral Reckoning*, p. 150.

349 Pius XII to German bishops, August 6, 1940, copy in *DA Regensburg*. Quoted in Guenter Lewy, *The Catholic Church and Nazi Germany*, p. 305.

350 Quoted in Perl, William, *The Holocaust Conspiracy*, p. 200.

351 See Guenter Lewy, *The Catholic Church and Nazi Germany*, p. 305 and John Loftus & Mark Aarons, *Unholy Trinity*, p. 19.

352 Owen Chadwick, *Britain and the Vatican during the Second World War*, p. 212.

353 Quoted in Ibid., pp. 212-213.

354 Quoted in Ibid., p. 213. Also see Michael Phayer, *The Catholic Church and the Holocaust*, p. 49.

355 Owen Chadwick, *Britain and the Vatican during the Second World War*, p. 214.

356 Guenter Lewy, *The Catholic Church and Nazi Germany*, p. 299.

357 Quoted in Owen Chadwick, *Britain and the Vatican during the Second World War*, p. 216.

358 Printed in *L'Osservatore Romano*, December 25, 1942, 1-3, 2. Quoted in Susan Zuccotti, *Under His Very Windows*, p. 1.

359 Quoted in Saul Friedländer, *Pius XII and the Third Reich: A Documentation*, pp. 141-142.

360 Quoted in Susan Zuccotti, *Under His Very Windows*, p. 112.

361 Quoted in Saul Friedländer, *Pius XII and the Third Reich: A Documentation*, p. 143.

362 Giovanni Battista Montini, "Pius XII and the Jews," letter to the British Catholic periodical *The Tablet*, reproduced in Eric Bentley, Storm Over "The Deputy," pp. 67-68. Quoted in Susan Zuccotti, *Under His Very Windows*, p. 169.

363 Saul Friedländer, *Pius XII and the Third Reich: A Documentation*, p. 145.

364 "La carità del Santo Padre," *L'Osservatore Romano*, October 25-26, 1943, 1. Quoted in Susan Zuccotti, *Under His Very Windows*, p. 2.

365 The speech was printed in *L'Osservatore Romano*, June 3, 1944, 1. Quoted in Susan Zuccotti, *Under His Very Windows*, p. 2.

366 Statement of Dr. Senatro on March 11, 1963, at a public discussion in Berlin. Quoted in Guenter Lewy, *The Catholic Church and Nazi Germany*, p. 304.

367 Daniel J. Goldhagen, *A Moral Reckoning*, p. 175 and reference in p. 324 n122.

368 John Loftus & Mark Aarons, *Unholy Trinity*, p. 29.

369 Alois Hudal, *Die Gründlagen des Nationalsozialismus; eine ideengeschichtliche Untersuchung*, Johannes Günther, Leipzig, 1937, p. 9. Quoted in John Loftus & Mark Aarons, *Unholy Trinity*, p. 30.

370 John Loftus & Mark Aarons, *Unholy Trinity*, p. 30.

371 Michael Phayer, *The Catholic Church and the Holocaust*, p. 166.

372 *Frieden, Krieg und 'Frieden,'* Maler, p. 322. Quoted in Uki Goñi, *The Real Odessa*, p. 233.

373 Quoted in John Loftus & Mark Aarons, *Unholy Trinity*, p. 28. See also Uki Goñi, *The Real Odessa*, p. 250.

374 Archbishop Siri was widely reported to be the hand-picked successor of Pope Pius XII.

375 Quoted in Daniel J. Goldhagen, *A Moral Reckoning*, p. 176.

376 Uki Goñi, *The Real Odessa*, pp. 240-241.

377 John Loftus & Mark Aarons, *Unholy Trinity*, p. 46.

378 Ibid., p. 47.

379 Pavelić was a devout Catholic. In a letter to Pius XII he wrote: "Holy Father! Since divine providence has made it possible that I take over the helm of my people and my homeland, I am firmly determined and wish fervently that the Croatian people, faithful to their laudable past, also in the future remain loyal to the holy apostle Peter and his followers and that our homeland, filled with the law of the New Testament, become Christ's kingdom. In this truly great work, I fervently ask the aid of Your Holiness. As such aid I first see that Your Holiness with Your highest apostolic authority recognize our state, then that You deign as quickly as possible to send Your representative, who will help me with Your fatherly advice, and finally that he impart to me and my people the apostolic blessing. Kneeling at the feet of Your Holiness. I kiss your sacred right hand as the obedient son of Your Holiness." Quoted in Vladimir Dedijer, *The Yugoslav Auschwitz and the Vatican*, p. 78.

380 British ambassador quote in British Ambassador to the Holy See, May 24, 1941, PRO FO 371 30174. See John Loftus & Mark Aarons, *Unholy Trinity*, pp. 71-73.

381 Gowen and Caniglia report of August 29, 1947, Pavelić CIC file, obtained under US FOIA, pp. 2-6. Quoted in John Loftus & Mark Aarons, *Unholy Trinity*, p. 83.

382 Quoted in John Loftus & Mark Aarons, *Unholy Trinity*, pp. 112, 114.

383 Ibid., pp. 96-98.

384 Quoted in Michael Phayer, *The Catholic Church and the Holocaust*, p. 35.

385 John Loftus & Mark Aarons, *Unholy Trinity*, pp. 99-100.

386 Ibid., p. 87.

387 Ibid., pp. 89, 58.

388 Monsignor Montini later became Pope Paul VI. Michael Phayer, *The Catholic Church and the Holocaust*, p. 173 & John Loftus & Mark Aarons, *Unholy Trinity*, p. 116.

389 To confirm it was possible to get false papers, a CIC agent simply paid someone with contacts at the International Red Cross, who examined the IRC files looking for "the name of a missing or dead person who fitted the description," and a couple of days later was given a name to apply with. He then needed two letters of identification, which the contact got from the Vatican and the Italian Red Cross. John Loftus & Mark Aarons, *Unholy Trinity*, p. 42.

390 See Ibid., pp. 91-96.

391 See Ibid., pp. 101-103.

392 Quoted in Ibid., p. 104.

393 Ibid., pp. 104-107.

394 Michael Phayer, *The Catholic Church and the Holocaust*, pp. 170-171.

395 John Loftus & Mark Aarons, *Unholy Trinity*, pp. 118, 119.

396 Exactly 25 years later, over 20,000 people perceived to be subversive elements by the Argentinean military government were murdered in concentration camps in Argentina. The military dictatorship that perpetrated these murders enjoyed the support of a Catholic Church that professed allegiance to the "Western and Christian way of life" and who proclaimed itself to be the "Moral Reserve of the Western World." As a result, young people, Jews, psychologists and other members of the Argentinean intelligentsia, very few of whom were actually subversive, became targets for extermination. Quoted in Uki Goñi, *The Real Odessa*, p. 246 & also see p. 247. Also see Emilio Fermín Mignone, *Witness to the Truth* (1988) for an account of the collusion of the Argentinean Catholic Church and the brutal military dictatorship that terrorized the country between 1975 and 1983.

397 The files of the International Red Cross were opened after the war. Uki Goñi, *The Real Odessa*, p. 248. Other clerics involved in the Vatican-sponsored emigration bodies were Monsignor Preseren (Assistant General of a powerful Jesuit Slovenian order with deep connections to the Pope), Bishop Bučko (re-

sponsible for helping the Ukrainian Galician SS Division), Father Cecelja and Father Gallov.

398 Michael Phayer, *The Catholic Church and the Holocaust*, pp. 173.

399 Uki Goñi, *The Real Odessa*, p. 321. On June 10, 1944, Colonel Juan Perón, at the time Vice-President and War Minister of Argentina, delivered the following pro-Nazi speech: "In South America, it is our mission to make the leadership of Argentina not only possible but indisputable. . . Hitler's fight in peace and war will guide us. Alliances will be the next step. We will get Bolivia and Chile. Then it will be easy to exert pressure on Uruguay. These five nations will attract Brazil, due to its type of government and its important group of Germans. Once Brazil has fallen, the South American continent will be ours. Following the German example, we will inculcate the masses with the necessary military spirit. . ." George I. Blanksten, *Perón's Argentina*, p. 48.

400 The same applied during the so-called Argentinean "Dirty War" of the 1970s, in which tens of thousands of people perceived to be leftist and/or dangerous to the state were "disappeared" by the military junta while a complicit Catholic Church looked the other way.

401 Uki Goñi, *The Real Odessa*, p. 237.

402 Tisserant to Argentine embassy, May 7, 1946, 3115 V, archive of the Argentine embassy in Rome. Quoted in Uki Goñi, *The Real Odessa*, p. 95.

403 La Razón, December 23, 1960. Quoted in Uki Goñi, *The Real Odessa*, p. 96.

404 Quoted in John Loftus & Mark Aarons, *Unholy Trinity*, pp. 42-43.

405 See Aarons & Loftus, *The Secret War Against the Jews*, Chapter 6. Quoted in John Loftus & Mark Aarons, *Unholy Trinity*, p. 49.

406 Uki Goñi, *The Real Odessa*, p. 380 n.444.

407 Quoted in John Loftus & Mark Aarons, *Unholy Trinity*, p. 43.

408 Quoted in Ibid., p. 48.

409 Ibid., pp. 192, 196.

410 According to a 1947 secret document of the British embassy at the Vatican, "His Majesty's Government have asked the Vatican to assist in getting the "Greys" to South America, although they were certainly wanted by the Yugoslav government." British embassy at Holy See to London, November 18, 1947, PRO, FO 371, 67402. Quoted in Uki Goñi, *The Real Odessa*, p. 238. See also John Loftus & Mark Aarons, *Unholy Trinity*, pp. 273-274.

411 Quoted in John Loftus & Mark Aarons, *Unholy Trinity*, p. 206.

412 Quoted in James Carroll, *Constantine's Sword*, p. 515. See also Daniel J. Goldhagen, *A Moral Reckoning*, p. 227.

413 Guenter Lewy, *The Catholic Church and Nazi Germany*, pp. 302-303.

414 See Daniel J. Goldhagen, *A Moral Reckoning*, pp. 48-49 for further analysis on the things the Pope did.

415 John Morley, *Vatican Diplomacy and the Jews*, p. 204.

416 See Daniel J. Goldhagen, *A Moral Reckoning*, p. 49 for further analysis on the things the Pope did not do.

417 Weizsäcker to the Foreign Ministry, October 28, 1943, PA Bonn, Inland IIg, 192. Quoted in Guenter Lewy, *The Catholic Church and Nazi Germany*, p. 302.

418 Susan Zuccotti, *Under His Very Windows*, p. 316.

419 For instance, when the Papacy came under French dominance in 1305, Pope Clement V moved to Avignon.

420 See Daniel J. Goldhagen, *Hitler's Willing Executioners* and Christopher Browning, *Ordinary Men.*

421 For a comprehensive defense of the Pope see Ronald J. Rychlak, *Righteous Gentiles: How Pius XII And the Catholic Church Saved Half a Million Jews from the Nazis* and David G. Dalin, *The Myth of Hitler's Pope.* For an effective exposé and counterarguments see Daniel J. Goldhagen, *A Moral Reckoning*, particularly pp. 45-57.

422 Garry Wills, *Papal Sin*, p. 9.

423 See Daniel J. Goldhagen, *A Moral Reckoning*, p. 259 and the Epilogue for more.

424 http://www.jcrelations.net/en/?item=926. See the Epilogue for further discussion on *We Remember.* A truthful and thorough moral reckoning is supported by one of the Church's own favorite theologians, St. Augustine: "Lying is not a lack of fidelity to the meaning of words but of the proper intention to another person"; "Lying is a particularly spiritual form of sin" and "Truthfulness is a heroic standard." Quoted in Wills, Garry, *Papal Sin*, pp. 284, 286, 287.

425 American judge Francis Biddle, *In Brief Authority* (Garden City, NY: Doubleday, 1962), pp. 480-481. Quoted in Norbert Ehrenfreund, *The Nuremberg Legacy*, p. 56.

426 This legal understanding stems from the European Convention on Human Rights, Article 7, adopted under the auspices of the Council of Europe in 1950 and which binds most European nations, and all European Union nations.

427 Quoted in Norbert Ehrenfreund, *The Nuremberg Legacy*, p. 55. For further discussion of the *ex post facto* principle and other objections to the Nuremberg Trial see op. cit., p. 58.

428 http://en.wikipedia.org/wiki/Defamation.

429 Catechism of the Catholic Church, parag. 2477.

430 This law is in Section 130 of the German Criminal Code (http://www.iuscomp.org/gla/statutes/StGB.htm#130) and was promulgated on November 13, 1998, more than fifty years after the Holocaust and many more after the centuries of hate speech emanating from Christendom toward the Jews. We must point out that the term "Hate Speech" was not used during the war.

431 Article II of the International Convention on the Suppression and Punishment of the Crime of Apartheid defines the crime of apartheid as follows:

a. Denial to a member or members of a racial group or groups of the right to life and liberty of person

    i. By murder of members of a racial group or groups;

    ii. By the infliction upon the members of a racial group or groups of serious bodily or mental harm, by the infringement of their freedom or dignity, or by subjecting them to torture or to cruel, inhuman or degrading treatment or punishment;

    iii. By arbitrary arrest and illegal imprisonment of the members of a racial group or groups;

b. Deliberate imposition on a racial group or groups of living conditions calculated to cause its or their physical destruction in whole or in part;

c. Any legislative measures and other measures calculated to prevent a racial group or groups from participation in the political, social, economic and cultural life of the country and the deliberate creation of conditions preventing the full development of such a group or groups, in particular by denying to members of a racial group or groups basic human rights and freedoms, including the right to work, the right to form recognized trade unions, the right to education, the right to leave and to return to their country, the right to a nationality, the right to freedom of movement and residence, the right to freedom of opinion and expression, and the right to freedom of peaceful assembly and association;

d. Any measures including legislative measures, designed to divide the population along racial lines by the creation of separate reserves and ghettos for the members of a racial group or groups, the prohibition of mixed marriages among members of various racial groups, the expropriation of landed property belonging to a racial group or groups or to members thereof;

e. Exploitation of the labour of the members of a racial group or groups, in particular by submitting them to forced labour;

f. Persecution of organizations and persons, by depriving them of fundamental rights and freedoms, because they oppose apartheid. http://www.unhchr.ch/html/menu3/b/11.htm.

432 http://untreaty.un.org/cod/icc/statute/romefra.htm.

433 In the 1976 California Supreme Court Tarasoff case, the court ruled: "When a therapist determines, or pursuant to the standards of his profession should determine, that his patient presents a serious danger of violence to another, he incurs an obligation to use reasonable care to protect the intended victim against such danger. The discharge of this duty may require the therapist to take one or more of various steps, depending upon the nature of the case. Thus it may call for him to warn the intended victim or others likely to apprise the victim of the danger, to notify the police, or to take whatever other steps are reasonably necessary under the circumstances." In this case the priest is no different from the therapist.

434 Brody, Acker and Logan, *Criminal Law*, pp. 537-539.

435 State ex rel. Attorney General v. Talley, 15 So. 722 (Ala. 1894). Quoted in Brody, Acker and Logan, *Criminal Law*, p. 539.

436 http://en.wikipedia.org/wiki/Accessory_(legal_term).

437 Brody, Acker and Logan, *Criminal Law*, p. 544.

438 See Daniel J. Goldhagen, *A Moral Reckoning*, p. 176 and *Catechism of the Catholic Church*, parag. 1868.

439 Universal Declaration of Human Rights: http://www.unhchr.ch/udhr/lang/eng.htm. The quoted law was promulgated by the U.N.'s International Tribunals for Yugoslavia and Rwanda (articles 7 and 6, respectively) in 1993: http://www.un.org/icty/legaldoc-e/basic/statut/stat02-2006.htm#7.

440 See Prosecutor v. Kvocka, Judgement, ICTY Trial Chamber, at para. 251, Case No. IT-98-30/1-T (Nov. 2, 2001): http://www.un.org/icty/kvocka/trialc/judgement/index.htm.

441 Daniel J. Goldhagen, *A Moral Reckoning*, p. 175 & Michael Phayer, *The Catholic Church and the Holocaust*, p. 175.

442 J. Demleitner, "Volksgenealogie," *Klerusblatt*, XV (1934), p. 503. Quoted in Guenter Lewy, *The Catholic Church and Nazi Germany*, p. 282. See also Daniel J. Goldhagen, *A Moral Reckoning*, p. 60.

443 Daniel J. Goldhagen, *A Moral Reckoning*, p. 156.

444 James Carroll, *Constantine's Sword*, p. 533.

445 The IBM punch card and card sorting system was provided to Hitler's Third Reich by IBM's German subsidiary, which operated independently but with the knowledge of the New York headquarters. The Hollerith punch card system (as it was known) was the machine that allowed the Germans to identify and target Jews for asset confiscation, ghettoization, deportation and ultimately extermination. More than two thousand of these machines were distributed throughout Germany, and thousands more throughout German-dominated Europe, including every major concentration camp. Some of the camps only operated the punchers and submitted their cards to a different location for processing. Identifying the Jews was accomplished by collecting information on national censuses and by searching communal, church and government records all across Germany and later the Nazi-occupied countries. The punch card systems were used to organize the systematic campaign of Jewish economic disenfranchisement during the 1930s, and then the massive deportation campaign into ghettos and concentration camps. When the Final Solution began and the Germans needed to coordinate the deportation of tens of thousands of people from ghettos and cities around Europe to the slave labor and death camps, the IBM machines were used to efficiently coordinate the transport of Jews along railroad lines. Edwin Black, *IBM and the Holocaust*, p. 8, 351.

446 Doris L. Bergen, Between God and Hitler: German Military Chaplains and the Crimes of the Third Reich, in *In God's Name*, edited by Omer Bartov, Phyllis Mack, pp. 128-130 & Daniel J. Goldhagen, *A Moral Reckoning*, pp. 62-63.

447 Doris L. Bergen, Between God and Hitler: German Military Chaplains and the Crimes of the Third Reich, in *In God's Name*, edited by Omer Bartov, Phyllis Mack, p. 134.

448 Doris L. Bergen, German Military Chaplains in World War II and the Dilemmas of Legitimacy. *Church History* 70(2), (2001) & Daniel J. Goldhagen, *Hitler's Willing Executioners*, p. 597 n.87 & Friedrich Heer, *God's First Love*, p. 319.

449 On Stangl, see Gitta Sereny, *Into That Darkness: An Examination of Conscience* (New York: Vintage Books, 1983) and Doris L. Bergen, German Military Chaplains in World War II and the Dilemmas of Legitimacy. *Church History* 70(2), (2001).

450 *Catechism of the Catholic Church*, parag. 1868 & St. Ambrose quoted in James Carroll, *Constantine's Sword*, p. 45.

451 For a complete analysis of the various acts of omission the Church may be guilty of, see Daniel J. Goldhagen, *A Moral Reckoning*, pp. 172-173.

452 Quoted in Ibid., p. 65. See also op. cit., p. 63.

453 Quoted in Daniel J. Goldhagen, *A Moral Reckoning*, p. 64.

454 Report of Michael Dov Weissmandl's conversation with the papal nuncio. It must be noted, however, that the papal nuncio used his influence to try to save Jews in Slovakia, so it is possible that in retrospect Weissmandl misattributed the statement to the wrong person. Even if that was so, the belief that Jews deserved to be punished was widely held by the episcopate. Michael Dov Weissmandl, *Min Hametzar* (1960; reprint ed. Jerusalem, n.d.), p. 24.

455 Quoted in Steven T. Katz, Shlomo Biderman, Gershon Greenberg, *Wrestling with God*, p. 502.

456 For further material on Slovakia see Daniel J. Goldhagen, *A Moral Reckoning*, pp. 63-65. and Michael Phayer, *The Catholic Church and the Holocaust*, pp. 88-91.

457 John Loftus & Mark Aarons, *Unholy Trinity*, p. 71.

458 Quoted in Michael Phayer, *The Catholic Church and the Holocaust*, p. 39.

459 Daniel J. Goldhagen, *A Moral Reckoning*, p. 66.

460 John Loftus & Mark Aarons, *Unholy Trinity*, p. 71.

461 London Charter of the International Military Tribunal, Article 6(c), Crimes against humanity: "Murder, extermination, enslavement, deportation, and other inhumane acts committed against any civilian population, before or during the war; or persecutions on political, racial or religious grounds in execution of or in connection with any crime within the jurisdiction of the Tribunal, whether or not in violation of the domestic law of the country where perpetrated."

462 Michael Phayer, *The Catholic Church and the Holocaust*, p. 170.

463 For more on a potential count of obstruction of justice see John Loftus & Mark Aarons, *Unholy Trinity*, pp. 282-283.

464 According to Stuart Eizenstat, the Undersecretary of Commerce who conducted a study of Nazi gold in 1997: "The Swiss National Bank . . . knew as the war progressed that the Reichsbank's coffers had been depleted, and that the Swiss were handling vasts sums of looted gold". Beir, Robert, *Roosevelt and the Holocaust*, p. 238. The most active Nazi depositing loot was Hermann Göring whose Swiss agents arranged for looted valuables, particularly paintings stolen from galleries and private collections across Europe, to be stored in Swiss bank vaults. Bower, Tom, *Nazi Gold*, p. 43. Walther Funk, the president of the Reichsbank, declared in his testimony at Nuremberg: "The other countries with which we still had business relations introduced gold embargoes. Sweden refused to accept gold at all. Only in Switzerland could we still do business through changing gold into foreign currency." Ibid., p. 46. To make matters worse, in more recent years, as Swiss complicity has been fleshed out, the Union Bank of

Switzerland ordered shredding all files from the 1930s and 1940s. Beir, *Robert, Roosevelt and the Holocaust*, p. 238, 239.

465 For further discussion on a potential count of receiving and profiting from stolen property see John Loftus & Mark Aarons, *Unholy Trinity*, pp. 284, 288, 289, 297, 299, 300.

466 See Ibid., pp. 284-285 for more on a potential count of abuse of diplomatic privileges.

467 Daniel J. Goldhagen, *A Moral Reckoning*, p. 165.

468 Jeremy Cohen, *Christ Killers*, pp. 213-214.

469 Ibid., pp. 225-226.

470 The play in recent years has become an immense source of revenue for the residents of Oberammergau. Ironically, as Jeremy Cohen says, "the play itself begins its tale of the Passion with Jesus' heated rebuke of Jewish merchants, profit-mongers who exploit the worship of God in the temple for their own personal gain." Ibid., pp. 215, 217.

471 H. Trevor-Roper (ed.), *Hitler's Table Talk*, 1941-1944, Oxford: OUP 1988 (repr.), p. 563, 5 July 1942.

472 Quoted in Friedrich Heer, *God's First Love*, p. 286.

473 Cited by the International Military Tribunal, Vol. V, pp. 114-116.

474 Closing statement for the prosecution at Nuremberg, January 10, 1946. http://www.nizkor.org/hweb/imt/tgmwc/tgmwc-04/tgmwc-04-31-09.shtml.

475 See Daniel J. Goldhagen, *A Moral Reckoning*, p. 164. Streicher was condemned to death by hanging by the Tribunal.

476 See the statements of General Rudenko, the Soviet Chief Prosecutor at the Nuremberg Trial of the major war criminals, Monday, 29th July, 1946. http://www.nizkor.org/hweb/imt/tgmwc/tgmwc-20/tgmwc-20-189-12.shtml.

477 Daniel J. Goldhagen, *Hitler's Willing Executioners*, pp. 223-232.

478 A pope is considered infallible when he solemnly declares or promulgates to the Church a dogmatic teaching on faith or morals as being contained in divine revelation, or at least being intimately connected to divine revelation.

479 Michael Phayer, *The Catholic Church and the Holocaust*, p. 224.

480 Even though as the war progressed the amount of available literature dwindled, in 1940 the Protestant Church had access to close to one hundred religious publications they could use in their pastoral care work with the armed forces. See Bergen, Doris L., "Germany Is Our Mission: Christ Is Our Strength! The Wehrmacht Chaplaincy and The 'German Christian' Movement." *Church History* 66(3), p. 528.

481 On July 1, 1946, an eight-year old Polish boy, Henryk Blaszczyk, was reported missing by his father Walenty. Two days later, the boy, his father and one
of their neighbors went to a local police station where Henryk falsely claimed
that he had been kidnapped by Jews (years later, shortly before his death in
1990s, he said he was told to lie by his father and the men from the secret police.
Henryk accused the Jews of killing children for their blood and keeping the bodies in the cellar of the Kibbutz (Jewish socialist collective community) on Planty
Street, among other alleged horrors. See Jan T. Gross, *Neighbors: The Destruction
the Jewish Community in Jedwabne, Poland* (2001).

482 Michael Phayer, *The Catholic Church and the Holocaust*, p. 181.

483 Ibid., p. 139.

484 Michael Phayer, "The Author replies," Commonweal, June 6, 2003,
http://findarticles.com/p/articles/mi_m1252/is_11_130/ai_104578578 & *The
Catholic Church and the Holocaust*, p. 164-5.

485 Michael Phayer, *The Catholic Church and the Holocaust*, p. 142.

486 According to historian Frank Buscher, "The number of prisoners in Lands-
berg's death row decreased from 28 to 7 due to sentence commutations." In the
end, High Commissioner McCloy let only five death sentences stand. See Ibid.,
p. 143.

487 Quoted in Ibid., p. 144.

488 Adolf Hitler, in a speech in the Reichstag on January 30, 1939.

489 Daniel J. Goldhagen, *A Moral Reckoning*, p. 200 & Daniel J. Goldhagen,
*Hitler's Willing Executioners*, pp. 453-454 and 597 n.86.

490 Daniel J. Goldhagen, *A Moral Reckoning*, p. 203 & Fisher, Tudin and
Tanenbaum, eds., *Religious Education Before and After Vatican II*, pp. 126-127.

491 Stated in a lecture given in Zürich, March 7, 1946. Not und Aufgabe der
Kirche in Deutschland. See also Daniel J. Goldhagen, *Hitler's Willing Executioners*, p. 114.

492 Michael Phayer, *The Catholic Church and the Holocaust*, p. 194.

493 Ibid., p. 206-207.

494 The Pope's Passion Sunday sermon earlier that year is hard to reconcile with
what he said after the Second Vatican Council: "The Jews must never be the
'object of our disdain or mistrust but the object of our respect, love and hope.'"
Ibid., p. 215.

495 Quoted in Ibid., p. 213.

496 Ibid., p. 214.

497 Quoted in Daniel J. Goldhagen, *A Moral Reckoning*, p. 214.

498 http://www.jcrelations.net/en/?id=1030.

499 General Audience Discourse of September 1, 1999; in *L'Osservatore Romano*, Eng. ed., September 8, 1999, 7. Quoted in James Carroll, *Constantine's Sword*, p. 394.

500 Catechism of the Catholic Church, parag. 1459.

501 See E. Rodocanachi, *The Holy See and the Jews*.

# Reference Bibliography

Arendt, Hanna. *Eichmann in Jerusalem: A Report on the Banality of Evil.* New York: Viking, 1965

Bacharach, Walter Zwi. *Anti-Jewish Prejudices in German Catholic Sermons.* Lewiston, NY: Edwin Mellen Press, 1993

Beck, Norman A. *Mature Christianity in the 21st Century: The Recognition and Repudiation of the Anti Jewish Polemic of the New Testament.* New York: Crossroad, 1994

Beir, Robert. *Roosevelt and the Holocaust.* Fort Lee, NJ: Barricade Books, 2006

Beschloss, Michael. *The Conquerors: Roosevelt, Truman and the Destruction of Hitler's Germany.* New York: Simon & Schuster, 2002

Black, Edwin. *IBM and the Holocaust.* New York: Crown Publishers, 2001

Blum, John Morton. *From the Morgenthau Diaries.* Boston: Houghton Mifflin, 1967

Bower, Tom. *Nazi Gold.* New York: HarperCollins, 1997

Brody, David C., Acker, James R., Logan, Wayne A., *Criminal Law.* Gaithersburg, Maryland: Aspen Publishers, 2001

Browning, Christopher R., *Ordinary Men: Reserve Police Battalion 101 and the Final Solution in Poland.* New York: HarperCollins Publishers, 1992

Carroll, James. *Constantine's Sword.* New York: Houghton Mifflin, 2001

*Catechism of the Catholic Church.* New York: Doubleday, 1995

Chadwick, Owen. *Britain and the Vatican during the Second World War.* Cambridge University Press, 1986

Cohen, Jeremy. *Christ Killers.* Oxford University Press, 2007

Cornwell, John. *Hitler's Pope: The Secret History of Pius XII.* New York: Viking, 1999

Coulombe, Charles. *Vicars of Christ: A History of the Popes.* New York: Citadel Press Books, 2003

Ehrenfreund, Norbert. *The Nuremberg Legacy.* New York: Palgrave Macmillan, 2007

Elliott, Lawrence. *I Will be Called John.* Collins, 1977

Fisher, Tudin and Tanenbaum, eds., *Religious Education Before and After Vatican II.* New York: Paulist Press, 1986

Freudmann, Lillian. *Antisemitism in the New Testament.* Lanham, Maryland: University Press of America, 1994

Friedländer, Saul. *Pius XII and the Third Reich: A Documentation.* New York: Alfred Knopf, 1966

———. *Nazi Germany and the Jews, Vol. 1.* New York: HarperCollins, 1997

Gallagher, Charles R. *Vatican Secret Diplomacy: Joseph P. Hurley and Pope Pius XII.* New Haven: Yale University Press, 2008

Gerlach, Wolfgang. *And the Witnesses Were Silent.* Lincoln, NE: University of Nebraska Press, 2000

Gilbert, Martin. *In Search of Churchill: A Historian's Journey.* New York: John Wiley & Sons, 1994

Goldhagen, Daniel J., *A Moral Reckoning: The Role of the Catholic Church in the Holocaust and its Unfulfilled Duty of Repair.* New York: Alfred Knopf, 2002

———. *Hitler's Willing Executioners: Ordinary Germans and the Holocaust.* New York: Alfred Knopf, 1996

Goñi, Uki. *The Real Odessa.* London, Great Britain: Granta Publications, 2002

Gutman, Israel. *Encyclopedia of the Holocaust.* New York: Macmillan, 1990

Gutteridge, Richard. *The German Evangelical Church and the Jews.* New York: Harper & Row Publishers, 1976

Heer, Friedrich. *God's First Love.* London, Great Britain: Phoenix, 1999

Hilberg, Raul. *The Destruction of the European Jews, Vol. 1.* New York: Holmes and Meier, 1985

Hirschmann, Ira. *Caution to the Winds.* New York: David McKay, 1962

Hitler, Adolf. *Mein Kampf.* New York: Houghton Mifflin, 1943

Isaac, Jules. *The Teaching of Contempt.* New York: McGraw-Hill, 1965

———. *Jesus and Israel.* Holt, New York: Rinehart and Winston, 1971

Kertzer, David. *The Popes Against the Jews.* New York: Alfred Kopf, 2001

———. *The Kidnapping of Edgardo Mortara.* New York: Alfred Kopf, 1997

Lewy, Guenter. *The Catholic Church and Nazi Germany.* New York: McGraw-Hill, 1964

Littell, Franklin H. *The Crucifixion of the Jews,* New York: Harper & Row, Publishers, 1975

Loftus, John & Aarons, Mark. *Unholy Trinity.* New York: St. Martin's Press, 1998

———. *The Secret War Against the Jews.* New York: St. Martin's Press, 1994

Morley, John. *Vatican Diplomacy and the Jews During the Holocaust.* New York: Ktav, 1980

Nietzsche, Friedrich. *Beyond Good and Evil.* New York: Random House, 1966

Passelecq, Georges and Suchecky, Bernard. *The Hidden Encyclical of Pius XI.* New York: Harcourt Brace, 1997

Penkower, Monty Noam. *The Jews Were Expendable: Free World Diplomacy and the Holocaust.* Wayne State University Press, 1988

Phayer, Michael. *The Catholic Church and the Holocaust.* Bloomington, IN: Indiana University Press, 2000

Poliakov, Léon. *The History of Anti-Semitism. Vol. 1, From the Time of Christ to the Court Jews.* New York: Vanguard, 1965

Rittner, Carol, Smith, Stephen D. and Steinfeldt, Irena, Editors. *The Holocaust and the Christian World: Reflections of the Past, Challenges for the Future.* New York: Continuum, 2000

Rodocanachi, Emmanuel. *The Holy See and the Jews.*

Roth, John K. and Rittner, Carol, Editors. *Pope Pius XII and the Holocaust.* Continuum, 2002

Rubenstein, Richard and Roth, John K., *Approaches to Auschwitz: The Holocaust and its Legacy.* Louisville: Westminster John Knox Press, 2003

Rubin, Barry. *Istanbul Intrigues.* New York: McGraw-Hill, 1989

Ruether, Rosemary Rathford. *Faith and Fratricide: The Theological Roots of Anti-Semitism.* New York: Seabury, 1974

Runes, Dagobert David. *The Jew and the Cross.* New York: Philosophical Library, 1965

Rychlak, Ronald J., *Righteous Gentiles: How Pius XII And the Catholic Church Saved Half a Million Jews from the Nazis.* Spence Publishing Co., 2005

Sachar, Howard M., *A History of Israel - From the Rise of Zionism to Our Time.* New York: Alfred Knopf, 1996

Taylor, Telford. *The Anatomy of the Nuremberg Trials.* New York: Alfred Knopf, 1992

Trachtenberg, Joshua. *The Devil and the Jews.* New Haven: Yale University Press, 1943

Wills, Garry. *Papal Sin.* New York: Doubleday, 2000

Wyman, David. *The Abandonment of the Jews.* New York: Pantheon Books, 1984

Zuccotti, Susan. *Under His Very Windows.* Yale University Press, 2000

# Image Credits

p. 144: Bayerische Staatsbibliothek München/Hoffmann.

p. 149: Bundesarchiv Koblenz, Bild 183-R70353.

p. 152: ullstein bild / The Granger Collection, New York.

p. 155: Carl Baer, public domain.

p. 157: United States Holocaust Museum Memorial, Washington D.C.

p. 160: Bildarchiv Preussischer Kulturbesitz / Art Resource, NY.

p. 162: Bayerische Staatsbibliothek München/Hoffmann.

p. 165: Bundesarchiv, Bild 183-H25547.

p. 167: United States Holocaust Museum Memorial, Washington D.C.

p. 172: Sister from Villa Nazareth, Rome. Used under the Creative Commons Attribution-ShareAlike 3.0 license. (*)

p. 183: Bayerische Staatsbibliothek München/Hoffmann.

p. 188: Public domain.

p. 191: Bildarchiv Preussischer Kulturbesitz / Art Resource, NY.

p. 211: United States Holocaust Museum Memorial, Washigton D.C.

p. 221: Photographer unknown. Public domain.

p. 256: Bundesarchiv, Bild 146-2005-0193, Henisch.

p. 261: Left, photograph published by the authorities of the Croatian NDH-state (1941-1945), public domain. Right, USHMM, Washington D.C.

p. 269: Der Stürmer Archive, Stadtarchiv Nürnberg, E39 neg. 10502, 10526 Nr.2247/11.

p. 272: United States Holocaust Museum Memorial, Washington D.C.

p. 280: United States Holocaust Museum Memorial, Washington D.C.

p. 282: Bundesarchiv, Plak 003-020-028-T1, Fips.

p. 299: Gedenkstätte Deutscher Widerstand (German Resistance Memorial Center), Berlin.

p. 301: Left, Bayerische Staatsbibliothek München/Hoffmann. Right, United States Holocaust Museum Memorial, Washington D.C.

p. 302: Peter Geymayer, public domain.

Cover: Foreground, Bayerische Staatsbibliothek München/Hoffmann. Background, United States Holocaust Museum Memorial, Washington D.C.

(*) You are free to share and make derivative works of this image under the conditions that you appropriately attribute it, and that you distribute it only under a license identical to this one.

# Acknowledgments

I am indebted to a large number of scholars whose work I consulted to provide the historical background material on which this book is based. I have included a bibliography of all the books I consulted so interested readers can learn more about the various topics covered in *Six Million Crucifixions*. However, I am particularly indebted to James Carroll, Daniel J. Goldhagen, John Loftus & Mark Aarons, Guenter Lewy, Jules Isaac, Michael Phayer, David Kertzer, Carol Rittner, Doris Bergen, Susan Zuccotti, Richard L. Rubenstein and John K. Roth. To all of them, and the other historians and scholars whose works I consulted for this book, I express my gratitude and admiration for their outstanding contributions to the literature. I hope this book helps in some way to further disseminate the information presented in the original scholarly works.

I am also grateful to various image archives for their help in finding and granting permission to use many of the images in this book. In particular, I would like to thank Martina Caspers from the Bundesarchiv in Koblenz, the Bildarchiv Preussischer Kulturbesitz, Tricia Smith from Art Resource and Silka Quintero from The Granger Collection in New York, Angelika Betz from the Bayerische Staatsbibliothek in Munich, Susanne Brömel from the Gedenkstätte Deutscher Widerstand in Berlin, the Stadtarchiv in Nuremberg, Miri Aumann from Yad Vashem in Jerusalem, Randall Bytwerk from the German Propaganda Archive and especially Caroline Waddell from the United States Holocaust Memorial

Museum, who tirelessly helped me track a large number of photographs.

I would also like to extend my gratitude to Jim Freedman, Denise Hummel and particularly to Professor William J. Aceves from California Western School of Law and Judge Norbert Ehrenfreund, whose insights helped me with the legal aspects of *Six Million Crucifixions*.

Marni Freedman edited and Ann Marie Houghtailing proofread the manuscript, and in the process transformed it into a more polished work. A number of friends and family members read drafts of the manuscript and provided input that made it better: my wife Yazmin Ghonaim Wilensky, my brother Javier Wilensky, and friends Richard Rosenblatt, Gabriel Morgulis, Juan Blumenkranz and Daniel Altbaum. I would like to especially thank my very good friend Marcelo Alé, whose extraordinary intellect influenced and challenged me during almost three decades of stimulating discussion on a myriad topics, and made me richer in the process. His comments and recommendations made a significant difference in this work. I will always be grateful to my parents for their nurturing and infinite support and to my uncle Jorge Herszlikowicz, who was instrumental in my becoming a bibliophile early on in my life.

Lastly, I would like to extend my gratitude to the scholars who read the manuscript and provided feedback and/or contributed an endorsement to the book: Michael Berenbaum, Geoffrey Cocks, Jonathan Friedman, Frederic Krome, Rochelle Millen, Carol Rittner, Thane Rosenbaum, Karl Schleunes, Robert G. Weisbord and others whose endorsements came after sending the book to the printer and to whom I am equally as grateful. I would like to especially thank John K. Roth, who contributed the foreword and was the first one to acknowledge this book had some merit. I will always be grateful to him for his support.

Gabriel Wilensky

# Index

Italicized page numbers indicate illustrations.

Lightning Source UK Ltd.
Milton Keynes UK
UKOW051911141111

182047UK00002B/24/P